THE
BODYWORK
BOOK

THE BODYWORK BOOK

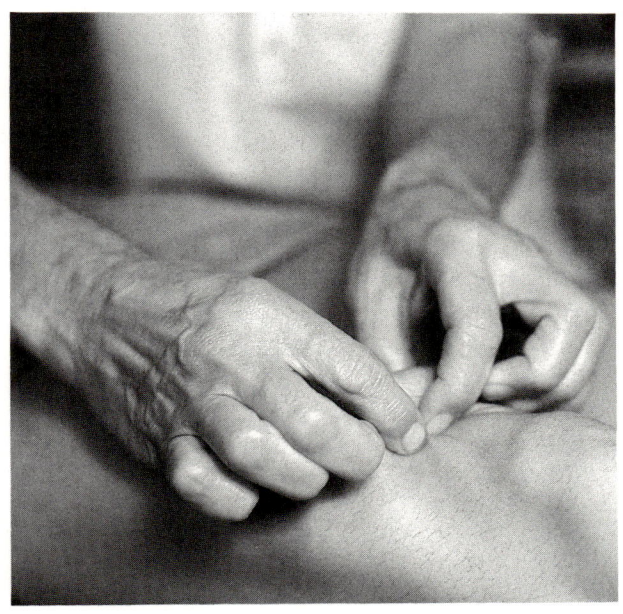

Edited by
NEVILL DRURY

PRISM ALPHA

THE BODYWORK BOOK
Copyright © 1984 by Nevill Drury
Copyright in individual chapters is retained by their authors.

All rights reserved. No part of this book may be reproduced in any manner without written permission except in the case of brief quotations embodied in critical articles and reviews. For information address: Prism Alpha Ltd., Church House, Half Moon Street, Sherborne, Dorset DT9 3LN, England

ISBN 0 907061 67 2

Distributed in the United States of America through Prism Alpha, P.O. Box 778, San Leandro, California 94577

613.7

Designed by Judy Hungerford
Cover photograph by Michael Cook
Printed in Singapore by Kyodo

CONTENTS

Foreword   *Nevill Drury*   7

1   SENSITIVE MASSAGE   *Ralph Hadden*   9
2   THE ALEXANDER TECHNIQUE   *Jeremy Chance*   20
3   THE TRAGER APPROACH   *Deane Juhan*   34
4   SELF-HELP CHIROPRACTIC   *Nathaniel Altman*   48
5   IYENGAR YOGA   *Carl Webster*   58
6   OKI YOGA   *Barbara Kimbrey & Carl Webster*   73
7   SHIATSU   *Daniel Weber*   82
8   TOUCH FOR BEAUTY   *Susan Roche & Helen Smith*   95
9   DEEP TISSUE MUSCLE THERAPY   *John Cottone*   118
10   REICHIAN AND NEO-REICHIAN THERAPY   *Lew Luton*   129
11   REBIRTHING   *Michael Adamedes & Alia Paulusz*   149
12   SHINTAIDO   *Alexandra Pope*   160

Acknowledgements   173
The Contributors   174
Bibliography   177

FOREWORD

With the development of holistic medicine and natural therapies, interest in bodywork has increased dramatically in recent years. There are several reasons why this should be so.

After wading so long in the mire of post-Victorian consciousness, modern western culture is now much more open about topics like sensuality, sexuality and interpersonal relationships than earlier generations were. It also seems apparent that the holistic philosophy of health — which focuses on both the physical body and the total inner person in promoting well-being — is somewhat different in emphasis from that of the Judaeo-Christian tradition. The latter led in earlier times to repression of interest in the body because of the connotation of sexual permissiveness, and regarded its main function as human reproduction. The concept that the body might provide wholesome pleasure, be a vital key to self-knowledge and creative expression, and might also reflect our emotional state was noticeably absent in the earlier view of the body but has attracted widespread public attention in recent times with the rise of the Human Potential movement.

Since the body is our vehicle of self-expression in the physical world it is the starting point for all paths of self-development. Even Yoga, meditation and guided imagery techniques depend on physical relaxation procedures and appropriate posture as an adjunct to the attainment of inner awareness.

To the extent that understanding more about the body is a crucial aspect of personal growth, the bodywork therapies present different techniques for attaining optimum physical self-expression. These range from exercises for general fitness through to procedures designed to free specific muscle spasms, correct inappropriate posture and maximise the flow of 'life-force' through the body. Some of the approaches — like Reichian therapy, Rebirthing and Deep Tissue Muscle Therapy — also include cathartic techniques which release emotional trauma trapped in the musculature of the body.

This book presents a variety of bodywork therapies with a view to making them accessible to the general reader. Many of the techniques have a self-help application which makes them directly applicable on a practical level, although in all cases we urge readers to proceed sensibly and, initially at least, with the guidance of a skilled practitioner.

The sequence of chapters does not imply a progression as such, although the therapies have been arranged in sequence as a reflection of their emphasis.

Massage is an ideal way of developing the awareness of touch, and this type of sensitivity is also applied specifically in the Alexander Technique and in Trager work

FOREWORD

— both of which are extremely subtle in their emphasis, while nevertheless very effective.

Chiropractic is very much an American bodywork system, but it does share with the Eastern systems of Iyengar and Oki Yoga a profound respect for the mechanical functions of the body and the development of optimum physical effectiveness.

Shiatsu and Touch for Beauty both draw on the acupuncture model in which the unimpeded flow of life-force (in China, *chi*; in Japan, *ki*) through the body represents the major determinant of health and becomes the key to a balanced lifestyle.

Reichian Therapy, Rebirthing and Deep Tissue Muscle Therapy explore the release of energy blockages in the body by freeing 'body armour' and allowing the subject to explore the intimate interplay between the emotions and physical activity. And finally, Shintaido has been included because like Tai Chi — which it superficially resembles — it expresses the Dance of Life and can lead us to a state of exultation and grace through physical expression.

It seems to me that the idea of presenting a variety of bodywork techniques in an accessible and practical format is both beneficial and timely. As we begin to take responsibility for our own health, it becomes obvious that the body is a good place to start.

Nevill Drury

CHAPTER 1
SENSITIVE MASSAGE
Ralph Hadden

INTRODUCTION

Massage is the simplest, most natural form of healing and has probably been used since the beginning of the human race. In ancient times, as well as in the modern era, a mother would rub a baby's tummy if it had colic, a friend would knead and squeeze your stiff shoulder muscles, and if you fell and bruised your knee you would hold the sore spot. Presumably someone in the tribe had a special knack for rubbing and squeezing the pain away and that person became the tribe's masseur — the founder of the ancient and honourable art of healing. Recently, with the growing popularity of health, fitness and personal growth, there has been an upsurge in the use of massage. Many people have a massage regularly for the maintenance of health and well-being. There has been a proliferation of styles — in fact as each masseur has his or her own way of doing a massage, there are as many massage styles as there are masseurs.

STYLES OF MASSAGE

Swedish Massage This is the commonest and most widely known massage style. It is actually more a European tradition of massage and is not specifically Swedish. The name probably owes its origin to a pioneer of massage, Peter Ling (1776–1839), who was from Sweden; he and others that followed influenced the development of massage in the 19th and 20th centuries. Swedish massage is fairly vigorous, aiming to stimulate the circulation of blood through the soft tissues, and uses rubbing or stroking (effleurage), kneading and squeezing (petrissage), slapping or pounding (tapotement) and some deep massage (friction). Other styles that have become popular utilise more adventurous and unorthodox methods:

Esalen Massage So called because it evolved at the Esalen Institute growth centre in California. It is based on Swedish massage, but is done in a slower, more flowing fashion. Esalen-style massage is not so much a specific set of techniques but more a philosophy of massage, where the emphasis is on treating the recipient as a feeling human being and producing a pleasurable, nourishing experience. *The Massage Book* by George Downing is an excellent introduction to this approach.

Rolfing Named after its founder, Dr Ida Rolf, this form of massage is also known as Structural Integration. It is a strong deep tissue massage which alters and aligns the structure of the body. Over ten sessions, visible changes in body posture and structure take place. Postural Integration and Deep Tissue massage are variations on this style.

Polarity Therapy This is not just a massage technique, because it also employs exercise, diet and a positive approach to life. The founder, Dr Randolph Stone, believed that an energy permeated the body, providing it with life, and that it flowed in certain pathways and directions and so had polarity. For example, energy is believed to flow out of the right hand and into the left hand and so, relative to each other, the right hand is said to have a 'positive' polarity and the left a 'negative' polarity. This flow of energy, however, can be obstructed through poor diet, where the person consumes more of a certain food than they can use or process, or through muscle tension, lack of exercise, or emotional distress. A polarity therapist will stretch the body and press on 'ouch points' where the energy is blocking to free up the flow of energy, and then just rest his (or her) hands on the body to balance and smooth that flow. This last technique, of just resting the hands, is surprisingly powerful in producing a feeling of deep relaxation and sometimes induces a dreamy trance-like state. In Polarity Therapy a person can also use stretching exercises, cleansing diets and positive thinking to free the flow of energy.

Reflexology/Zone Therapy This is a special massage for the feet which reflexologists claim can be used to diagnose and treat the whole body as there are reflex connections in the feet which link to the rest of the body. A problem in the body will show up as a sore spot on the foot (when pressed on firmly), and the complaint is treated by massaging that sore spot. Reflexology can also be applied to the hands, though this is not so common. Reflexology along with Iridology and Auricular Acupuncture works on the assumption that, as with a hologram, the part reflects the whole — the state of one part of the body (in fact any part) indicates the state of the whole of the body.

I first realised there was something to it when I gave a friend a foot massage. Geoff was quite healthy except for a problem of ringing in the ears (tinnitus). I pressed firmly all over the foot, with nothing remarkable happening until I came to an area on the sole of his foot, near the bases of the third and fourth toes. Geoff gave a yelp as I pressed — the point was the one corresponding to the ears, and was quite tender!

Shiatsu/Acupressure These are Oriental styles of massage which, in contrast to Swedish massage which uses oil for sliding stroking, instead uses pressure applied mainly with the tips of the thumbs or fingers. This massage is applied to specific pressure points and tends to be shorter and sharper and leaves one feeling energised (see Chapter Seven).

Intuitive Massage Often we know intuitively what to do, although there seems no rational reason. And in massage, if we trust our intuition, often we'll be doing what is just right for the client. We might, for example, feel drawn to starting the massage on the feet, and the client will say it felt right to start there! In massage there is an interplay between set techniques and intuitive work. Allowing our intuition to lead us keeps the massage fresh and alive and lifts it out of the routine so that it is much more enjoyable both for the masseur and the recipient. The basic techniques provide a structure which allow for improvisation, just as a jazz trumpeter may use his basic technique and a standard tune to spontaneously create a wonderful musical experience.

Sensitive Massage My own style of massage I call Sensitive Massage, as it requires of the practitioner both a sensitivity and an awareness — a sensitivity to the physical and emotional state of the recipient and to the practitioner's own state. The techniques are mainly a blend of Esalen, Polarity and Intuitive massage, along with methods I have developed myself. A sensitivity and flexibility is important, as different clients require different sorts of massage — gentle or firm, slow or fast — and the same client may require a different massage at different times. Even during a single massage the mood

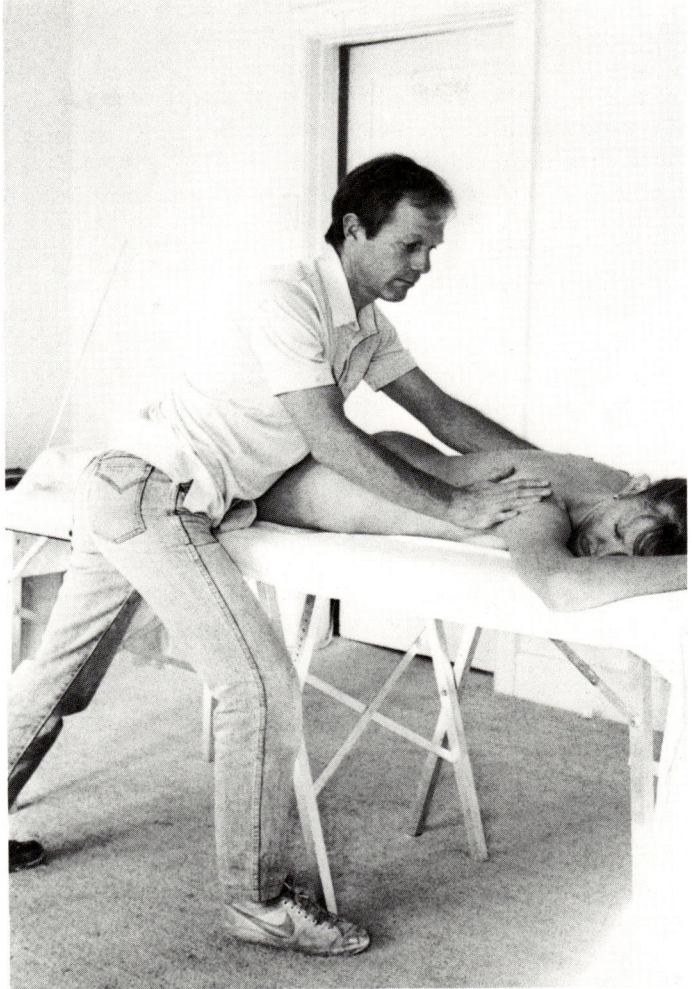
Performing a Sensitive Massage

may change and the sensitive practitioner should also change to be in harmony with the mood of the moment, like water in a stream changing with bends, rocks, trees, deep and shallow stretches.

PERSONAL EXPERIENCES WITH MASSAGE

Why is massage becoming as popular as it is? What are the benefits to the recipient? Before I answer these questions, I'll give some examples of my experiences with massage.

Michael came for massage at a particularly stressful time in his life. His father had died, and a long term relationship with his girlfriend had come to an end. Some massages at that time provided him with extra support and caring that was needed, so that he felt stronger and was better able to work through the crisis in a constructive way.

David is a counsellor, a very sensitive, aware person, and a regular client. In one session, relaxing into the massage, he found that he was experiencing himself as a two year old, in his parents bed. Sunlight and the scent of spring blossoms streamed through the window and he experienced again the feeling of utter joy and contentment. The massage, and his openness to the experience, had enabled him to contact a rich, warm memory.

Celia is a violinist and her work involves many hours of concentration while holding her body in the correct position for playing. Regular massage helps her to keep her body free and mobile, which means she enjoys her work more and plays better as well.

BENEFITS OF MASSAGE

As can be seen by these examples, sensitive massage can help people in many ways — physically, emotionally and mentally. The benefits that sensitive massage provides can be classified as: relaxation, nourishment and awareness. I'll now go into these in more detail.

Relaxation is the most obvious benefit and, in a world where many people are over stressed, the relaxation that massage provides is very important. Our bodies have two modes of physiological activity — active and resting. In the active mode the physiological priorities are for muscular activity, movement and strength, so that we can do things effectively in the world. In the resting mode the physiological priorities are for healing and repair of tissue, digestion of food, and elimination of waste materials, so that we restore and rejuvenate ourselves.

Sensitive massage is one way of providing deep relaxation, thereby shifting the body from the active to the resting mode. Of course there are many ways of relaxing, including meditation, stress management programmes, taking a bath, listening to some restful music or even taking a sedative! I like massage for relaxation because it's safe and natural, and requires no effort — I just lie there and someone else does all the work; the lazy person's way to relax!

But we have come a long way from the jungle in which our physiological systems evolved and with the noise and speed of traffic, telephones ringing, high pressure business and the many other stimuli which bombard our senses we often find it difficult to shift from the active mode to the resting mode. Under tension, our bodies age and decay much more rapidly than is natural. In the relaxed state the body heals and repairs itself and clears out the debris. There's also a feeling of cleaning out mental debris — I often find when I receive a massage that, as my worries and frustrations are soothed away, my mind becomes clearer and many creative thoughts and ideas float up to the surface.

One interesting phenomenon I've observed in my massage classes is the effect relaxing massage has on a person's energy level. After a day spent in a massage workshop, where the students give and receive relaxing massage in a friendly nurturing atmosphere, they come back the next day and usually report one of two experiences. Either they go home feeling pleasantly relaxed but very tired and go to bed early and sleep soundly, or else they go home feeling pleasantly relaxed but full of energy and spend the whole evening with friends, wining, dining and dancing into the early hours!

It seems that in the first case the relaxing massage peels off the surface layer of tension that somehow keeps them going while unaware of their real state, and underneath they discover how really tired they are, and how they really do need a rest, and are ready to take it. Any Sensitive Massage practitioner will tell you that it is a regular occurrence for highly tense people to fall asleep halfway through a good, relaxing massage.

In the second case the relaxation released energy that was locked in muscular tension and being wasted, and gave those people the feeling of abundant energy that was rightfully theirs.

Another benefit of the relaxation in massage is that it can become habitual. Usually after a good massage the recipient will feel relaxed, alive and happier than usual for several days afterward, then slowly the everyday tensions will creep back. But with the regular experience of relaxation, this relaxed, alive state becomes routine and debilitating tension becomes a rarity.

Apart from any other benefits the feeling of deep relaxation experienced in massage is rewarding in itself. The body feels loose, open to pleasure, supple, floating and there is a feeling of deep contentment. The mind drifts in and out of dreamy sleep and ideas and images float through the field of awareness. It is a feeling which is rarely experienced otherwise apart from, say, the post-orgasmic state, the time between contented sleep and waking, or the feeling of deep meditation — which are all experiences that approximate the relaxing massage experience.

Nourishment Massage provides physical and emotional nourishment. To live well we need not only the essential nutrients — food and water — but also pleasure and positive input. In fact there should be a balance in our lives between output and input. Output is the energy we give out to the world — cooking the meals, cleaning the house, answering the phone, doing work. Input is anything that feeds in to us, nourishes us, such as any physical or emotional pleasure, satisfaction gained from work done, and of course food and drink. Massage is a strong input: the recipient lies completely passive as the masseur feeds in pleasure, relaxation and caring. For people who feel they are giving out a lot to the world a regular massage helps to redress the balance.

Many of my clients are in the helping professions — doctors, psychologists and social workers — who in their work are constantly giving out and helping others with their problems. They find a massage lets them feel looked after for a change, and they go away feeling replenished and that they've then got more to give. (These helpers, I feel, are the enlightened ones in their professions. Unfortunately many in the helping professions are compulsive helpers. They always want to help others and not be helped themselves and inevitably they feel burnt out and resentful of those they help.)

Touching itself is an essential nutrient for living well. If this is not obvious enough, there are many scientific tests to prove it, from laboratory rats (those that are handled and stroked are healthier than those that receive no touching) through to human babies. As Dr Ashley Montagu mentions in his book *Touching*,

Dr. J. Brenneman established the rule in his hospital that every baby should be picked up, carried around and 'mothered' several times a day. At Bellevue Hospital in New York, following the institution of mothering on the pediatric wards, the mortality rates for infants under one year fell from 30 to 35 per cent to less than 10 per cent by 1938. What the child requires if it is to prosper, it was found, is to be handled, and carried, and caressed, and cuddled and cooed to.

A certain amount of caring touching is vital for adults as well, and sensitive massage is one powerful way of providing it.

Awareness Massage generates a tremendous awareness of the self. The masseur touches practically the whole surface of the body when doing a 'whole body' massage, and will squeeze and press into any tight spots where tension is being held. The recipient thus becomes aware of all the places he or she is holding tension. Many people get up from their massage saying 'I didn't realise how tense I was!' This is not

SENSITIVE MASSAGE

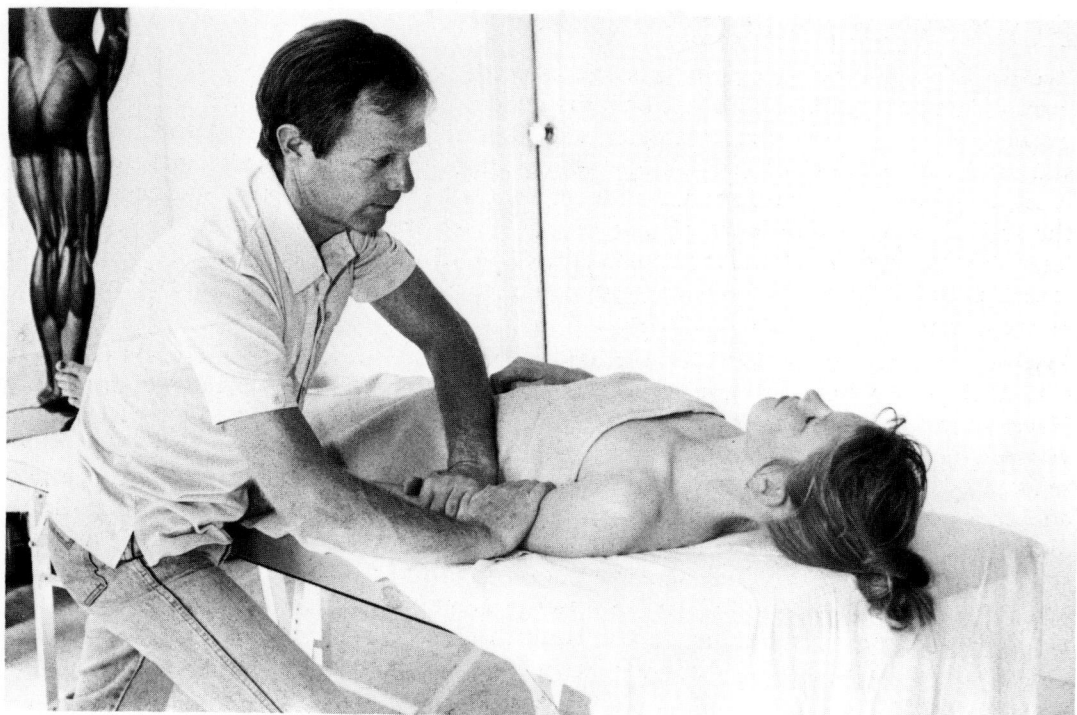

The arm being massaged

as discouraging as it sounds because through becoming aware of the tension areas the person is more conscious of tensing up in that area the next time it happens and can consciously let go of the tension, or change the situation causing it. For example George, a businessman, discovers during the massage that there is a lot of painful tension held in his shoulders. The massage helps to ease that tension and give him a feeling of looseness and ease in his shoulders. The next day while dealing with some problem in his work he notices the tension — which he was previously unaware of — returning to his shoulders and he realises he is responding to the problem by storing tension in his body. With this awareness George can choose to respond differently to the problem, in a way which will not damage himself.

Through skilled sensitive massage, deeper levels of awareness and understanding are also possible. Mary initially came for massage for the relaxation and nurturing, seeking a time in her busy life to simply be still. But she also found that the massage was helping her contact many vivid memories and feelings from her past. At one time as I massaged her foot she felt as if she were a baby and her foot was the rubbery and tiny foot of a baby. Each part of her body, when massaged, brought back feelings and images from particular times in her life. Mary found that what was happening now was a repeat of some circumstances in her earlier life, including childhood. The massage would bring to her awareness the early experiences, and give her a greater understanding of what was happening now.

So massage brings an increase in self-awareness, and this is a very powerful tool for living, as the more awareness and understanding of ourselves we have, the more information we have at our disposal when we make choices in our lives. These choices, in turn, can then be more positive and constructive.

HOW TO MASSAGE

I've listed the main benefits of massage as being relaxation, nourishment and awareness. There are, of course, further benefits I could have gone into, such as mobilisation of the body and alleviation of medical and psychological problems. However, at this stage it is important to present some practical suggestions on how to do massage. While it is not possible in a single chapter to present all the skills of professional massage, the following are some ideas to start with. These are usually contained in the first lesson of the Sensitive Massage course at my school, and will teach you a few practical massage techniques with which you can give some relaxation, nourishment and awareness to your friends and family.

Experiencing Touching For this activity, as with any massage, you should choose a time and place where you can work with a partner quietly and without disturbance. Have your partner lie face down on something soft, and get comfortable. Position yourself beside your friend and take a few moments to make yourself comfortable, relaxed and settled. Shake your hands loose so that you let go of any tension in them and then hold them, loose and relaxed, about an arm's length above your partner. Slowly, as if settling your hands into a pool of water without causing any disturbance to the water, let your hands float down to eventually rest gently on your partner's back and be still. Be aware of what you experience as you make contact. How do you feel, and how does your partner feel to you through the contact you have? Be aware of the contact between your hands and your partner's body. Similarly, your partner should be

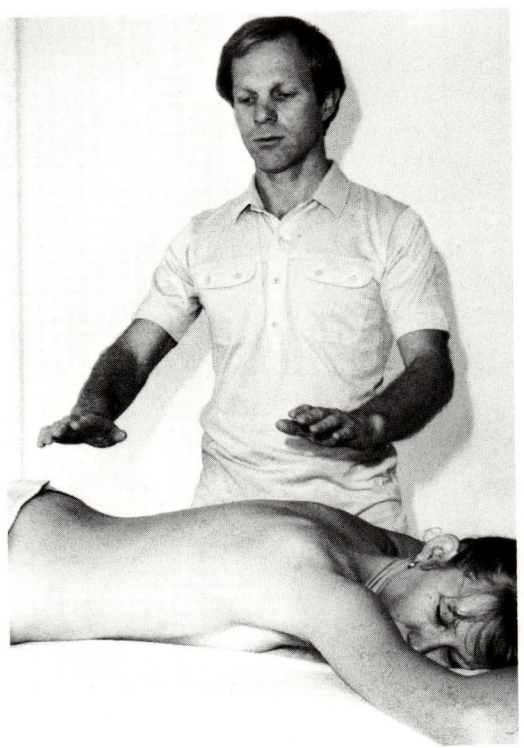

Floating the hands down to the body

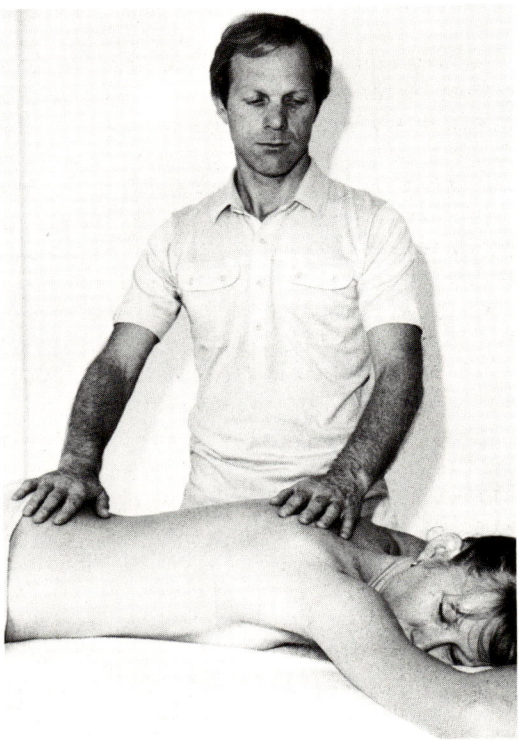

Making contact, being still . . .

SENSITIVE MASSAGE

aware of what he or she is experiencing — but don't talk. You can, and should discuss this afterwards, but don't distract your awareness now while you're doing this exercise.

After a minute or two slowly lift your hand away from your partner, floating up through the 'pool'. Once again, be aware of any changes as you break contact. For a further minute or two, both you and your partner should rest, relax and be aware of how you feel. Then you can discuss your experiences and if you wish, change places and do it again.

This may seem like a simple, or even trivial, exercise, but it is very useful for developing the sensitivity and awareness that is so important in massage. Students in our class report that they can sometimes feel the hands approaching and that there is a definite change in feeling when contact is made. Try it with a few different people, and notice how each person feels different under your hands.

Once you have explored this activity, use it as a way to start and finish a massage. Start by relaxing yourself, settling the hands slowly onto your partner, and being still. Then perform the massage, come to a finish by being still, float your hands away, and relax.

The Three Levels Practise this on a friend's arm or leg. Begin by making contact as described earlier, then start with a flowing stroking of the skin — slowly and smoothly as if warming the skin. Let you and your partner be aware of contours and textures of the arm or leg surface. This is a 'Level One' surface level stroke.

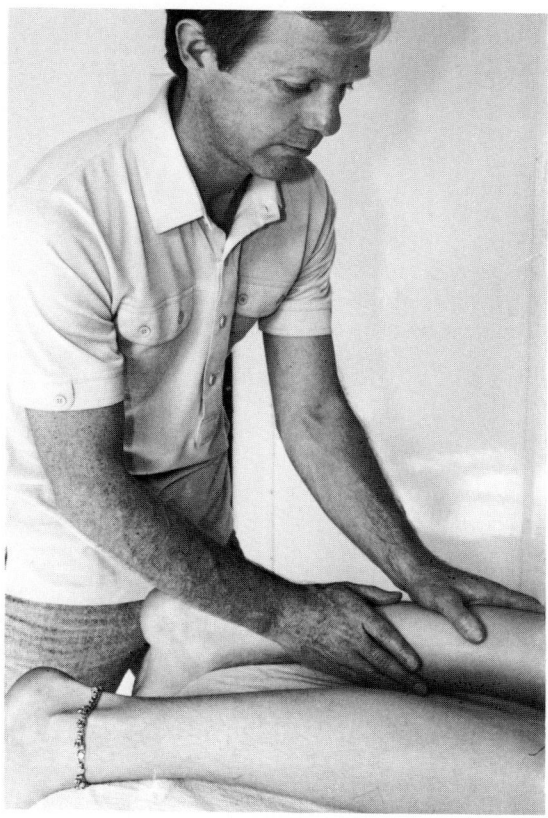

Level One: *surface stroking*

SENSITIVE MASSAGE

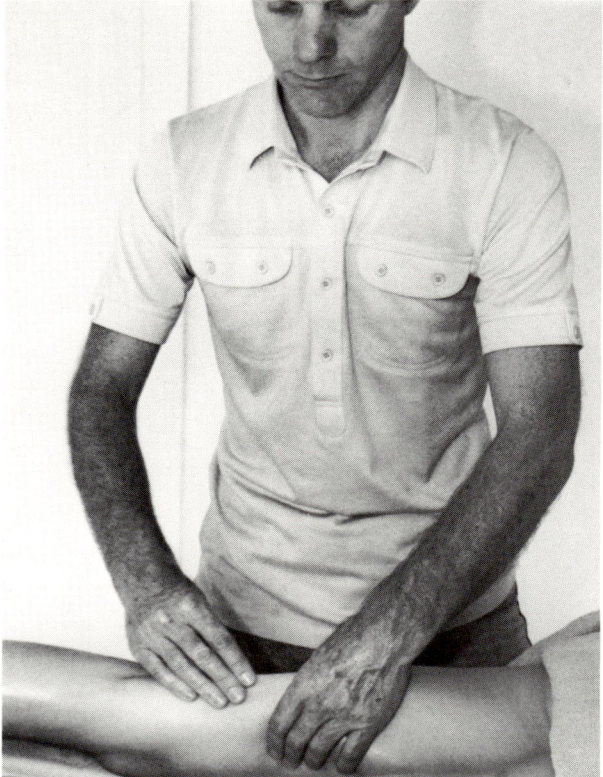

Level Two: *kneading*

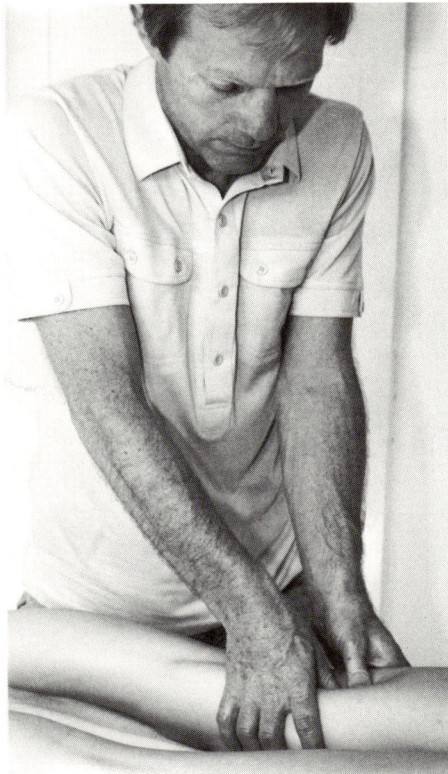

Level Three: *deep pressure*

Stay in contact the whole time and proceed now to knead and squeeze. Feel the muscles under the skin and imagine that they are like sponges — you are squeezing the moisture out of them, and then releasing to allow the moisture to flow back. Work smoothly and firmly, with broad pressure from the hands. This is the 'Level Two' intermediate level stroke. When you are first learning to massage ask your partner to tell you how firmly he or she wants to be squeezed.

'Level Three', the deep level, involves using your thumb or fingers (or even your knuckles, elbow, knee or foot!) to press firmly and deeply into the muscles. Levels One and Two have accustomed your partner to your touch, and warmed up the area ready for the deeper massage. Now begin to press in more deeply, aiming for a feeling of a satisfying deep massage of the muscles.

Caution With this deep massage, only press in to soft tissue that is yielding to your touch, and talk to your partner. Find out what feels good as you're doing it, and only do what feels comfortable. Never massage in a way that your partner doesn't like — the aim is to work in harmony with your partner, not to create discord. Pressing on tension areas may cause some pain, but it should be a comfortable pain that the recipient is able to relax into. If your partner is tensing up in response to the pressure, you are defeating the purpose of the massage. You need to lessen the pressure you are using or, if that's not the problem, ask your partner about the source of discomfort. Whether we are beginners or advanced masseurs, we all have a lot to learn from the recipients of our massage.

SENSITIVE MASSAGE

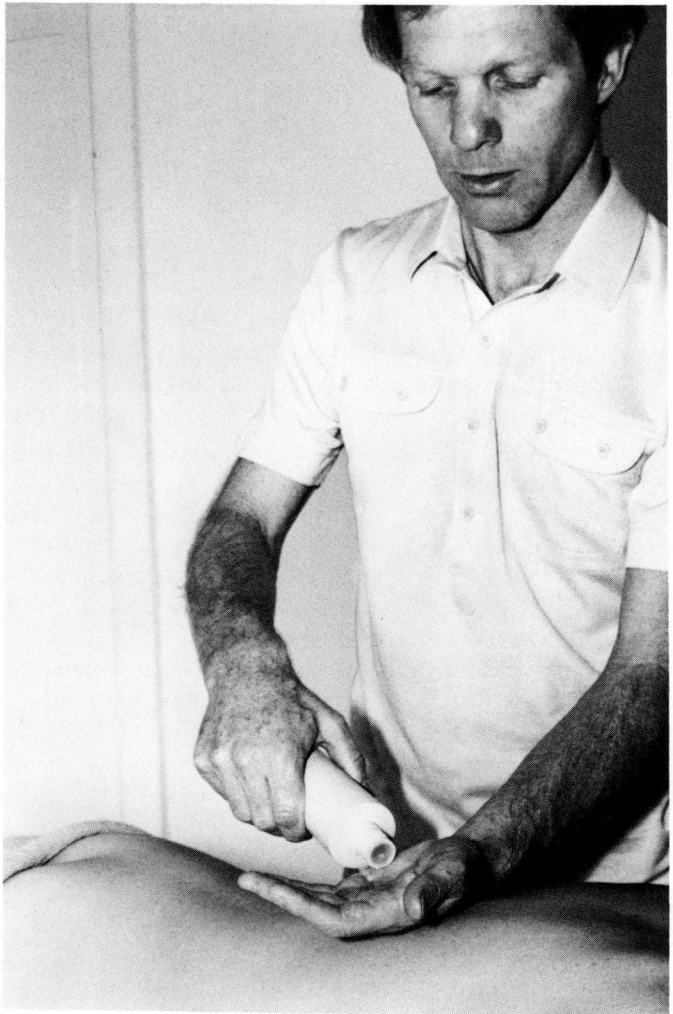

Pouring oil onto the hand while making contact

Having done some deep level massage, return to the Level One stroke to sooth and smooth out the person's arm or leg. Then come to a finish as described.

The first few times you try this, don't try to be fancy or impressive, simply do it to get the feeling of three levels of pressure, stroking all over the arm or leg, or any other fleshy part of the body, taking a minute or two at each level. You can then build up to doing a whole body massage, as the three levels work on all parts of the body, except for the face where it is best to use just the Level One stroking. Remember that different people and different parts of the body will tolerate different pressures, so be sensitive and aware of your partner's responses, and adjust your massage accordingly.

HINTS

1 Massage works best with some type of oil as a lubricant. You can use a vegetable oil with a few drops of essential oil, such as rose, jasmine or cinnamon, to give it a pleasant smell. Pour the oil onto your hands and then spread onto the body part you are massaging.

2 To do a whole body massage using the simple three level strokes, do one body part at a time. For example when doing the back of the body, begin by contacting the back, proceed through the three levels and then go back to Level One on the back. Pause a moment, flow down to a leg and massage it, pause and then flow onto the other leg and massage it in turn. Finish the whole back with a Level One stroke that flows over the whole length of the body, then finish as suggested. Ask your partner to rest for a minute or two, then turn over. Continue similarly on the front of the body.

3 Generally stroke or squeeze towards the heart, to assist the venous return of blood.

4 Maintain a continuity of contact, so that there is always some part of you touching your partner throughout the massage, apart from breaking contact when you finish one side and your partner turns over.

5 Enjoy it: make sure you are relaxed and comfortable and enjoying yourself while doing massage, and your partner will enjoy it too.

It has only been possible here to provide a brief outline of the benefits of sensitive massage and how to perform it. If you are seriously interested in massage I suggest you investigate the available publications on the subject and track down the local practitioners. Most districts have some professional masseurs and a school of massage. Your first step after all, should be to go and receive some professional massage. Remember, however, that massage is an intimate experience and you need to be sure that your masseur is someone you can trust and feel safe with. It is best if you have a friend who can personally recommend someone that they've had a massage from, but if that is not possible, look under 'Masseurs' in the telephone directory, talk to several, asking them what sort of massage they do, and then choose someone that you feel completely at ease with.

Massage is a wonderful gift to give yourself. If you have the time and money, and a skilled masseur you trust, then a massage every week is to be recommended. You will be rewarded with ever improving health, well-being and self-awareness.

CHAPTER 2
THE ALEXANDER TECHNIQUE
Jeremy Chance

'I consider that Alexander's work is probably one of the most underrated achievements of the 20th century. I think it is surprising how relatively unknown and unrecognised it is, because I am convinced that it will prove to be as important to humanity as the work of Newton, of Einstein and particularly of Darwin.'

W. H. M. Carrington
Centenary Memorial lecture in honour of F. M. Alexander, 1969

'This story of perceptiveness, of intelligence and of persistence, shown by a man without medical training, is one of the true epics of medical research and practice.'

Professor N. Tinbergen
The Nobel Prize Oration for Medicine, 1973

The Alexander Technique offers an unusual experience. It comes to us from an even more unusual man — an actor and scientist whom many now consider to be one of the great thinkers of our time. And yet many more, unfamiliar with his work, find him an enigma — was he a true scientist or simply a charismatic actor with a few bold ideas? Perhaps he was both. The answer lies in his discovery, a discovery that is drawing increasing attention from all those who are concerned with achieving better health for the human being. For Alexander's Technique can help us achieve a state of health and well-being that some of us still dream of.

AN ALEXANDER LESSON

The experience of this now deceased man comes to us in a short 30 minute activity called an 'Alexander lesson'. Our 'Alexander' teacher will have completed a full-time three-year training consisting almost entirely of practical work: for 1600 hours the training student will have practised and perfected an activity, either alone or with their teacher, as simple as getting in and out of a chair. For 60 years Alexander taught the likes of Lillie Langtry, George Bernard Shaw, Aldous Huxley and John Dewey what was involved in this so seemingly simple activity. It is not simply how to get in and out of a chair that is the object of all this attention, but how to bring 400 million years of postural development under our conscious direction.

Alexander taught good body use. His technique, based on a concept of mind-body unity, involves becoming aware of those habits that disturb our poise. The immediate effect of undoing these harmful and unnecessary habits will be an overall improvement in the way you move: with increasing lightness, fewer aches and enhanced fluidity. You are being taught to respond to gravity with greater ease.

ALEXANDER'S BACKGROUND

Alexander was born in Tasmania in 1869. A poor constitution in his early years, a bad temper and a precocious intelligence led to his removal from the village school and he was subsequently taught privately by an old Scottish schoolmaster. It was through him that Alexander began his lifelong passion for Shakespeare which in turn drew him to a career in the theatre by the time he was in his early teens.

From his earliest days Alexander showed considerable dynamism and determination — he worked hard from the age of 16 to 19 in order to save enough to move to Melbourne and begin his professional training as an actor. Within six months he had formed an amateur dramatic company while taking lessons in elocution, dramatic art and the violin. He soon had his career on a professional footing and it was then that the first stirrings of an ugly problem with far reaching implications began to interfere with his success. Time and time again Alexander would have to cut short, postpone or cancel a performance due to hoarseness in his voice. With typical determination, and failing to gain outside help, Alexander initiated a long series of experiments and observations of himself and so, over a ten year period, the 'Alexander Technique' was born.

When Alexander set out on his task he had very little to go on. His one observation had been that, while his voice worsened while he was reciting, it improved during the periods when he was not performing. On the strength of this he decided to observe himself — first while speaking, then while reciting — to see if he could detect any differences between the two. He soon noticed that, in response to the idea of using his voice, he brought into play a whole series of muscular contractions around the neck and head which were more pronounced during reciting than they were during speaking. He experimented by changing these patterns but found this more difficult than he had originally anticipated. Through careful observation he concluded that while he could change these patterns by doing more — that is, increasing the tension — it did not help him. Relief only came about by doing less, but this proved far more difficult to achieve. The real problem, he slowly realised, was that he felt impelled to make all these movements with his head and neck when all the evidence of observation suggested that they were harmful. It is a conflict we have all faced when trying to change harmful habits: we can consciously realise that our habit is doing us harm and yet we still keep doing it because our feelings impel us to. We must recognise that we need to change our experience of the habit but this is hard because our experience of the moment is totally contrary to doing that. 'You can't change a thing by an instrument that is wrong', Alexander once said. He felt this was due to the faulty sensory perception of ourselves, that what we feel is right may only be what is *habitual* to us and not necessarily what is *good* for us.

Alexander coined the phrase 'faulty sensory perception' to describe this phenomenon, and this concept is central to an understanding of the Alexander Technique. A simple way of illustrating the concept is to try the following experiment: Stand with your eyes closed and, place the legs so that the sides of the feet are parallel to each other without touching. Nine times out of ten, people are unable to do this because their *feeling* is that their feet are pigeon-toed when in fact they are parallel. This illustrates

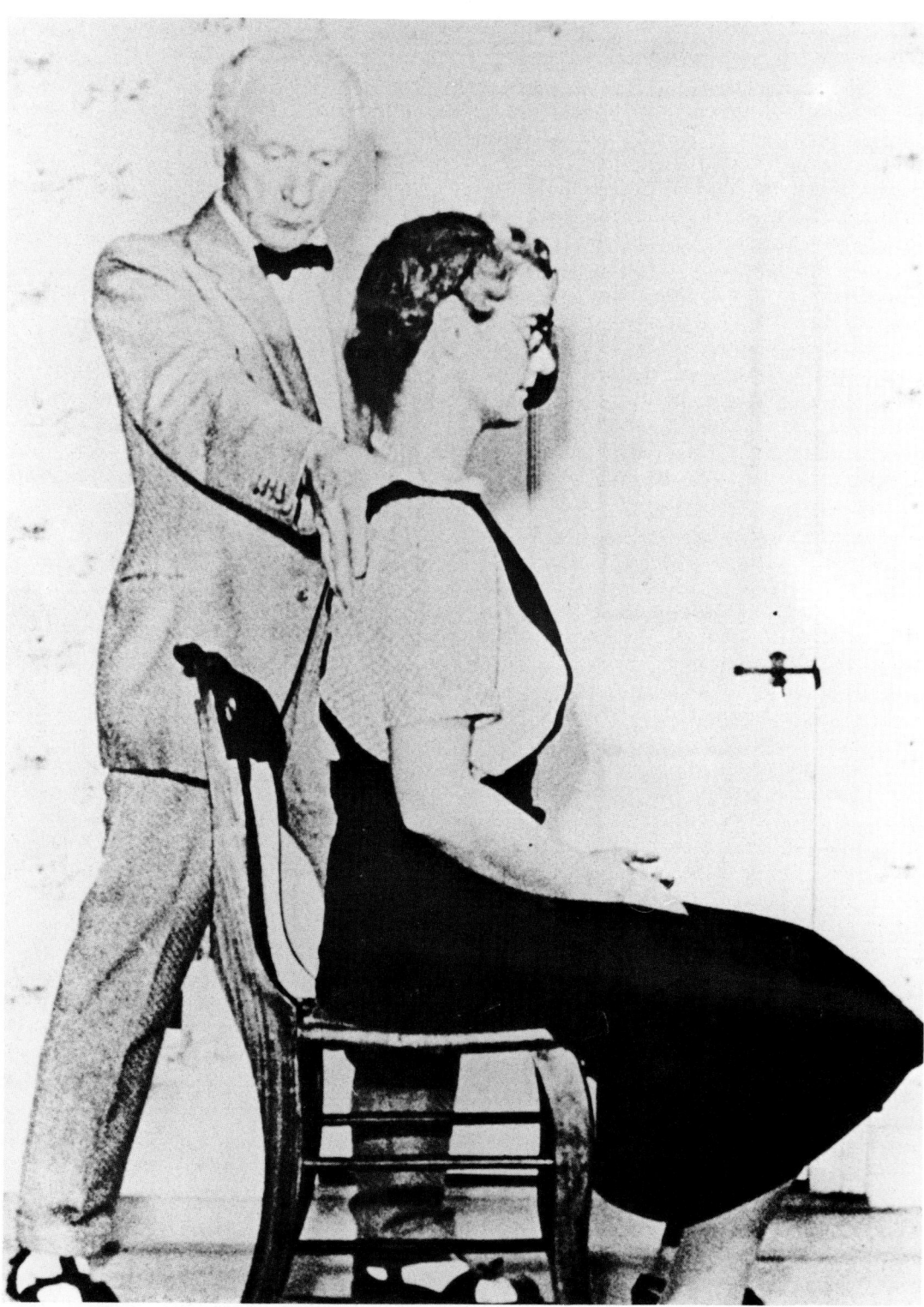

Plate 1 *Alexander at work*

in a minor way the same faulty sensory perception of ourselves that can lead to unwarranted neurotic tendencies and harmful habits that we find ourselves unable to change.

When Alexander began to teach he realised that this discovery of the faulty sensory perception of ourselves meant that he would have to devise a direct means, through the use of his hands, for providing his pupils with an experience of the new body use that he was advocating. The change that took place in them could be totally unexpected and quite at odds with their idea of what was necessary to achieve 'good posture' in themselves. For this reason Alexander developed a non-verbal 'hands-on' technique for changing bad habits of body use and it is this unique touch that is the hallmark of the modern Alexander teacher.

In the beginning it was an accident that Alexander ever taught at all. It was not his original intention to teach but even the early results of his investigation — his improved body stature, voice and breath control — had provoked the attention of his peers, who were curious to know how he had brought about such improvement. Within three weeks of setting up practice Alexander was teaching nine hours a day and within three years he had pupils who were prominent in the fields of medicine, law, religion, government, education and, of course, the stage. By this time it was clear that Alexander had discovered something of universal importance. With the special encouragement of Dr McKay, a man with an international reputation at the time, and the added assistance of £750 won on a horse, Alexander left Australia in 1904 bound for London and keen to introduce to the world his revolutionary discovery.

In those days, a lesson with Alexander was a curious affair. You were expected to take at least 30 lessons, and often more if yours was a serious problem. He would see you daily for two months, then less frequently until such time that he considered that you possessed sufficient understanding to carry on using yourself in an improved manner. Regardless of your particular 'problem' he would insist that he was not curing you; that this was an education not a treatment; that you were a pupil not a patient.

The lesson itself, though designed in part to redistribute your muscular effort, involved no exercises. Alexander was always against 'postural' exercises. He insisted that a 'postural' problem was never simply caused by a weakness in a certain group of muscles but that that weakness was in itself caused by a misuse of the way a person was generally co-ordinating themselves *as a whole*. What use then, he argued, in exercising a specific group of muscles if we continued to co-ordinate ourselves in the same bad old way as we did it!

Alexander mounted many criticisms of the medical profession because he considered that they did not take into account the way a person used themselves as a whole when diagnosing and treating disorder and disease. His constant attacks did not win him many friends, yet there was a small but significant minority of doctors who began to realise the soundness of his approach. In 1937, nineteen of them signed a letter that was published in the British Medical Association's Journal *The Lancet*:

We are convinced that Alexander is justified in contending that 'an unsatisfactory manner of use, by interfering with general functioning, constitutes a predisposing cause of disorder and disease,' and that diagnosis of a patient's troubles must remain incomplete unless the medical man, when making the diagnosis, takes into consideration the influence of use upon functioning.

THE ROLE OF 'USE'

Alexander developed a concept of 'use' over his sixty years of teaching which implies an understanding that we are whole, indivisible beings. Our 'use' of ourselves is built up over many years. Our environment, our early relationships, our hopes and disappointments, all have a place in developing that particular walk of ours, the way we laugh and hold our head — all the unique characteristics that form our personality. 'Talk about a man's individuality and character — it's the way he uses himself,' Alexander would say. The tendency to treat our problems as separate things that afflict us is a dangerous thread that weaves its way insidiously through the fabric of Western society. Normally we would never make a statement like 'I am giving my back problems' but rather blame the back instead, complaining 'My back is giving me problems'!

In his lessons, Alexander would ask his pupils to become aware of what they were doing to themselves as they got in and out of a chair. You can try observing this for yourself. Begin by sitting in a chair with the posture illustrated in Plate 1. Ask someone to observe closely what movement is occurring in the head/neck area whilst you are standing up from a chair. Ensure that you have devised a very reliable means, either through the use of two mirrors or another, sharp-eyed person, to detect any movement of the head and neck in relation to each other and both in relation to the torso. Observe both *carefully* and *patiently* for as many times as is necessary to arrive at one of the following three choices:

DURING THE MOVEMENT

1 neither the head nor the neck moves in relation to each other, nor do they move in relation to the torso. (Plate 2)

2 the head remains in its starting relationship to the neck but both head and neck drop forward and down in relation to the torso. (Figure 1)

3 the head tilts backwards in relation to the neck while the neck drops forward and down in relation to the torso. (Figure 2)

For the majority the result will fall into either the second or third categories but very rarely the first. You may have been able to assume a movement which seems to look the same as the movement illustrated in Plate 2 but your effort to do so might well involve more tension than when you stand up ordinarily. Herein lies the secret of the Alexander Technique and the thing most difficult to communicate by the written word. The Technique teaches you something about your posture that any number of photographs showing the 'right' and 'wrong' way could not. When you try to copy a posture illustrated by a photograph or through the written word the thing that you will

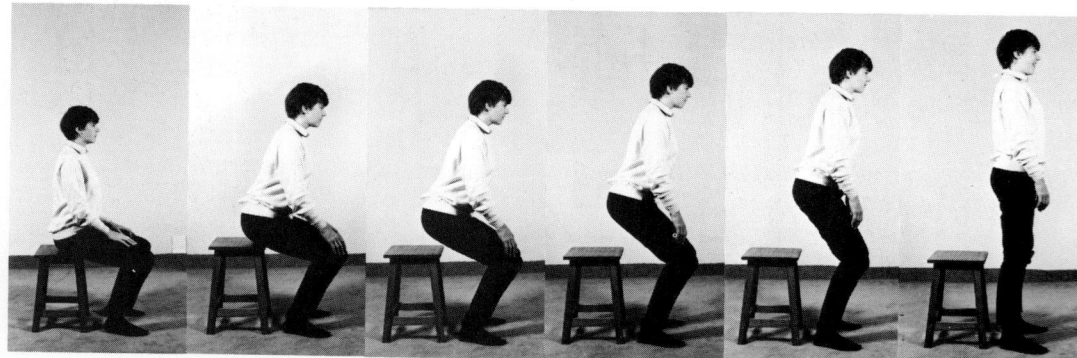

Plate 2 *This pictorial sequence shows good body-use in motion*

not be taking into account is the 'instrument' that is guiding your body musculature to do what you ask of it. This 'instrument' is the sensory appreciation of what your body is doing, and is more commonly known as the kinaesthetic sense. A bad 'instrument' will accept high levels of tension as normal, will accept a twisted spine as straight or a raised shoulder as level. Before making any change in the outer external shape of yourself a subtle, inner change must first occur. So if you ask yourself 'How can I bring myself into an erect posture when my inner perception of it is a crooked one?' you should recall Alexander's teaching. 'Sensory appreciation conditions conception — you can't know a thing by an instrument that is wrong.'

Much of our early life is involved with destroying the reliability of this instrument. At school we soon know what it means to curb our free inquiring spirit and sit and learn many things which we would not, by choice, be interested in. Boredom is the frequent result of this schooling process and boredom leads to a collapse in our posture and a deadening of our senses. Soon our spine no longer knows how to function in the upright position and slumping becomes normal. Finally we find ourselves leaning on our elbows, crossing our legs and fidgeting about uncomfortably as we try to study. Reading and writing also contribute to this misuse as evidenced by the boy in Plate 3(a). The end result is a poor state of co-ordination. As we grow older we load our weakened system with the stress of having to do well, of dealing with our awakening sexuality, of having to cope in a world where love is very often hard to come by. This all combines to distort the original harmony and grace of our uprightness, replacing it with a new guiding 'instrument' that bases its function on all the erroneous and unconscious tensions that we have acquired during our early years. It is this 'instrument' that guides us in our attempts to copy 'good posture', ensuring that our attempts will be misguided ones. The Alexander Technique restores the reliability of this sensory 'instrument' through a direct experiential process. (Plates 4 and 5)

Plate 3   *(a) Poor adaptation to the requirements of study   (b) Taking a sensible approach*

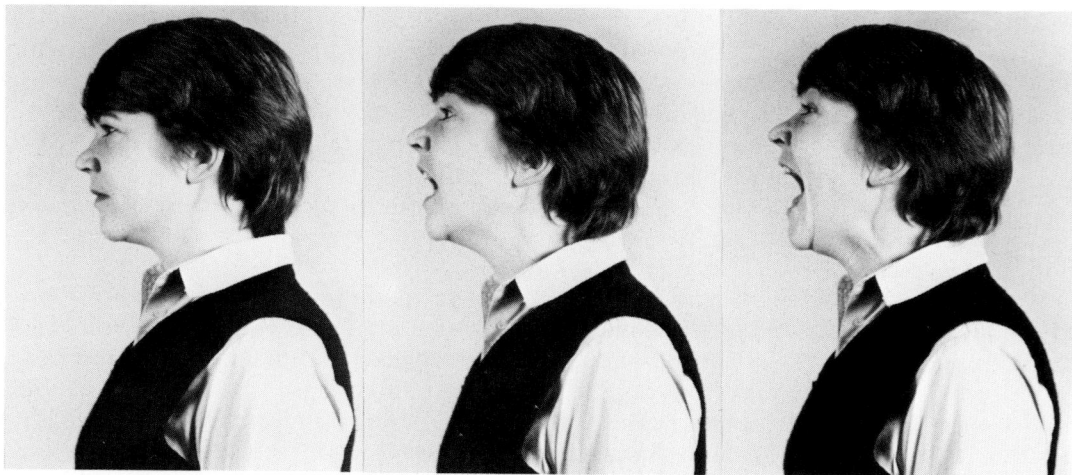

Plate 4 *The tendency to pull the head back on the neck is one of the primary features of misuse*

SELF-AWARENESS OF THE BODY

Restoring a reliable picture of ourselves is the first task of the Alexander teacher. To do this it is necessary first to become aware of the tensions, twists and distortions that already exist in us. We may know intellectually and visually that we have a twist but it is a very different thing to *feel* this kinaesthetically, to know in our bodies what it is that we are doing. Very often we simply don't stop long enough to observe ourselves, so intent are we on getting a good result. It was Alexander's chief complaint about the Western approach to postural defects that when a thing was wrong we set out to find something that we could do to make it right. Surely, he argued, if a thing is wrong then it will be because we are doing something to interfere, so that we must first discover what that is and stop doing it!

Much of Alexander's work during the initial ten years of observing and experimenting with his own body was concerned with discovering how he interfered with the balanced relationships between different parts of his body as he spoke or when he was at rest. This did not involve finding the right 'position' or 'posture' (Alexander avoided the use of those words) but finding the right tendencies for our busy musculature while standing, sitting, or moving. For Alexander, this implied that, whatever we are doing, as long as we are even partially upright we are always involved in a process of balancing ourselves within the gravitational sphere. We are never in a fixed position. Practically, to achieve this subtle inner balancing in the relationship of all our moving parts, Alexander would first restore a good relationship between the head, neck and back. He named this relationship the Primary Control mechanism and maintained that unless a good relationship was restored between these parts they would continue to adversely affect the posture generally.

THE 'PRIMARY CONTROL' AND 'STARTLE PATTERN'

Alexander discovered this when, as an actor, he had begun to meticulously observe the way he used his voice to find a solution to his hoarseness. What he initially observed

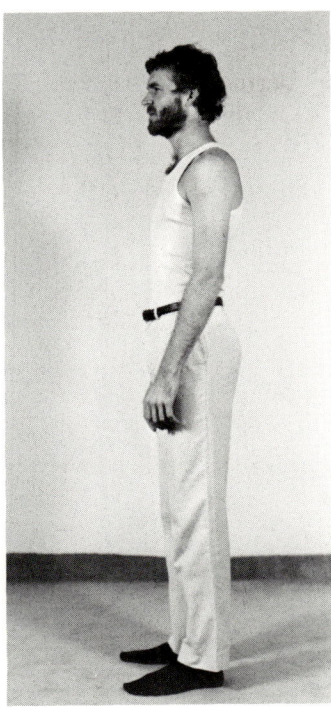

Plate 5 *Subject standing in a balanced way*

was a retraction of the head on the spine as illustrated in Plate 6. Watch yourself or a partner yelling and see if this is also the case with you — for ninety percent of the time this will be what is happening. The tendency to pull back the head from the neck is one of the primary features of misuse. It happens not simply while we yell or speak but, as Alexander discovered, it is a universal constant occurring while we sit, stand, walk, eat, sleep, work and play in our everyday lives.

It is an ancient response to stress, evidenced in most mammals and associated with fear called the fight-or-flight response. Anyone who has sat through a Hitchcock movie has experienced this response in themselves. It also occurs when we are bored or depressed. It is operating when people remark 'you look down to-day' — our head and neck are quite literally pushing us down. Eventually it ceases to be a response to events outside us and becomes a continuous harmful habit inside us, a habit very difficult to reverse. Alexander taught that a consideration of this 'Primary Control' mechanism was vital when approaching any problem brought on, or aggravated by, postural defects.

The 'startle pattern' is associated with the fight-or-flight response (Plate 6) and is the classic manifestation of a misuse pattern in the Primary Control. It is never the same from one individual to the next and yet for each individual it will closely correspond to their own patterns of misuse. Compare the posture of the man in Plate 5 with that of Plate 6. In Plate 5 he is standing in a position of balance, in Plate 6 we note his reaction to a starting pistol. A condition of poise and balance has been instantaneously transformed into one of stress and contraction. This is an extreme example of misuse and it is not always as evident to the unskilled eye. However, for most of us it is always there, subtly and constantly exerting an influence for the worse on the general gait by compressing our spines, reducing our thoracic capacity for the intake of air, pushing

THE ALEXANDER TECHNIQUE

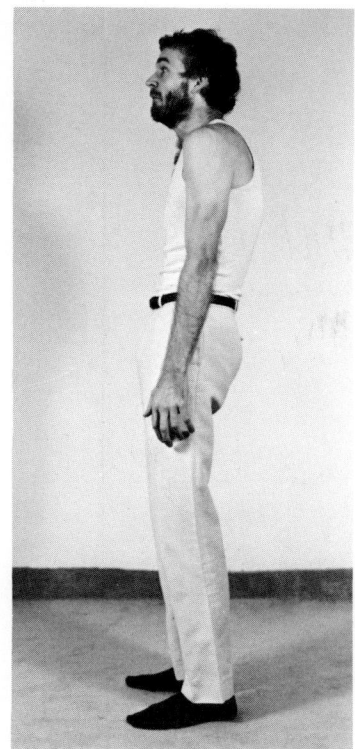 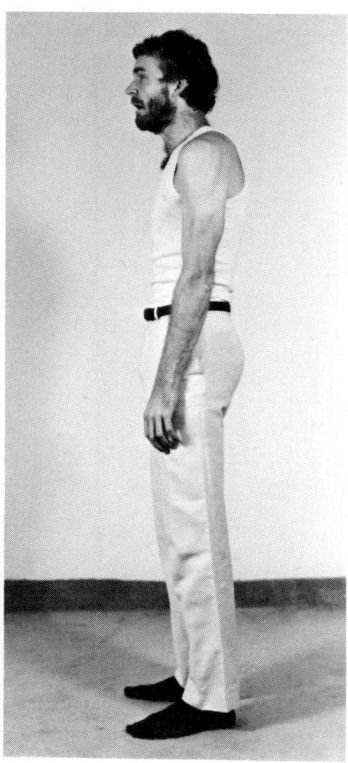

Plate 6 *Subject's reflex reaction to an unexpected noise, with the head and neck initiating the response*

down into our abdomens and causing a general increase of tension throughout our bodies. Stopping this response, at will, is extremely difficult and sometimes may produce fixed, stiff-necked 'Alexandroids' who are trying to *do* something which should be the result of *undoing*. Those people are thinking in terms of the right position rather than the right condition, which is that the neck should be free and the head light. If you experiment with this, bear in mind the principle of *non-doing* which must underline your approach.

THE AFTERMATH OF THE 'STARTLE PATTERN'

The pattern of misuse initiated by the 'startle pattern' (Plate 6) does not end in the Primary Control area but ripples on down the body — distorting the shoulders and arms, shortening the length of the torso, and increasing the tension in the legs. Initially the effect is transmitted through the spine and can result in an increasing curvature taking any of three general forms — 1. Lordosis (Figure 3) 2. Kyphosis (Figure 4) or 3. Scoliosis (Figure 5). Normally the curvature is a combination of all three whether slight or serious. It is at this point that it becomes difficult to ascertain what it is that we must 'undo' in our body musculature to create more poise and freedom in our movements. The possible variations of these three conditions of the spine, in combination with the misuses of the Primary Control, are virtually limitless — and we have not yet even begun to consider the effects that the arms and legs will also be having on the whole.

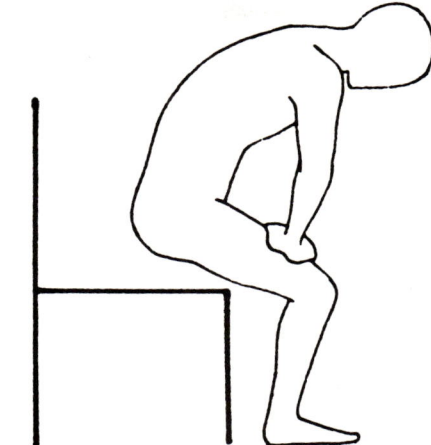

Figure 1 Dropping the head and neck

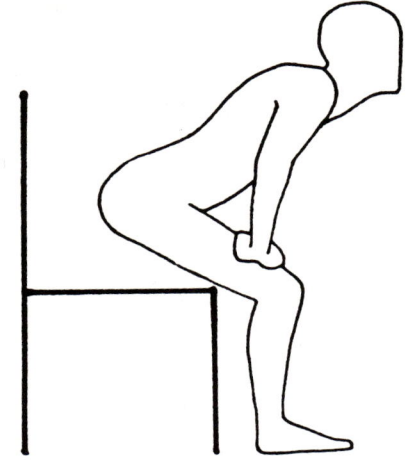

Figure 2 Pulling the head back on the neck

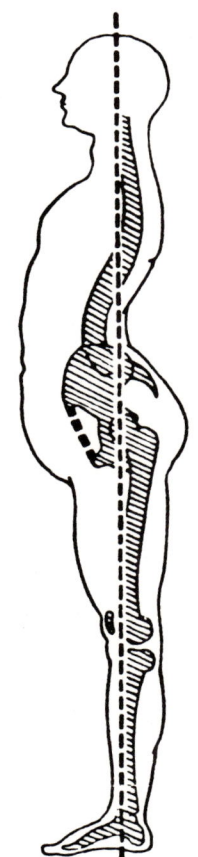

Figure 3 Hollow back, or lordosis

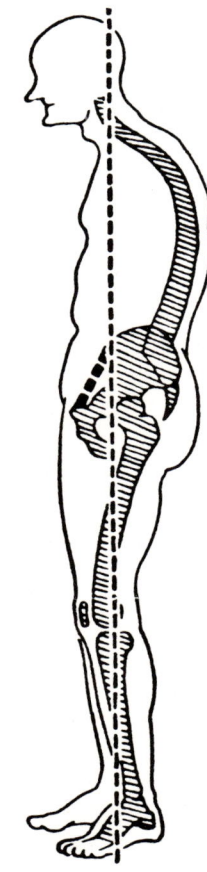

Figure 4 Round back, or kyphosis

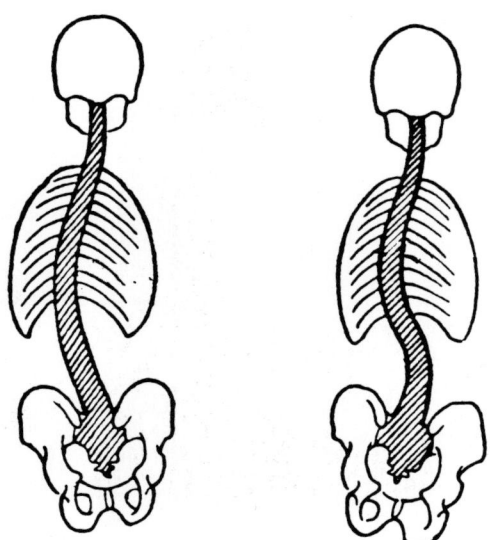

Figure 5 Two types of scoliosis

SEMI-SUPINE POSITION

Where specialist help is not available there is one procedure that can benefit enormously if practised regularly and that is to lie in the semi-supine position (Plate 13). In this position gravity realigns the body. There are three particular points to make about the physical orientation of this position:

1 The head has been placed on a pile of books, not a cushion. This is to give firm support to the head and bring both it and the neck into a normal relationship to the body. The height depends very much on the roundedness of the upper spine and shoulders. To assess the correct height of the books stand in your 'normal' posture against a wall and have a friend measure the distance between the back of your head and the wall. This should roughly equal the height that the books should be.

2 The legs are bent up — this is to relieve pressure on the lower back and is essential if any benefit is to be obtained. The legs should be positioned so there is no strain in keeping them there — if there is a strain, or if they are constantly falling out, the solution is either to knock-knee them in slightly, or to place a very large cushion under each knee.

3 The hands are placed separately on each side of the torso roughly at hip level. This is better than having them stretched out full length by the side, since it reduces drag on the shoulders.

The aim of the semi-supine position is to lengthen and open out our tightened bodies. It is therefore important that we pay some attention to *how* to lie down in the first place. To begin, place the books behind you on a firm surface (not a bed) and stand the distance of your body length away from them. Drop down onto one knee and then the other (Plate 7). From this kneeling position sit back on the legs (Plate 8). Sit with your legs to one side, placing both arms behind the hip joints to give some support to the weight of the back (Plate 9). Bend the knees, bringing the heels up close to the buttocks (Plate 10), giving full support for the back through the two arms. The heels should not

THE ALEXANDER TECHNIQUE

Plate 7 *Plate 8* *Plate 9*

Plate 10 *Plate 11*

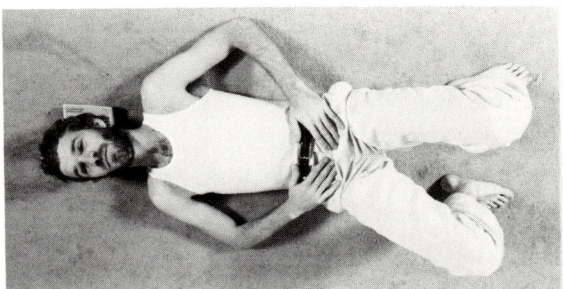

Plate 12

Plates 7–12 *Give attention to the means by which you arrive in the semi-supine position*

Plate 13 *Semi-supine position*

be close together but apart as they would be when one is standing (Plate 11). Finally, roll down onto the books, dropping the head from the top joint of the spine just before you do and imagine a lengthening effect through the whole torso as you allow the spine to make contact with the ground (Plate 12).

If this has been done well the back should now be firmly in contact with the floor. Sometimes there may be a slight arch in the lower back. In this case do not attempt to push the lower back down — the principle remains to *undo* the wrong, not to *do* the right — but let gravity slowly do its work as you think of lengthening along this area. Once down keep the eyes open: this encourages a wakeful kind of awareness. You can now begin to become aware of the following areas:

1 Allow the full weight of the head to drop onto the books. Imagine a softening of all the muscles around the head, neck and shoulders.

2 While remaining aware of this Primary Control area, begin to think of releasing along the two columns of muscle on either side of the spine.

3 While allowing the back to continue lengthening and broadening, open out any tightening that you may feel in the front of the torso from the tummy to the throat. Allow the front to be supported down into the back.

4 Continue with the previous procedures and become aware of your arms connecting through the shoulders and into the back. The weight of the arms can be allowed to drop down through the elbows to the ground.

5 While continuing to be aware of all the previous suggestions imagine releasing along the legs from the back to the knees. You could imagine a line passing out through the knees and into the sky so that the legs are releasing out of the tummy and lower back — the whole midriff area.

The semi-supine position should be attempted daily for 10 to 15 minutes. It is better to do it towards the end of the day as this is when our spines are most tired and strained. If we follow this procedure faithfully we can restore some health to our old and aching spines.

THE PRACTITIONER

The Alexander Technique heralds a new kind of practitioner that defies comparison with other exponents of bodywork and is only truly understood through a direct 'hands on' experience. This experience involves linking the nervous system of the teacher with that of the pupil and in the process the pupil experiences a restoration of the anti-gravity reflexes. The effects are often pleasant, involving a reduction of general tension and an increase in height and breadth. Breathing becomes fuller and indirectly all the systems of the body, from digestion to circulation, are given a better context in which to perform their various functions.

The Alexander teacher also conforms to the old adage 'Physician, heal thyself', for the training of Alexander teachers is centred almost completely on the improvement of their own use. It is only by improving *themselves* that they will be able to pass on this improvement through their teaching hands. The Alexander Technique is a kinaesthetic re-education of postural mechanisms that is effected through a conscious process of observation and change under the direction of teaching hands. The teacher is trained to a high standard, yet the Technique is so simple in its approach that its form is easily counterfeited. Be wary of those who claim to teach it, and they are many, and ensure that they have completed the full-time three year training.* Much of the subtlety and content of a trained teacher's hands are not so easily duplicated by the novice of 30-odd lessons or more.

Alexander teachers are destined to multiply rapidly as the Technique approaches its first century of healthy existence. Alexander has taught us how to use the powers of our conscious minds to master and direct the use of ourselves. It is not a cure-all or panacea but an organised, common-sense method of restoring better practical use of the human instrument that is Nature's gift to us all.

---

* For details of available training in the Alexander Technique see 'A Note on Contributors'.

CHAPTER 3

THE TRAGER APPROACH: Psychophysical Integration and Mentastics

Deane Juhan

'There is no tracking until the pupil is brought into the same state or principle in which you are; there is a teaching, and by no unfriendly chance or bad company can he ever quite lose the benefit.'

Ralph Waldo Emerson

Trager Psychophysical Integration was the discovery of a single individual, Milton Trager, M.D. He first encountered its simple principles and its surprising effects intuitively, and almost accidentally, at the age of 18. He then spent the next 50 years, first as a lay practitioner and later as a medical professional, expanding and refining his discovery. This long and successful career as a therapist was behind him before he tried to teach anyone his innovative form of bodywork, so that in spite of its almost silent incubation and development, Dr Trager's work reached his first students at a very ripe stage, with a wide variety of demonstrably successful applications.

Dr Trager's manner of manipulating the body is not a technique or a method, in the sense that there are no rigid procedures which are claimed to produce specific symptomatic results. There is no formula, no recipe, no standardised practical procedure. Rather, it is an *approach*, a way of learning and of teaching movement re-education. He stresses that his patients should come to him ready to absorb a lesson, instead of ready to simply receive a treatment. His concern is not with moving particular muscles or joints *per se*, but with using motion in muscles and joints to produce particular sensory feelings — positive, pleasurable feelings which enter the central nervous system and begin to trigger tissue changes by means of the many sensory-motor feedback loops between the mind and the muscles.

The Trager therapist does not change the condition of tissue with his hands but uses the hands to communicate a quality of feeling to the nervous system, and this feeling then elicits tissue response within the patient. When a body *feels* lighter, it begins to stand and to move as though it *were* lighter.

THE ELEMENTS OF A TRAGER SESSION

A session of Trager Psychophysical Integration takes from 1 to 1½ hours. No oils or lotions are used. The client wears swim trunks or briefs and lies on a well-padded table in a warm, comfortable environment. During the session, the practitioner makes touch-contact with the body of the client — both as a whole and in its individual parts

THE TRAGER APPROACH

Milton Trager, M.D.

— in such a gentle and rhythmic way that the person lying passively on the table actually experiences the possibility of being able to move each part of the body freely, effortlessly, and gracefully on his own. The practitioner works in a relaxed meditative state of consciousness which Dr Trager calls 'hook-up'. This state allows the practitioner to connect deeply with the recipient in an unforced way, to remain continually aware of the slightest responses, and to work efficiently without fatigue. After getting up from the table, the client is given some instruction in the use of 'Mentastics', a system of simple, effortless movement sequences developed by Dr Trager to maintain and even enhance the sense of lightness, freedom, and flexibility that were instilled by the table work. 'Mentastics' is Dr Trager's coinage for 'mental gymnastics' — a 'mindfulness in motion' — designed to help his patients recreate for themselves the sensory feelings produced by the motion of their tissue in the practitioner's hands. It is a powerful means of teaching the patient to recall the pleasurable sensory state which produced positive tissue change, and because it is this *feeling* state which triggered positive tissue response in the first place, every time the feeling is clearly recalled the changes deepen, become more permanent, and more receptive to further positive change. It is evident, based upon most recipients' experiences, that the effects of a Trager session penetrate below the level of conscious awareness and continue to produce positive results long after the session itself. Changes described have included the disappearance of specific symptoms, discomforts, or pains, heightened levels of energy and vitality, more effortless posture and carriage, greater joint mobility, deeper states of relaxation than were previously possible, and a new ease in daily activities.

THE TRAGER APPROACH

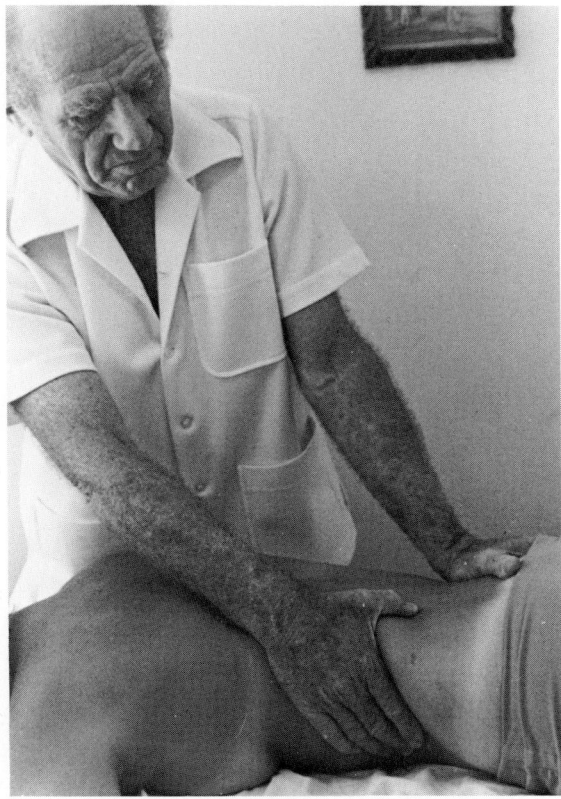

*'When a body **feels** lighter, it begins to stand and to move as though it **were** lighter'.*

And because these benefits are cumulative, the results of a learning process, patients often profit considerably from a series of sessions or from occasional 'reminders'.

Unlike the many forms of massage, the Trager Approach uses no oils or lotions, no long, broad strokes over the surface of the body. Unlike various techniques of deep-tissue manipulation, it does not utilise extreme pressures or rapid thrusts to create structural change, and it does not produce pain as a necessary adjunct to its effectiveness. Unlike many movement re-education therapies, the patient has no task to perform, but rather becomes increasingly passive to the steady, rhythmic motions imparted by the practitioner's hands. But perhaps what most distinguishes Tragering from other bodywork disciplines is the particular focus and intent of the Trager practitioner's manipulations. Most other methods direct their attention to one or another of the body's tissues — the skin, the fascia, the muscles, the joints, the lymph and blood circulation, overall structural relationships, and so on — and the various properties of these tissues determine the sort of touch and manipulation required by the practitioner. But even though his hands must inevitably contact them when he works, Dr Trager's focus and intent are not specifically directed towards local conditions in any of these tissues. As Dr Trager says,

My work is directed towards reaching the unconscious mind of the patient. Every move, every thought communicates how the tissue should feel when everything is right. The mind is the whole thing, that is all I am interested in. I am convinced that

THE TRAGER APPROACH

for every physical non-yielding condition there is a psychic counterpart in the unconscious mind, corresponding exactly to the degree of the physical manifestation. Tragering consists of the use (not the laying on) of the hands to influence deep-seated psycho-physiological patterns in the mind, and to interrupt their projection into the body's tissues. These patterns often develop in response to adverse circumstances such as accidents, surgery, illness, poor posture, emotional trauma, stresses of daily living, or poor movement habits. The purpose of my work is to break up these sensory and mental patterns which inhibit free movement and cause pain and disruption of normal function. My approach is to impart to the patient what it is like to feel right in the sense of a functionally integrated body-mind. Since the inhibiting patterns are affected at the source — the mind — the patient can experience long-lasting benefits. The result is general functional improvement.

This is to say that rather than working for local tissue changes which eventually accumulate to influence physical and mental function, the Trager Approach seeks to specifically influence the feeling states in the sensory and the unconscious elements of the mind which most directly control tissue response, metabolism, postural habits, and behavioural patterns. Of course, as with all other kinds of bodywork, the goal of the therapist determines the manner in which he works: in seeking to produce particular kinds of feelings, the Trager practitioner can only contact the tissues in ways that will actually stimulate those specific sensory and emotional responses. In an hour-long Trager session, there are several thousand light, rhythmic contacts, and each and every one of them is an opportunity to create and to deepen the feelings of lightness, freedom, relaxation, ease, and peace. When the Trager practitioner encounters stiffened limbs or hardened muscles, his response is never to bear down upon them, to work harder to soften them, or force them to stretch. On the contrary, his response is immediately to become lighter, more sensitive, more searching. He never asserts his idea of how soft or free an area should be; he deliberately retreats from such assertions and instead projects through the motions of his hands the questions, 'What can be lighter and freer than that? Yes. And lighter than that? Fine. And freer than *that*?' And so on.

Tragering avoids undue pressure and effort so that the manner of working will be wholly consistent with its goal of creating sensations of lightness, freedom, and ease. In the first place, heavy pressure on spasmed muscles or forced stretching of stiffened joints normally causes a painful response; the involved area is usually hypersensitive in the first place, and is already braced against painful motions. This generation of pain is precisely the opposite sensory effect of the desired response, and it seriously interrupts the repetitive rhythmic flow of pleasurable sensations to the mind. More than that, pain inevitably triggers reflex contractions, and this merely produces *another* defensive pattern rather than dispersing the ones that are already there. Secondly, the feelings of lightness and effortlessness simply cannot be imparted by means of heavy pressure and hard work on the part of the therapist. Dr Trager holds that the moment the practitioner *tries* to relax the tissue he is doomed to failure. Trying is effort, effort is tension, and relaxation is quite the opposite. The practitioner, then, must be as light as the feelings he wishes to instil. The point is not to impose a preconceived structural or functional model upon the patient's body, but to transmit a pleasurable and continual questioning, 'What is freer, what is lighter?' The point is not to arrive finally at a specified goal — after all, we don't know what 'freest' or 'best' might be — but to instil in the mind of the patient the constant renewal of the question, 'What is better, and what is better'. This is not the imposition of a postural or behavioural model, but rather the initiation of an open-ended development process, both for the therapist and for the patient.

This developmental process is also of primary importance to the Trager practitioner himself. These questionings and these feelings have to be established in his character, have to be a part of his mind and body, before he can successfully project them into another person's sensibilities. No one can give what they do not genuinely have. This is why the cultivation by the practitioner of the mental state Dr Trager calls 'hook-up' — a relaxed, meditative alertness — is crucial to effective Tragering. The state of 'hook-up' is not fundamentally different from a state of deep meditation, even though the practitioner in 'hook-up' is physically active. Achieving this state of active meditation is not an incidental addition to Dr Trager's work, it is of the essence. 'Hook-up' is the practitioner's source of the enriched and relaxed feelings which he projects, his own contact with the qualities of gracefulness, effortlessness, and non-intrusive presence. 'It is,' Dr Trager says, 'like floating in a vast ocean of pleasantness,' and it is the gentle rocking of that ocean which is imparted to the patient's body. Dr Trager maintains that the attributes of mind and body are holistically interrelated in the whole energetic force field that composes all matter and life:

We are surrounded by a force which sustains everything. You don't have to go beyond the surface of your skin to get it. But people are blocked within themselves, so negative, so tense, that this force cannot enter their consciousness. Once this force comes into them, they are changed people, and will function differently and much better than they have ever done before.

It is the conscious contact with this force, this ocean of pleasantness, which gives the practitioner the pleasurable feelings he projects through his motions into the sensations of the patient, and as the patient's consciousness is opened to these feelings it is this force which becomes the active source of vitality and health. Dr Trager often tells his students —

'Hook-up' is like measles. You catch it from someone who's got it. I want you all to experience the subtle thing of your mind asking, 'Well, how free is that? We-e-e-ll?' ... pause a moment, come deeper into this state ... and, 'Well, what's freer than that?' Technique — forget it. It's what you have developed in your mind. That's why every moment of every treatment, every second, every thought, should be this 'Well?' Every time you do it you develop ... just you and this feeling going hand in hand, 'Oh yes, what is finer, what is finer, what is finer?' Take them to this state, take them, take them, bring them along, give them something more so that they can be different. We are lulling, we are lulling, and that is a wonderful state to be in. Compare on the other side of the fence the turmoil of daily living, the stress, the frustration, the trauma. You can help people in this turmoil with this feeling — they can be different because they have felt, have experienced something different. Many times in my treatments I will find myself saying 'Thank you,' and 'thank you'. I would say it all the time. It took me many years to realise that I wasn't thanking the patient for responding, I was thanking this 'hook-up' thing that was doing so much for me. My big helper.

The principle is elegantly simple: We learn to love by being loved, we learn gentleness by being gentle, we learn to be graceful by experiencing the feeling of grace. The goal of a Trager session is no more complex than this — to bring to the surface of consciousness an awareness of this force, and of the pleasurable and positive feelings that are inherent in it. These feelings will do the rest. As the Maharishi Mahesh Yogi said to Dr Trager in 1958, 'It is natural for the mind to want to go to the field of greater

THE TRAGER APPROACH

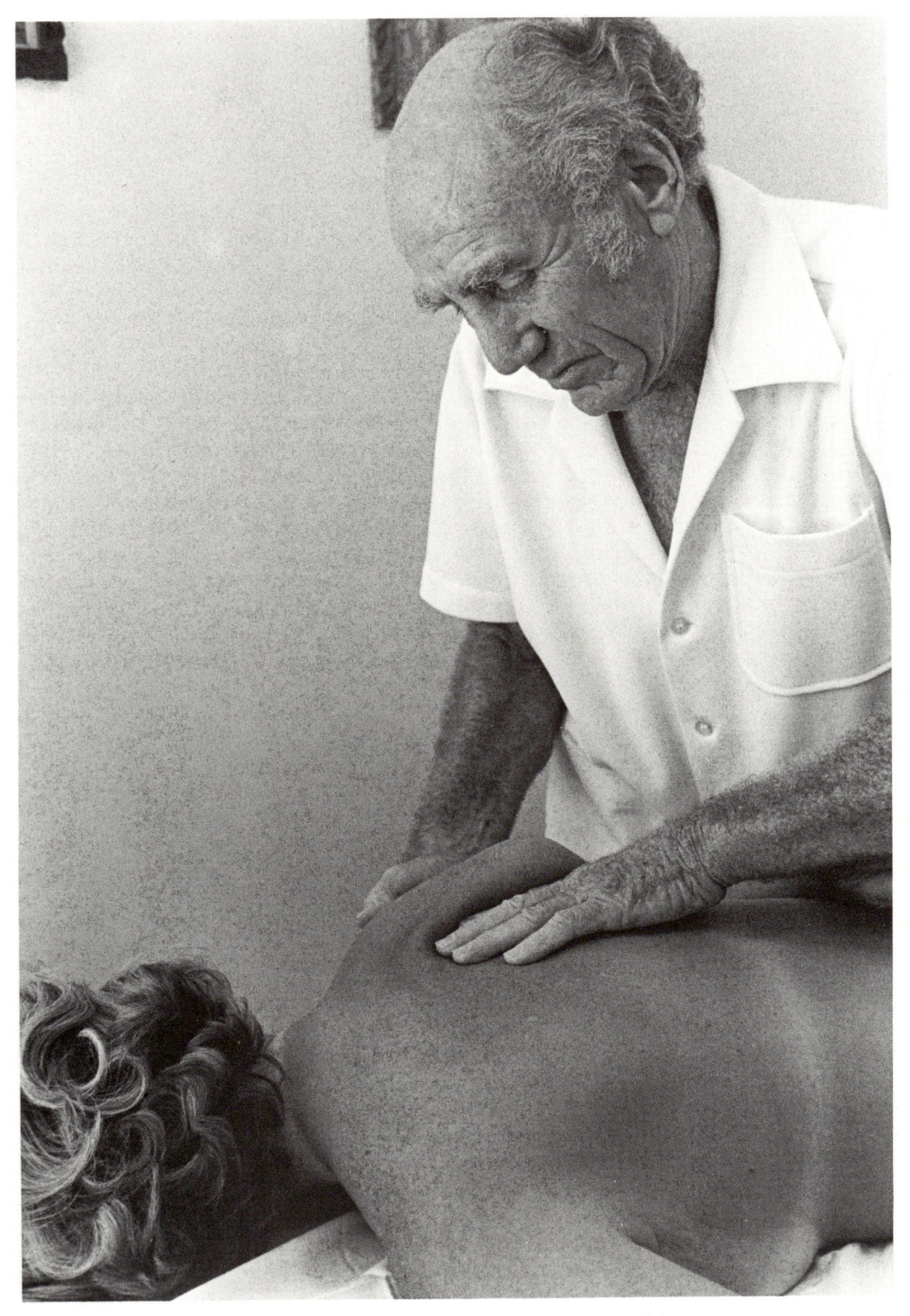

'We learn to love by being loved, we learn gentleness by being gentle'.

happiness,' towards deeper understanding, towards expansiveness, towards connecting with the sources of our being. Tragering was developed as a sensory means of redirecting the footsteps of someone who has lost the way.

DEVELOPMENT OF THE TRAGER APPROACH

Milton Trager was born in Chicago in 1908. He grew up there until he was 16, when he moved with his family to Miami. By the age of 18 he was training in Miami to be a professional boxer. Mickey Martin, his trainer, used to give him a rubdown after each training session. One day Mickey looked tired, and young Milton said, 'Come and lay down on the table, Mickey. I'll work on *you*.' After he had been working for about two minutes, Mickey turned around to him, a little stunned, and asked,

'Hey, where did you learn to do that?'

'You taught me, Mickey,' Milton said. 'I've never done anything like this in my life.'

'I never taught you this, kid. But I don't care. Let me tell you, you got hands.'

Milton was elated. When he went home, he approached his father, who had been suffering from acute sciatica for two years. 'Lay down, Dad,' he said, 'I think I can fix your legs up.' The sciatic pain eased considerably that first session and two sessions later Mr Trager was completely free of his symptoms. They never recurred. Milton was more than elated. He started going around his Miami neighbourhood and down to the beach, looking for aches and pains to work on. He had no idea what he was doing or why it worked, but he got results. People began to seek him out, and Tragering was born.

He quit boxing so that he could take care of his hands. He worked as a dancer and as an acrobat. And he Tragered. When Milton was 19, his first polio victim walked in — a 16-year-old boy who had been paralysed for over four years. From then on, he thirsted to find problems, to work with those who could find no relief through conventional medicine. For many years he worked only on abnormal, unhealthy bodies, and his results continued to improve.

After eight years of this pursuit, he felt he wanted more formal training and the certification necessary for him to establish a professional therapeutic practice. In 1941 he received his Doctorate of Physical Medicine from the Los Angeles College of Drugless Physicians, and was certified by the California Medical Board as a Drugless Practitioner that same year. During the war, he worked in the Physical Therapy Department of the Navy in San Diego and in Africa. After this duty, he continued working in Los Angeles with neuromuscular disorders caused by the war.

At this time he was entitled as a veteran to financial aid to continue his education. He had long wanted to become an M.D. so that his work would be accepted by the medical profession, and he knew that it was now or never. He applied to 70 American medical schools, but they all turned him down because they felt that at 41 he was too old to warrant training. He was finally accepted into the University Autonoma de Guadalajara in Mexico. When he arrived there, they asked him what he did in physical medicine, and he told them that he specialised in polio. He had not been there long when, one day, he was called into a treatment room lined with doctors, professors, and the Mother Superior with some of her nuns. On the table was a four-year-old girl, a victim of a polio epidemic who had been paralysed from the waist down for two years. They all wanted to see what he could do for her. He worked on her for about forty minutes, and by that time she could move her foot and twitch her leg in four directions. Dr Trager turned around to see all the nuns, including the Mother Superior, on their knees crossing themselves. He said to himself, 'How can a Jewish boy in a Catholic university fail with all this feeling coming through?' In three weeks, with additional treatments, the girl walked. The university organised a clinic for Milton, and he continued to treat polio victims throughout his years of study there.

He received his M.D. in 1955 and went to Hawaii, where he did his year of internship at St Francis Hospital in Honolulu. This was followed by a year's residency there, and then two years of residency in psychiatry at the Territorial Hospital in Kaneohe, Oahu. In 1958 he was initiated in Transcendental Meditation by the Maharishi Mahesh Yogi; his wife-to-be became the Maharishi's confidential secretary for several years, and was instrumental in opening the Los Angeles Transcendental Meditation centre. In 1959, Dr Trager started his private practice in general medicine and physical rehabilitation in the Waikiki Medical Building, which he continued for the next 18 years.

Then in 1974 and 1975 a series of events brought Dr Trager and his work out of his private office. One evening at a social gathering, a psychologist asked him what this thing was he did. Dr Trager simply had him lie on the floor, and he worked on his neck for ten minutes. Something must have happened in those minutes, because the psychologist wrote enthusiastically to Will Schutz at Esalen Institute in California, and two weeks later Dr Trager received an invitation to demonstrate his work there. He missed that first appointment at Esalen, because, while he was on his way, he was called in to work on a muscular dystrophy patient in Los Angeles. As he was leaving after the treatment, the patient asked him if he could show his regular therapist how to do the same thing for him. Dr Trager did not have much hope. Every time he had tried to show others how to do it, it had never really worked out. But he gave it a go. The therapist was not getting it, and Dr Trager was about to quit when he had a moment of inspiration: he told the therapist to cover his hands lightly as he did his work, and he could tell that in this way the therapist was finally getting some feeling for it. Then he had the therapist place his own hands on the patient while Dr Trager worked on top of them. To his joy, he could feel the other's hands responding — he had hit upon a way to transfer his own feeling to a student. He let the therapist go to work by himself, and the patient finally cried, 'That's it, Doctor, he's got it! It almost feels like you were doing it!' When they got back to their hotel, his wife Emily looked at him and said, 'Do you realise that you were teaching someone else your work?' It was too late to get to Esalen in time, but a turning point had been reached.

Later in 1975 Dr Trager finally got to Esalen, where he did his first public demonstrations. There he met group leader Betty Fuller, who was complaining after one of her class sessions of a stiff and painful neck. He told her to lie on the carpet so he could work on her. 'Nobody is going to touch *my* neck,' she replied. He promised not to hurt her, and her misery made her give in. She was up in a few minutes asking, 'How do you do that?' She convinced the Tragers to go with her to her home in San Francisco so that she could learn more from him about his work. Dr Trager found that he could teach her to treat parts of the body in the same fashion that he had taught his patient's therapist. She proceeded to arrange for his very first training workshop back at Esalen, and recruited a group of friends and colleagues as students. She followed him to Honolulu and pestered him until she became the first one to learn an entire treatment. She immediately recognised the significance of what he was doing, and also came to realise that he was too content in his Honolulu practice to take up the task of creating a training programme. She persuaded him to let her form an organisation that would learn and spread his work. Thus the Trager Institute, located in Mill Valley, California, was founded, with Betty Fuller as its director. By 1977 Dr Trager closed his private practice to devote all his time to his growing number of students. At present, there are well over 2000 students throughout the world, more than 200 accomplished practitioners, and seven instructors.

Dr Trager has since demonstrated his work in many hospitals, medical schools, and training centres in the United States and Europe. He is currently a member of the American Medical Association, the Honolulu County Medical Society, and the North American Academy of Manipulative Medicine. He teaches, lectures, and demonstrates in Honolulu, Mill Valley and Europe.

APPLICATIONS OF THE TRAGER APPROACH

The appeal of the Trager Approach is broad. Many kinds of people have been attracted to the work, all of them searching for more effective ways of producing more immediate and more lasting results in psychophysical and neuromuscular conditions. Classes have drawn students from such disciplines as holistic health care, psychology, counselling, medicine, nursing, physical therapy, massage, sports, and performing arts, among others which regard movement as a primary means of learning and an integral part of existence. Ever since his early success with paralysis, Dr Trager's particular interest has been the application of his approach to severe neuromuscular disturbances which do not respond well to conventional therapies. However, both he and the practitioners he has trained do achieve excellent results with a wide range of conditions that are more common and less overwhelmingly debilitating — the aches, pains, depressions, poor postures, limited movements, and aging processes which plague many daily lives to one degree or another. Most of these troublesome and inhibiting conditions do not respond any better to drugs and surgery than do many kinds of paralysis and spasm, but they often prove to be very responsive to the soothing sensory intervention of Tragering.

Tense muscles can be caused by many things, but the pattern of the tension is in the mind. Dr Trager recalls

I was doing my internship at St Francis Hospital in Honolulu in 1955, when an indigent patient, a man about 75, was brought in for abdominal surgery. I watched him walk, and he was so stiff that if you called to him, he'd have to turn his whole body to look at you. He couldn't just turn his head. But under a general anaesthetic, it took eight people to roll him over on an operating table without dislocating his joints — he had become so limp and loose. Then I had to watch him while he recovered from the anaesthetic. It was interesting to observe what went on as he gradually came to himself. By degrees his body progressively returned to its original pattern of stiffness. Seeing this, I began to realise that the stiffening and the aging processes are not just tissue involvement. This experience, and others similar to it, were germinal to my realisation that we are the sum total of all the adverse happenings in our lives which cause this kind of phenomenon. The pattern of stiffness and of aging exist more in the unconscious mind than in the tissues.

Since birth, we have in our day-to-day lifestyle brought to the mind many good and bad experiences that have shaped us physically and psychologically. Every individual carries within themselves an exceedingly intricate computer system, a recorder that has no erase button. Whatever experiences have been put there will always be there, influencing every function of the mind and body. Since it is not possible to avoid a variety of traumas, and since none may be erased once they have occurred, therapy should be directed towards bringing appropriate *positive* feeling experiences to the patient. These help directly to influence the mind and body, so that the physical patterns can be alleviated. We are all familiar with the *degenerative* effects that nega-

THE TRAGER APPROACH

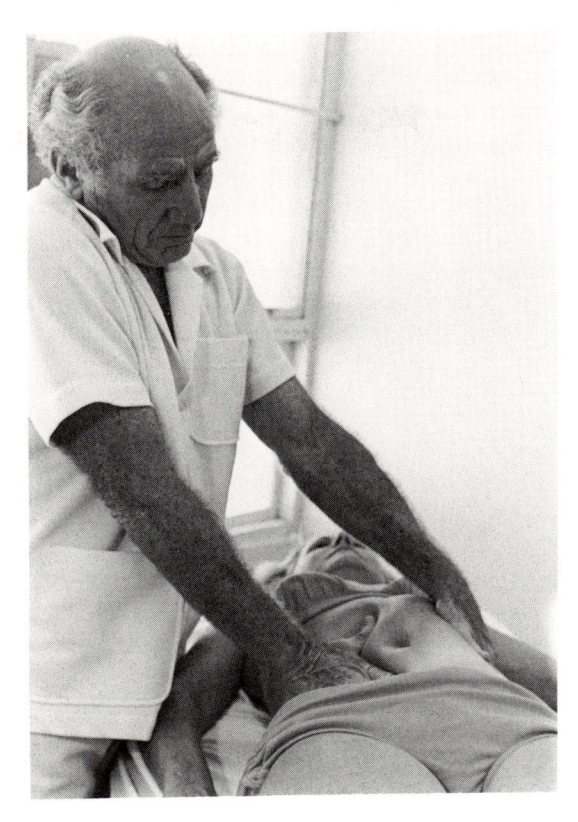

'... therapy should be directed towards bringing appropriate **positive** feeling experiences to the patient'.

tive feelings and attitudes can have upon the body but it is possible to turn this potent force of feelings to a constructive purpose as well.

Although Tragering can deal effectively with a wide array of common discomforts and limitations, it is through the dramatic results achieved in some of the more serious cases that we begin to understand more clearly how it works and how wide its perimeters of effectiveness may be. J. A. is a patient with multiple sclerosis who has experienced a long series of sessions from a Trager practitioner. Before she began her treatments, J. A. felt overwhelmed by the burden of her disability — there is as yet no cure for her degenerative condition. But as her Trager experience progressed, she found new ways to be lighter, freer, and more positive in her outlook. She describes the process as follows

Until the cure comes, our primary focus should be to make ourselves feel good. It is difficult in the face of continual bodily destruction to maintain a feeling of confidence towards our physical selves, and yet it is with our physical selves that all interactions with others take place. My concern has been to build an image of myself, something that radiates from within and then works to move my body with less effort.

A. B. is another multiple sclerosis victim who found her way into Trager training. When she began, her fellow students could not even touch her feet, they were so sensitive and painful. As a result of the work she received during the training, the acute sensitivity in her feet disappeared, the aching that had plagued her legs diminished dramatically, and she began to feel spontaneous activity in her weakened left thigh. Her overall symptoms went into remission, and she was able to postpone the clinical testing and treatment for which she had been scheduled. She states that

Most of the issues that came up for me during the Trager class had to do with not belonging, and with the fear that things would always recur as they had in the past. I came away with a new awareness that things do not always repeat as they have in the past. It's like the reason my toes and feet were so painful is because every time in the past that my feet and toes have been in those positions I always got a cramp, and it was always painful. My body thought that every time my toes pointed, they'd cramp. By re-educating my body that this is not always true, some other things started loosening up in my head.

T. M., a psychologist, is a muscular dystrophy patient who has received twelve treatments from Dr Trager, and many additional sessions by his own physical therapist, who has been trained by Dr Trager especially for his condition. He writes

The Psychophysical Integration sessions accomplished the removal of emotional blocks such as frustration resulting from muscle weakness, fear of progressive muscle weakness, and depression resulting from feeling helpless and hopeless. My belief system was changed in the direction of a 'positive' expectancy of health and muscle strength away from the 'negative' expectation of progressive muscle weakness conditioned by the medical prognosis that 'your muscles will continue to become weaker no matter what you do.'

In T. M.'s case, this renewed ability to think positively about himself created changes considerably beyond his subjective attitude towards his disease

On a physical level, I have gained twenty pounds. Previously, I was unable to gain weight no matter how much I ate. I feel that this weight-gain indicates a change in my metabolic processes. Two weeks before, and two months after seeing Dr Trager, I had isolated muscle strength tests done by the registered physical therapist working with the Muscular Dystrophy Association. The tests showed that 12 out of 18 muscles improved in strength, four stayed the same, and only two became slightly weaker. Also, the hearing in my left ear improved 10–20% as measured by an audiologist. Before I saw Dr Trager, my doctor was considering surgery to improve my hearing. After I returned from Honolulu, my doctor decided not to perform surgery because of the hearing improvement. I attribute the above physiological, emotional, and physical changes to the process of being put in touch with what 'healthy' tissue feels like, and the neurological patterns of 'healthy' tissue. In this respect, my body, through Trager movements, re-educated my mind to perform the necessary neuromuscular and metabolic functions of healthy tissue. On the spiritual level, I feel much more aware of the vibrational frequencies correlated with 'healthy' muscle response.

These sensory and emotional feelings associated with healthy response to stimulation may be blocked by social or psychological difficulties as well as by disease or trauma. Because this is true, Tragering has produced dramatic instances of success in helping psychological as well as physical pathologies, including autistic, schizophrenic, and even criminal behaviour patterns.

Marilyn Kreuger is a Trager practitioner in Minneapolis, Minnesota, where she is the Treatment Director of a community corrections programme, an alternative to incarceration for adult male felons. As Marilyn began to use Tragering and Mentastics more and more in her treatment programme, she found that

THE TRAGER APPROACH

It became clear to me that this work added a special component to our therapy programme. Although we learn by seeing and doing, feeling is the real truth, and Tragering and Mentastics gave our clients a new way of being, new feelings in their bodily selves to go along with the changes in behaviour. We observed changes in behaviour becoming more consistent, and frequently these changes took place without the traditional progress in verbal therapy preceding them. In fact, it appeared that the Trager work facilitated work in the verbal therapeutic area. It has become obvious to me that holding patterns in the body contribute to the behaviour of the person, that changes in the body then contribute to changes in behaviour, and that Trager sessions and Mentastics frequently contribute more to behaviour changes than any form of traditional therapy does.

These kinds of behavioural changes can be elicited in many varieties of psychological and physical conditions. N. B. was oxygen-deprived at birth. She is 39 years old, but she has a mental age of about three. After her first Trager experiences, she demonstrated major behavioural changes. Her repetitious chattering ceased, and her conversational abilities increased noticeably. She began to climb stairs one after the other, instead of one at a time. She began — for the first time in her life — to chew her food. Her father wrote to Dr Trager and to Betty Fuller on one New Year's Eve as follows

Our daughter has responded in so many ways, showing improvement in walking more confidently; chewing her food; also, for the first time, being able to swallow in a normal pattern; releasing tensions and frustrations in actual conversations, showing determination to communicate with family members. All of these changes are evident in the improvement of skin-tone, hair problems, physical and social happiness. These successes have been noticeable to all family members and friends during this holiday season.

N. B. has continued to improve. She is now learning to reach out and touch people.

Dr Trager contends very firmly that he is not a 'healer' or a manipulator of esoteric energies, and that his successes have nothing of the 'miraculous' about them. The kinds of reflex responses, tissue changes, and behavioural changes he is able to elicit are possible because of the intimate neurological associations between sensory stimulations, emotional feelings, attitudes and concepts, and the body's motor responses to all of them. At this time no one can say with certainty just exactly how these sensations, feelings, and actions are materially interrelated, but the fact that they profoundly influence one another is abundantly clear. And it is equally clear that the unconscious forces which control their relationships may be turned back from a vicious circle into a fruitful one.

Dr Peter Levine, a neurophysiologist, took one of Dr Trager's early trainings, and discussed possible mechanisms of Psychophysical Integration with him. Dr Trager told him that he felt it had a sound scientific basis, but that it was difficult to explain it and have it accepted. Dr Levine's response was, 'If an accepted scientific theory cannot explain a particular phenomenon, it is not because the phenomenon is unscientific, but because science itself is not appropriately refined.' Dr Trager's is a subtle and intuitive approach to the elusive and complex problem of the physiological manifestation of psychological distress, and all degrees of this distress and its manifestations have the positive potential for improvement just as long as the nerve circuits themselves are not destroyed by disease or trauma.

Dr Trager is able to give us some concrete insights into how his approach works in the following description of a particularly challenging case. In 1976, while giving a workshop at Esalen Institute, Dr Trager was asked to see a 46-year-old physician who had come there to lecture. While in residence at Esalen, this man had suffered a terrible car accident; he sustained many fractures, including one at the base of the skull with a spinal fluid leak and severe concussion. Dr Trager describes his symptoms

When I came to see him, his tissues were so painful and tender that he could not bear to be touched. At first, in his semi-conscious state, he showed anger when I tried to touch his hand or foot. I started by just holding his foot very gently; even this caused pain. His skin felt like it was adhering tightly to the bones. It was bluish-white in colour. I just sat there, making no apparent movement with my hands, yet something was happening. I could feel the pads of his foot changing. I knew what was occurring. There was a transmission from my mind, through my hands to the patient's tissues, and then to his mind. At that moment, unbeknownst to him, he became the therapist and sent the message to his tissues. I felt this nutritive change in my hands, and a complete circuit was established. His tissues were then able to receive stimuli from the central nervous system, to establish reflexes, and bring movements to the limbs. Very soon after this, and before I finished the treatment, I was satisfied that this had happened, and that he could recover most of his physical function. I gave him a treatment every day for six days. The last morning, he walked into the Esalen dining hall on his own, to the cheers of his friends. I saw him a year later, and he told me that he had recovered almost 90% of his physical activity. I feel that this case was not one of paralysis caused by actual lesion of the nerves, but by disruption of the autonomic patterns. The manner in which I worked influenced this system, bringing the skin and muscle changes.

It is this manner of working, this evocation of a particular feeling state, which is responsible for Dr Trager's many successes. Out of over 5000 painful lower backs that he has treated in over 55 years as a therapist, he asserts that 90% have had notable and lasting relief from a single session and continued use of Mentastics. Dr Trager explains

The success I have had with low back pain is not because the tissue in the lumbo-sacral area were manipulated in a special way. It has come because I have succeeded in reaching the psycho-physiological components. I never tell my hands what to do. I hook up, and I go. My job is to impart to my patient what it is like to be right in the sense of a functionally integrated body-mind. This is transmitted, I feel, through the autonomic nervous system from the therapist's mind, through his hands, to the involved area. This feeling is picked up in the patient's mind because of the manner in which the tissues are worked, creating the feeling of relaxation. In this way, the sensory feedback which maintains the psychic component of muscle spasm is broken. Until this feeling reaches the patient, no lasting results can be expected. It is the manner in which I work, not necessarily the technique that I use, which brings about the change. Every move, every pressure of my hands, every thought, is directed towards bringing new feeling experiences to the unconscious mind of how the affected area should feel. The holding pattern is then broken.

And these holding patterns may be massive or minor, old or relatively new, generated by psychological or by physical trauma, overwhelmingly debilitating or merely uncomfortable and inhibiting. The psycho-sensory mechanism of their release is similar in all cases, and relies only upon finding the appropriate manner of stimulating the tissues.

The Trager Approach is not in itself a medical treatment. It is actually a learning experience. You are learning how your body can move. You are learning what it is like to be freer and lighter. It is really a learning approach to using yourself well, to being

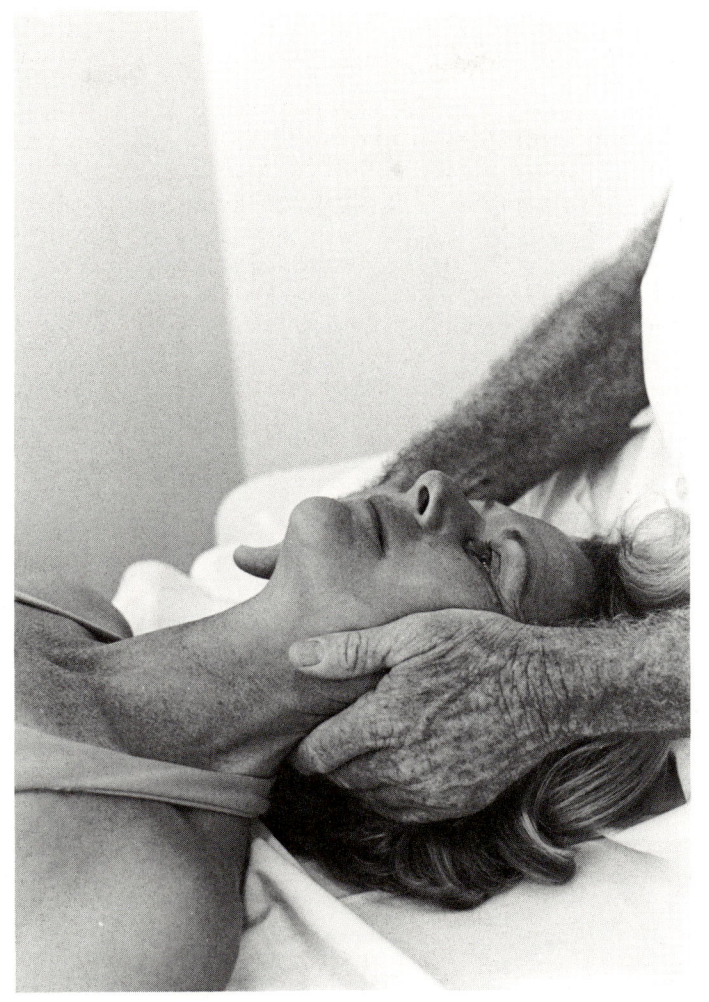

'I never tell my hands what to do. I "hook up", and I go'.

a whole person, to having all your pieces and parts well integrated and coordinated, to feeling yourself connected to the energies which sustain you. All of it is directed towards the mind. In the final analysis, people do not respond to a technique or a procedure; they respond to the skill with which it is used. And what constitutes skill for Dr Trager is, more than anything else, the ability to *be* there with the patient, to be 'hooked-up', open to his or her needs, intimately aware of responses, intimately *responsive* to responses. Any technique may be applied with little or no connection to the actual awareness of the patient, and with poor results. It is this *connection* that Dr Trager strives above all to impart to his patients and to teach to his students. And it is this feeling of calm, peaceful connectedness that is indeed the essence of the Trager Approach. 'Not until we experience it is it more than just words,' he tells his students. 'After we experience it, there is no need for words. The importance of words is to stimulate the desire to experience. Feeling is experience, and by this experience we develop.'

CHAPTER 4

SELF-HELP CHIROPRACTIC Exercises for a Healthy Spine

Nathaniel Altman

Chiropractic teaches that overall health is just a measure of the well-being of the spinal column. In addition to correcting misalignments, many chiropractors recommend regular exercise. Any programme can increase our strength, stamina, and coordination, but unless it also strengthens the back and neck to reduce the possibility of subluxations, the benefits are limited.

Like healthy intentions and a nutritious diet, a programme of exercise, posture development, and proper lifting can promote constructive survival values in our lives and keep us on the road to good health.

EXERCISE: POINTS TO CONSIDER

Every form of exercise provides some benefits, but not all offer the same advantages. Jogging, skiing, football, rugby, wrestling, dance, and the martial arts are excellent body conditioners, but, from a chiropractic point of view, may be too strenuous on joints, ligaments, and the spinal column.

Jogging, for example, reduces tension, improves our ability to deliver oxygen to all parts of the body, increases muscle tone, and improves blood circulation. However, it jars the body, particularly the spine, and can be a cause of vertebral subluxation. Sports like snow skiing, football, and wrestling often lead to strains of the spinal muscles and bruising injuries to the spinal column itself. Chiropractors generally do not discourage their patients from practising these forms of exercise, but advise that sports equipment should be in good order, overexertion should be avoided, and complete spinal examinations should be received to determine if there are any physical limitations that could make such exercise dangerous. They also recommend an immediate visit after experiencing any mishaps.

For those who enjoy a sport like jogging but suffer from its jarring effects, a growing number of chiropractors recommend a small trampoline-like device made of a strong steel frame to which a resilient mat is attached by heavy springs. The mat on which you run or jog sits about seven inches off the floor. Research by a testing firm in Houston revealed these joggers produce only about 39 per cent of the trauma experienced when we run on the floor.*

---

* You can write to one of the following companies for more information:
THE JUMP 'N' JOGGER, Jump 'n' Jogger International Corp., 230 Central Park South, New York, New York 10019
THE REBOUNDER, Trim Way Corp., PO Box 77113, Seattle, Washington 98133
SKIP JOGGER, Skip-Hellen Enterprises Inc., 11259 Virginia Avenue, Lynnwood, California 90262

STRETCH FOR SPINAL HEALTH

Stretching exercises are among the finest body conditioners and are favoured by chiropractors for themselves and their patients. When performed with knowledge and care, they are excellent for firming and toning the muscles of the arms, legs, shoulders, neck, and back. They also firm up abdominal muscles which are directly involved in preventing spinal disorders. According to Thomas Pipes and Paul Vodak, authors of *The Pipes Fitness Test and Prescription:* 'When your abdominal strength and endurance are poor, the lower intestines, which are contained in a supporting membrane that attaches to the lower spine, protrude outward, causing disruptive stress on the spine. With continued stress, the backbone eventually distorts, pinching various nerves.'

The most popular stretching exercises are featured in the ancient practice of Hatha Yoga. Chiropractors recommend yoga because it helps us relax, improves muscle tone, strengthens the abdominal and spinal muscles, and enables the spine to be more flexible and respond better to everyday stress and strain. There are a number of fine courses on Hatha Yoga available in book and record stores. Classes in yoga and other stretching exercises are offered in most communities. If taught by a qualified instructor, the benefits can be great. A chiropractor from Pittsburgh offered the following advice: 'Don't overdo it, and don't force the exercises by straining the muscles or by making sudden movements. Your body is made to move gracefully and you don't have to force it into positions that cause pain and discomfort.'

NINE DAILY EXERCISES FOR SPINAL HEALTH

Each chiropractor tailors an exercise programme to the individual needs of the patient, often drawing the best features from different exercise systems. The following ones were created by a chiropractor and are especially designed to strengthen the muscles of the neck, abdomen and back. They reduce tension while improving muscle tone and strength, and are intended to minimise the onset of vertebral subluxations and improve the effectiveness of chiropractic adjustments. Perform these as often as you like, although twice a day is considered ideal. Each can be done by itself or as a group, but all nine should be performed in order to obtain maximum benefits.

Before starting any exercise programme, speak to your chiropractor about any possible physical limitations you may have. Those offered here should not cause any pain and can be performed by people of all ages. However, if one or more of the exercises causes discomfort, it may indicate a spinal problem.

NECK EXERCISES

1 Cervical (Neck) Extension In a standing position, slowly nod your head backwards until you feel a firm pressure at the base of the head (as opposed to letting your head drop as far as it will go). Hold this position for a slow count of three. Slowly bring your head to an erect position once more. Repeat five times. Increase the number daily until you can do 20. Like the following exercise, the cervical extension helps strengthen neck muscles and improve their general tone.

2 Cervical Flexion In a standing position, gently nod your head forward on your chest to the count of three. Make sure to avoid any strain of the neck muscles. Hold this position for another count of three. Slowly bring your head erect. Repeat five times. Slowly increase daily until you can do 20.

3 Cervical Left and Right In a standing position, turn your head slowly to the left without straining or rolling your head up or down. Hold this position for three seconds.

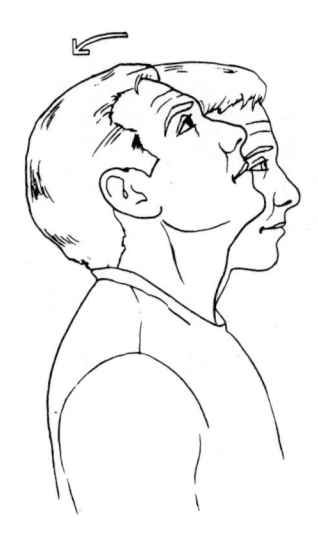

Figure 1 Cervical Extension

Figure 2 Cervical Flexion

Figure 3 Cervical Left and Right

Figure 4 Cervical Tilt

Bring your head back to the centre, and rest. Then slowly turn your head to the right, hold, and bring your head back to centre once more. Repeat five times. Gradually increase daily until a count of 20 is achieved. The goal of this exercise is to increase the lateral range of motion of the neck and improve muscle tone.

4 Cervical Tilt The cervical tilt is designed to strengthen shoulder muscles in addition to those of the neck. First, tilt your head slowly to the left until you feel the muscles on the right side of your neck tighten. Hold this position for three seconds. Bring your head erect again. Repeat by tilting the head gradually to the right until you notice the tightness of the muscles on the left side of the neck. Repeat this right and left tilt three times, and gradually increase daily until you can do 20.

SELF-HELP CHIROPRACTIC

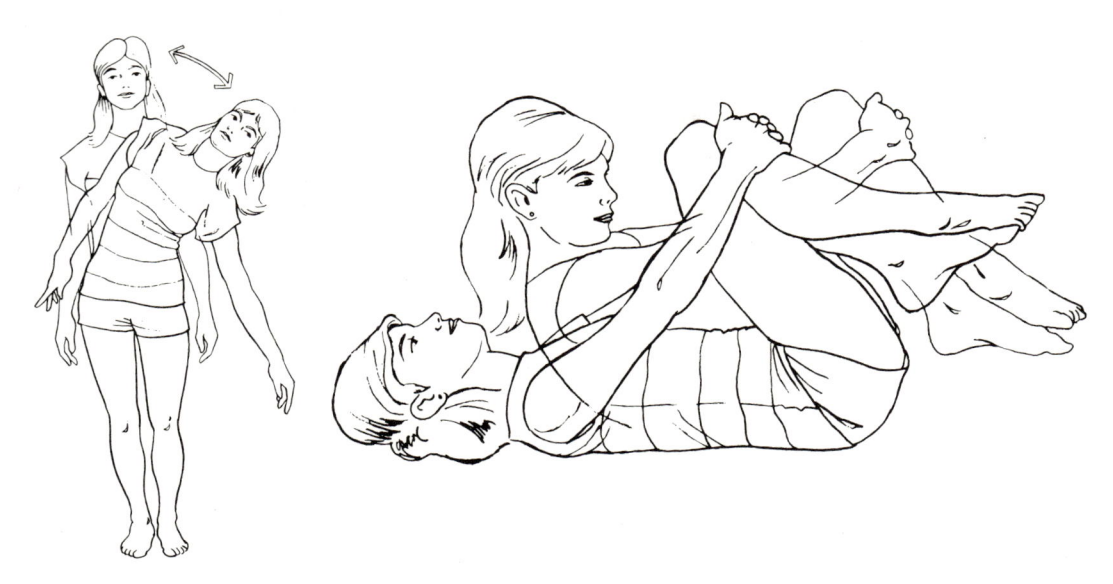

Figure 5 *Thoracic-Lumbar Lateral Flexion*   **Figure 6** *Thoracic-Lumbar Flexion*

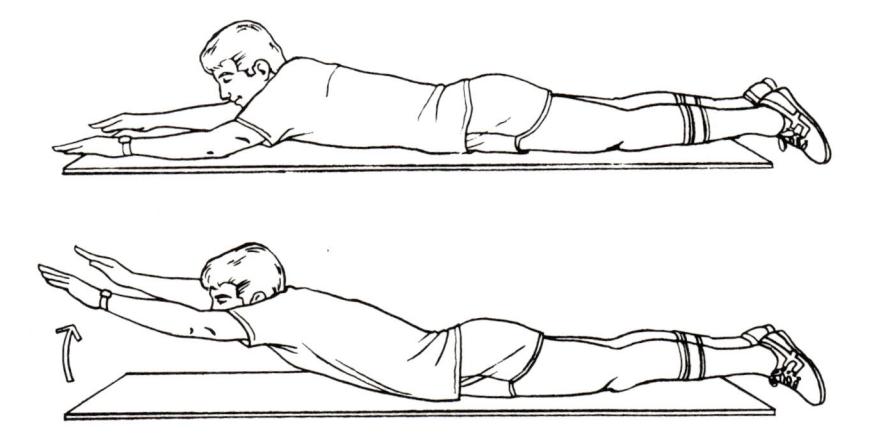

Figure 7 *Thoracic-Lumbar Hyperextension*

EXERCISES FOR THE MID AND LOWER BACK

5 Thoracic-Lumbar Lateral Flexion Stand erect with your feet six inches apart and arms at your sides. Slowly lean to the left until your body is angled at approximately 20 degrees or so. You should begin to feel some muscle strain in your right side. Hold this position for five seconds. Slowly stand erect again. Repeat the action by bending slowly to the right. Gradually increase this exercise daily until a count of 20 is achieved. In addition to increasing general body flexibility, this exercise is useful for strengthening the muscles of the middle and lower back.

6 Thoracic-Lumbar Flexion Lie flat on your back. Flex your knees towards your chest — they don't have to touch — and lock your hands around your knees. Gently

SELF-HELP CHIROPRACTIC

Figure 8 *Thoracic-Lumbar Extension*

roll backward and forward letting your head move with the motion; don't try to keep your head flat on the floor. Be sure to lie on a mat, carpet, or other suitable padding, since the flexion will increase the prominence of the vertebrae. Gently roll backward and forward about five times, breathing in when you go backward and out when you roll forward. Gradually increase this number daily until you can do 20. In addition to toning up the muscles of the middle and lower back, this exercise strengthens the abdominal muscles and increases blood circulation.

7 Thoracic-Lumbar Hyperextension Lie face down on a carpet or mat with your arms outstretched in front of you. Keeping your arms straight, gently arch your back and slowly raise your arms, head, and shoulders by tightening your back muscles. Raise yourself up, hold for a few seconds, and then lie flat and relaxed. This is a strenuous exercise that will greatly increase the strength of the lower, mid, and upper back, shoulders, neck, and arms. Repeat this exercise five times, and gradually increase daily until you can do 12.

8 Thoracic-Lumbar Extension This is one of my favourite exercises for relieving muscle tension brought about by typing for long periods of time. Kneel down on your hands and knees, with your arms supporting your shoulders. Don't worry about your feet — you can either rest on the backs of your feet or have them lie with the top of the feet touching the ground. Relax your back and slowly slump forward. Hold this position for a second or two and then arch your back to where the spine is rounded. Roll your pelvis forward when slumping, and backward when arching. This is a good exercise to help you correct some of your own subluxations (you may hear several 'cracks' or 'pops' as you do the exercise) and tone up the back, abdominal, and shoulder muscles. Repeat this exercise five times, and gradually increase daily until you reach a count of 20.

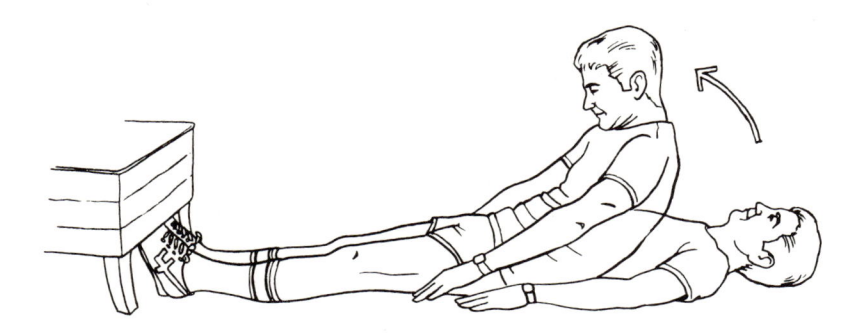

Figure 9 *Abdominal Flexion*

EXERCISE FOR THE ABDOMEN

9 Abdominal Flexion Lie flat on your back with your arms at your sides. Anchor your feet beneath a sofa or a friend. Gently tighten your abdominal muscles and raise your body up slowly from your waist, making sure to keep your hips on the floor. Hold for a moment, and then slowly lower yourself again to a position flat on your back. Repeat three times. Gradually increase this count daily until a series of 12 is achieved. This exercise — a variation of the 'sit-up' — will strengthen the muscles of the abdomen, upper chest, and legs.

WHAT ABOUT POSTURE?

Good posture is one of the goals of chiropractic. The profession has taken a leadership role in educating parents and children on its benefits for more than fifty years.

Although we were taught that good posture looks attractive and is necessary for coordination, chiropractic points out it also keeps us healthy. When the human structure is out of balance, it can produce distortions of the spine. The resulting curvature may change the position of our internal organs and cramp the lungs, stomach, and intestines which may lead to shallow breathing, faulty digestion, and poor elimination. However, the most serious result is vertebral subluxation which may alter the function of various organs by affecting specific spinal nerves.

There are many reasons for poor posture. Excessive weight, negative emotional attitudes, visual impairment, injury to joints, bones, and ligaments, faulty nutrition, improper sleep support (soft or sagging mattresses), poorly designed chairs, and vertebral subluxations are all common contributors to poor posture. High-heeled shoes, badly-designed seating in cars and trucks, and just plain laziness follow close behind.

Disturbances of body balance may show themselves as a slight tilt of the head to the right or left, one shoulder (or hip) may be slightly higher than the other, or there may be an abnormal curve of the spine (known as lordosis or 'swayback') or an abnormal backward curve of the spine (known as kyphosis or 'humpback').

Bad posture does not always involve subluxation of the spine, although it usually does. Sometimes spinal curvature may not produce a subluxation and sensitive spinal nerves may not be impaired. However, your chiropractor, as a specialist in spinal care, is qualified to determine the nature and extent of your postural problem. He or she will thoroughly examine your spine, correct vertebral subluxations if needed, and advise how you can develop habits to promote healthy posture.

On Your Feet: Standing and Walking Human beings are one species of a small group of animals that are bipeds — who stand erect and walk on two legs. This position gives us more agility than other animals, enables us to lift heavy objects, and enjoy greater mobility. It also creates structural demands which can become spinal disorders. For that reason, chiropractors believe learning how to stand and walk properly is essential, reducing the inherent gravitational and structural stress endured every day.

When you stand, point your toes straight ahead. Place your body weight primarily on your heels. Shift your upper chest slightly forward so that it protrudes farther out than the abdomen. Bend your knees slightly. This is not standard military posture, but an easy, relaxed position that reduces forward pull on your back and limits the possibility of strain and subluxation. If you stand for long periods of time, wear low-heeled shoes to reduce muscle strain in the lower back.

When walking, keep the toes pointed straight ahead. Keep your chest uplifted in a natural, unforced way. Be sure to lift your knees so that you are flexing the muscles of the legs and lower back. Wear low-heeled, comfortable shoes with padded soles. They keep your body closer to its natural centre of gravity and reduce jarring and fatigue.

At Ease: Sitting and Sleeping From childhood on, we are told to sit up straight to avoid spinal curvature and other results of poor posture. Although slouching in a chair is a major cause of curvature of the spine, the ideal sitting position is with the shoulders slightly rounded and the knees higher than the hips to prevent back strain and forward curvature of the spine (known as lordosis).

What is the 'ideal chair'? According to Hyman Jampol, a physiotherapist who is Director of the Beverly Palms Rehabilitation Hospital in Los Angeles, a good chair fulfils the following three requirements:

1 The seat should be inclined slightly backward for improved lower back support.

2 The back support should be level with your shoulder blades to eliminate stress on the shoulders and neck.

3 Your thighs should be comfortably supported so that sharp edges (like the thin seats of deck chairs) will not cut off blood circulation. If necessary, add pillows to chairs which cause back strain, or cut an inch off the rear legs of a sofa or chair which does not provide adequate low back support. Be sensitive to your body's needs. Learn to avoid chairs and sofas which cause back pain.

Some chiropractors recommend rocking chairs because the backward and forward motion relieves pressure on the spinal muscles and prevents cramping. A small footstool is recommended for keeping the knees higher than the hips. It will take pressure off your lower back and help straighten out the lumbar area of your spine.

All chiropractors agree that a soft, sagging mattress is extremely harmful to the spine. It leads to back pain and vertebral subluxation. Since we spend approximately one-third of our lives in bed, a firm mattress with good back support is an excellent investment in health and comfort.

There are many good beds available in any furniture store. Select one that is really comfortable for you: a mattress that is too soft may allow your back to arch too much. One that is too firm may cause pain and subluxation from too much pressure. A recent survey by the *New York Times* found that most people preferred an 'orthopaedic' mattress (the King Koil® mattress has received the endorsement of the International Chiropractors Association) with water beds coming in a close second.

The best sleep position is on your back, because sleeping on the stomach arches and strains the lower back and neck. Sleeping on your side is a good idea, especially if you bring both knees up toward the chest to reduce muscle tension in the spine. Conventional pillows often contribute to neck strain, so use a small, soft pillow or special cervical pillow which provides additional support to the neck. Many chiropractors actually sell them although they may also be found in any surgical supply store.

Gezundeit! A strong sneeze can bring more back injury than almost any other cause. It forces the upper part of the body to bend vigorously. Resisting the sneeze suddenly stops the upper body's natural forward motion, resulting in a powerful muscle contraction that can cause painful subluxation and lead to an increased lumbar curve. In his book *The Weekend Athlete's Way to a Pain Free Monday*, Hyman Jampol offers the following simple advice: 'To prevent injury *bend your knees* so that you are in a half squat and do not resist the sneeze. Relax and let go.'

HOW TO LIFT WITHOUT RUINING YOUR BACK

Improper lifting is a leading cause of subluxation. It strains the spinal muscles which can pull one or more vertebrae out of alignment and cause severe pain. We tend to place excessive weight on the lower back instead of the legs which are designed to support far more than our body weight. We lift with a quick, jerking motion and bring about sudden strain. Instead of holding an object close to our bodies, we hold it away from the natural centre of gravity, throwing the entire body, especially the spine, out of balance and causing injury and pain.

Learning how to lift properly is not a difficult task. The National Safety Council has recommended the following six steps:

1 Your feet should be approximately twelve inches apart. One should be placed alongside the object you are lifting. The other should be located slightly behind the object. This will provide you with greater balance and stability. You will have greater strength for lifting. If you need to change positions in order to lift, move your feet instead of twisting your body.

2 Keep your back straight in a nearly vertical position. This reduces some of the pressure that builds up in the abdominal region and keeps your spine and body in proper alignment.

3 Keep your chin tucked in. This will reduce injuries to the neck and aids in spinal balance.

Figure 10 *Feet parted — one alongside, one behind the object you are lifting*

SELF-HELP CHIROPRACTIC

Figure 11 *Keep your back straight, chin tucked in, and grip the object with the whole hand. Keep elbows and arms tucked in.*

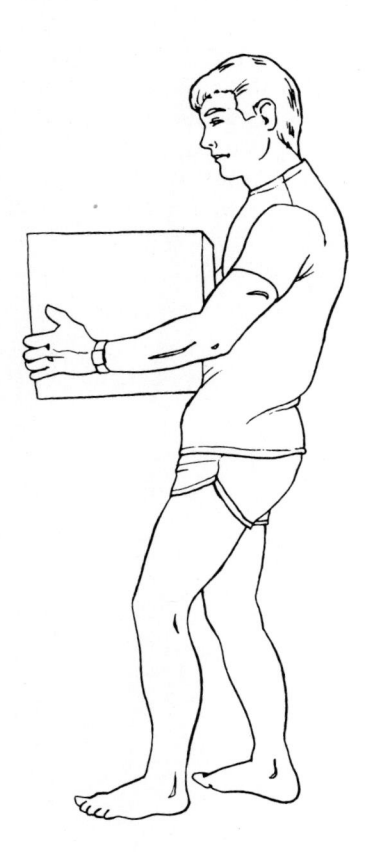

Figure 12 *Make sure that body weight is directly over the feet.*

4 Grip the object with your whole hand. This prevents it from slipping, which causes a sudden shift in weight and perhaps back strain or other injury.

5 Keep your elbows and arms tucked in. Bring the object as close to your body as possible. With a closer centre of gravity, lifting will be easier and your spine will remain balanced and free from strain.

6 Make sure your body weight is directly over your feet. This will help your body to balance the weight of the object and will give greater strength for lifting and carrying.

WHAT IF YOU SUFFER A BACK INJURY?

The purpose of this chapter is to help you avoid back sprains, strains, and subluxations. However, despite precautions, accidents do happen — a fall in the bathroom, reaching into a low cabinet, a sudden sneeze — which can injure the spine and cause intense pain.

When a back injury occurs, lie down immediately in a comfortable position and apply an ice pack directly to the injured area for ten minutes. Call a chiropractor and arrange to see him or her as soon as possible. Often the cause of back pain, a vertebral subluxation, can be removed with only one adjustment and save you much pain and discomfort. Follow your chiropractor's advice about how you can facilitate recovery.

Through a programme of preventive exercise, you can avoid many common spinal problems which cause pain, limit activity, and open the door to ill health. It can even be a pleasure. If you do every exercise described in this chapter, you do not need to devote more than fifteen or twenty minutes a day. Performed to music and in attractive surroundings, daily exercise can be a pleasure looked forward to and shared with family and friends.

Chiropractic works to preserve the integrity of our bodies and keep us healthy, active, and strong. With a personal programme of daily exercise and increased awareness of correct posture and proper lifting, you can greatly enhance the benefits of chiropractic care. Take greater responsibility for your health in these and other ways described earlier and work as a partner with your chiropractor to keep healthy.

CHAPTER 5
IYENGAR YOGA
Carl Webster

Yoga has often been rejected as being just for the spiritually inclined, or too passive to be a real test of fitness. It is true that some forms of yoga don't require much except chanting, meditating or watching the breath. However, yoga, as bodywork, offers the chance of getting supremely fit, coupled with an increase in self-awareness that can literally transform your life. And one man has transformed yoga into a dynamic and exhilarating discipline worthy of the most ardent fitness adept.

BACKGROUND

B. K. S. Iyengar of Poona, India, began yoga in his mid teens and received only minimal instruction, before being told to teach the beginners' class. Faced with his own lack of knowledge he began practising 10–12 hours a day and noting his mental and bodily responses to the yoga *asanas* or postures. Now in his sixties, Iyengar has elevated yoga to the refinement of a true art and the precision of a science. In addition, he has added his own personal qualities of dynamism and intensity to make his style of yoga a total experience of health.

B. K. S. Iyengar was first introduced to the west in the early 1960s by his pupil Yehudi Menuhin, the famous violinist. Such is the dedication and integrity of Sri Iyengar that he now has thousands of pupils world-wide and his exacting, scientific approach to yoga has earned him a reputation as one of the greatest exponents and teachers of yoga in the world today.

Iyengar has brought yoga down to earth, out of the clouds of mysticism and philosophy and onto the *terra firma* of realised physical experience. 'If you cannot master the body,' he says 'how can you master the mind?' The substantive difference between Iyengar's teachings and those of other masters has been the precision and concentration demanded of the student in doing the simplest of yoga poses. In this way the body and mind are toned up and sharpened, and perception is vastly increased. Again, unlike many yoga teachers, Iyengar demands that one 'goes to the limit' — for only by confronting one's physical and mental limitations can one progress through, around, and beyond them.

A major problem faced by the average person in improving his or her health is overcoming stiffness, dullness and weakness, which have a tendency to creep into the physical and mental framework as age increases. Yoga is a dynamic activity and Iyengar states emphatically that it must be practised dynamically in order to overcome lethargy, gain strength and reach a state of balance and purity.

Parsvokonasana — *a side stretch pose for loosening up the body. Iyengar Yoga pushes its practitioners to their personal limitations.*

Because yoga works through the mental and physical body, or the inner and outer body, increasing not only strength but also total awareness, the benefits are tremendous, and limited only by one's efforts.

Iyengar Yoga offers a great opportunity to anyone seeking to understand and master their mind and body. Western civilisation and education has tended to focus on the mind, the power of rational thought and logical thinking, in order to develop our potential and overcome both our individual and societal weaknesses. The intuitive, receptive, sensitive 'lateral thinking' brain has become associated with 'the arts' or 'the emotions' and even our appreciation of these subjects is often intellectual, at the expense of an outlook which can encompass both a critical and a sensitive awareness.

We need to become more flexible in order to widen our appreciation of both our own nature and our relationship with others. Too often we witness the split in roles and attitudes in a family relationship. For example, one partner may go out to work full-time and bring back a hyper-critical mental attitude relating to the situation, say, between the other partner and the child, where the relationship should ideally be based more on feeling and understanding.

Iyengar Yoga offers a way of bringing together these two outlooks by strengthening the mind and intellect while allowing recognition and acknowledgement of the receptive, feeling-based side of the human character.

Through the practice of Iyengar Yoga the ego is challenged and shown its tendency to dominate and overrule the senses. The emotions are allowed expression through the practice of postures and, rather than being indulged, are harnessed as a source of power based on sensitivity rather than aggressiveness.

Yoga is about creating mastery of mind and body and mastery of the intellect and emotions, not through suppression but rather by increasing awareness and understanding. While many yoga paths concentrate on the mind, Iyengar believes the body provides a solid starting point for self-study, building a foundation of strength and suppleness. With the dynamic and intense practice of Iyengar postures, the mind also begins to learn these attributes of firmness and flexibility. Moreover, our body is our source of energy — our vehicle on the road of life — and we do well to look after it and keep it road-worthy. Iyengar calls the body a temple which must be kept in shining order so that the spirit may flourish.

Every posture can be treated as a meditation in itself and through combining strength on the outside with gentleness on the inside, many of the benefits of meditation can be realised much faster and more substantially than by sitting cross-legged with the eyes closed.

GUIDELINES FOR PRACTISING

Whether you wish to do yoga to lose weight, gain strength, flexibility or become a more aware person, the effectiveness of your effort depends on your application. Yoga is about learning to experience your mind and body as a whole, and to practise it we must use 100% effort and commitment even if only practising 10 minutes a day.

Nature has provided us with a guide to prevent injury, in the form of breath. When breathing becomes difficult or jagged, then one should proceed slowly. One should seek one's maximum stretch in the postures through cultivating awareness rather than by using force or aggressiveness. Breathing is generally through the nose, but can be through the mouth if the nose is blocked, or breathing becomes difficult. Progress can be difficult without a good teacher, but an invaluable teacher is the clock — seeing how long one can hold a posture and then gradually extending the limit. Difficult postures should be held for a shorter period and repeated more often, easy postures *vice versa*.*

YOGA RELIEVES STRESS

Stress is a constant factor for most people, whether it comes in the form of noise, pollution, looking after children, or working long hours. Yoga teaches us how to reduce the energy spent in holding onto stress and adopting defensive postures with mind and body. Yoga provides a safe space for subjecting ourselves to a form of 'therapeutic' stress — stress that stretches us and allows us to let go and experience a sense of freedom. While doing yoga we can notice our 'normal' reactions to stress and learn new ways to dealing with it — correct breathing, strengthening our legs and lower back rather than holding on with the chest and shoulders. However, one should be wary of practising yoga 'stressfully'. It is better to take a short rest before doing yoga if one has been working hard or is feeling tired. For this reason, the morning is a good time to practise because the body is rested and refreshed. However, the time of day may be chosen to suit your own schedule. In the morning before breakfast the body has more energy but is generally less supple, before supper you may relieve the tension of the day and regenerate for the evening, and before going to sleep yoga can help you relax and enjoy a deep slumber. You should only practise yoga on an empty stomach, 3–4 hours after a main meal, ½–1 hour after a snack.

Aim to begin with some general warming-up exercises — shaking hands and feet, rotating the waist and pelvis, making arm circles and squatting. Then rest for a few moments taking a few deep breaths before beginning the *asanas*.

Allow the posture to dictate your breathing. If you find it difficult to breathe through your nose, feel dizzy, stuck or generally weak don't hesitate to try breathing in and out through your mouth. Always exhale fully to allow yourself to let go into the posture — the 'in' breath can look after itself. As you get stronger, breathing will come easily and more naturally through the nose.

What follows is a selection of ten basic *asanas* with guidelines on their physiological and psychological effects. The order of presentation is fairly arbitrary and it is worth experimenting with. Generally, standing-up poses are a good warm-up for sitting-down ones, and the more difficult postures are often best done in the beginning or middle of practice, when one has more strength and determination. Remember to lie down and relax at the end of the session — this allows the body and mind a chance to absorb the new experiences and enjoy the sense of energy and space created.

UTTANASANA (or 'Touch the floor!')

Directions
Place the feet 4–8 cm apart, with heels turned slightly out, making sure both feet are symmetrical (don't have one foot in front of the other). Bend forward, with the knees locked and the kneecaps pulled up. The arms may be folded above the head and lifted away from the legs to facilitate spinal arching. Dropping the arms down to the floor is easier and the hands (if they reach) should have the palms upturned on either side

---

* It is wise to heed the following cautions:
Women having their periods should not practise inverted postures and those with high blood pressure should pay particular attention to their breathing, keeping it slow and relaxed at all times. If you have had a recent back injury or disc displacement be sure to seek advice and/or a good teacher. Generally with such a problem you should not attempt forward bending postures without advice.

of the feet. To increase the stretch rock forward slightly on the soles of the feet. Hold 1–5 minutes. Turn the front thighs inwards and the back thighs outwards.

Comment
The way this posture is held illustrates the distinct difference between yoga and calisthenics. Rather than 'bouncing' up and down, the student holds the pose and allows the hamstring muscles to fully extend (*Uttanasana* literally means 'intense stretch'). Holding the pose for 1–3 minutes allows the muscles to stretch, experience resistance, relax and stretch a little more.

While 'bouncing' creates a sense of working, in fact the student may never get to touch his toes. Working in the yoga way allows progress to be made relatively swiftly at first and then more slowly. Notice the condition of the abdomen and diaphragm — allow them to relax and soften. The tension of the legs must be counteracted by letting go in the upper body. After a few days or weeks practice even a stiffer person should be able to touch the floor.

Benefits
By surrendering the head to a forward bend position, the brain gradually relaxes and the heart and lungs are rested. The initial pain and discomfort experienced in the legs reflects the 'holding-on pattern' and tightness in both the leg muscles and the lower back. The major nerve and blood supply to the legs are tonified and re-charged by this pose. As performance improves, the benefits extend into the pelvis, hip joints, coccyx (tail bone), sacroiliac and lumbar spine.

This is an excellent posture for anyone experiencing ache and tiredness in their legs and lower back. It is also good for those who suffer from head and neck tension and have a tendency to get hyperactive.

TRIKONASANA (Triangle Stand)

Directions
Right side: Position the feet 3–3½ feet apart as shown, right foot out, left foot in. Raise the arms to the level of the shoulders and extend the fingers. Pull up the kneecaps, tuck in the tailbone, and lift the chest. On an exhalation, stretch out to the right, allowing the pelvis to tilt sideways but not twist. Place the right hand below the right knee and look up at the upstretched left hand. Stretch the fingers, keep the knees straight, and rotate the chest up towards the upper arm. To feel the correct position try doing the posture with the back against a wall. Stay 15 seconds–1 minute and then repeat on the left side, turning the feet in the opposite direction.

Comment
Iyengar has revolutionised this classic yoga posture, making it a test of balance and stamina. Pay particular attention to the feet position since this helps to create a good stretch on the inside legs as well as teaching control of the body in balancing. The weight of the trunk is kept vertically over the right thigh (as though pressed against a wall) and one begins to understand the relationship between the upper torso, hips and legs. Like all Iyengar's 'standing poses' *Trikonasana* creates a sense of power and freedom, though one is forced to tackle weaknesses in the leg muscles before noticing this.

Benefits
The Triangle Stand stretches the legs fully and opens the hip joints, increasing mobility and circulation to the whole body. The lower back in strengthened and the chest capacity is developed.

Trikonasana *(Triangle Stand)*

VRKSASANA (Tree Pose)

Directions
Stand with the feet together and the legs straight. Focus the eyes on a point on a facing wall or floor and become calm. Lift up the right leg and place the sole of the foot high up on the left groin. Extend the Achilles tendon into the groin to prevent the foot slipping. Keep the left leg straight and first balance with hands on hips. When you are ready, inhale and extend the arms over the head. Placing your palms together and keeping your arms straight, stretch the fingers and lift the chest. Make sure the chest is facing forward (and not turned to the side) and at the same time extend the bent leg out to the side. Hold 30 seconds–1 minute and then repeat with the left leg.

Comment
This pose creates a sense of balance and poise in the body which is also reflected in the mind. Holding this pose stimulates one-pointedness as we learn to focus the mental and physical energies on one point. The pose has all the dignity and gracefulness of a tree and in order to balance one must certainly cultivate one's roots in the shape of the feet and ankles!

Benefits
The post strengthens the knees, legs and ankles, and lightens the body through stretching up. The back is strengthened and the shoulder joints and upper chest are opened and stretched.

Vrksasana *(Tree Pose)*

VIRABHADRASANA (Warrior Pose)

Directions
Right side: Place the feet 4–5 feet apart, right foot out, left foot in on a line. Hold the arms over the head, gripping by the thumbs, straighten the elbows and lift the chest. Turn the hips, waist and chest clockwise to the right and on an exhalation bend the right knee until the shin is vertical. Stretch the fingers, keep the back leg straight, and open the chest. Keep the eyes wide open. As your stretch increases take the feet wider until the right thigh is parallel with the floor. Hold 15 seconds–1 minute. Repeat on the left side.

Comment
The Warrior Pose, as its name implies, is a powerful *asana* for increasing the strength and will-power of the student. The essence of *Virabhadrasana* is an expression of controlled power and courage, the arms extending to the universe and the front bent leg expressing flexibility and movement. This posture brings clarity to the mind and senses, and the spirit is drawn into the eyes.

Holding the posture at first taxes the student's strength and the time limit should be increased gradually. To rest, keep the feet apart but the toes turned in and bend forward and hold the ankles, keeping the insteps lifted and the legs straight. If the head touches the floor bring the feet closer together.

Benefits
The Warrior Pose strengthens the inside legs and quadriceps on the upper thighs, creating stamina and endurance. The student learns to harness his energy to sustain the activity of the legs while keeping the chest open, the spine fully extended and the arms pushing upwards. A degree of flexibility between the spine and pelvis is also created and the heart and lungs are strengthened. The pose defies gravity and heaviness in the body, and the nervous system is invigorated.

URDHVA PRASARITA PADASANA (Leg Lifts)

Directions
First Stage: Lie on the back with the heels stretched and the arms extended over the head. On an exhalation lift the right leg as near vertical as possible, keeping the leg straight. Turn both knees slightly in (working the left leg too), breathe normally and hold 15 seconds up to 2 minutes. Lower on an exhalation. Repeat with the left leg.
Second Stage: In the same starting position raise both legs on an exhalation, keeping them straight and squeezing the inner ankles, knees and thighs together. Aim at eventually getting the legs vertical, with the kneecaps turned in and the backs of the legs turned out. Hold 15 seconds up to 2 minutes (or longer). Lower on an exhalation.
Third Stage: Follow Stage Two and then practise lifting and lowering both legs to a half-way position, holding, and then raising or lowering. Intermediary angles of the legs will work on different areas of your abdomen.

Comment
This pose is often very difficult and tiring as we find out the stiffness and weakness in our legs, abdomen and lower back. Remember that practice will improve things! For those with a very weak lower back, with injury or acute pain, practise longer with one leg before attempting with both. Again let the breath guide you — if you cannot exhale and lift, keep building up your strength using one leg and other postures.

Leg lifts are one of the simplest, most effective and therapeutic yoga exercises one can do as they tone up the abdomen, legs and lower back muscles.

Often we hide and suppress stress in our thighs, hips, abdomen and diaphragm, and leg lifts work to correct this pattern and even out the energy-flow between the upper and lower torso. When the body is working well this *asana* can be sustained for minutes at a time in a relaxed fashion. Again, do not be discouraged and keep practising.

Benefits

In addition to those outlined above, this *asana* is excellent for reducing abdominal fat and flaccidity. It also aids those suffering from digestive troubles. Anyone suffering from back-ache whether upper or lower, left or right, should also witness some improvement through some continued practice. This posture may also help sufferers of asthma as improved performance gradually teaches the diaphragm to relax, which may aid the tightness and constriction experienced during attacks of wheeziness.*

USTRASANA (Camel Pose)

Directions

Kneel on the floor keeping the knees as close as possible, with the feet slightly apart and the toes pointed in. Lift the chest, tuck in the tailbone, and bend backwards to place the hands on the feet. Keep your eyes open and on the exhalation push the body weight forward onto the knees, while opening the chest.

Comment

Back-bends often feel like 'back-breakers' and in fact this difficult pose is done to break us out of our rigid patterns (characterised by a stiff spine) and open us up to change and a new experience of ourselves. The chest is fully expanded, which allows us to express and open the heart centre. The posture also makes the strong energetic connection between the head and genital regions, increasing the flow of energy

Ustrasana *(Camel Pose)*

* Because yoga makes us aware of stress patterns in the body, asthmatics may experience a slight attack of asthma when beginning yoga. Rather than reaching for the inhaler it is recommended to slow down but keep practising a range of postures. The author's experience has been that many of these initial attacks will pass in 15–20 minutes. Obviously do not prolong continued stressful breathing and use your own judgement to gauge your response.

between the intellectual and sexual centres. Very often a student may experience fear, dizziness and panic when first attempting this pose, and in this case it is advisable to first lift the head, get used to the feelings of openness and extension, and then drop the head back.

Those suffering with weakness or injury to the lower back should best work with a teacher to prevent excessive strain in this region. However, the Camel Pose is recommended for many back and spinal problems as the curvature actually pushes the individual vertebrae into correct alignment.

Benefits
The Camel Pose corrects kyphosis (round back) and hunched, rounded shoulders by lifting and opening the chest. The central nervous system in the spinal column is purified and energised and, occasionally, coming out of the posture may lead to a slight headache due to stress being released. (If this happens sit on your heels and bend forwards.) The pose increases flexibility in the back and opens the chest, aiding the lungs in working towards full expansion.
Caution: Back-bends do not actually strengthen the back and this practice should always be balanced by doing other postures described in this chapter.

VIRASANA AND SUPTA VIRASANA

Directions
Sit on the heels and gradually widen them until the buttocks rest on the floor. If this is too difficult practise sitting on a cushion or a pile of magazines and gradually lower down to the floor. Try to turn the heels out and curl the toes around the buttocks. Use a thick blanket to help cushion the feet. Straighten the back and stretch the arms over the head.

For *Supta Virasana* gradually lie back onto the elbows, the head and finally the upper back — taking the arms over the head. Tuck the tailbone under, and relax. Stay in the pose up to 10 minutes.

Comment
Although pain may be experienced at first in the ankles, knees and thighs, it is well worth breaking through this barrier to enjoy the benefits of this pose.

Virasana teaches us that mobility and flexibility begin in the ankles and feet. The posture literally grounds or earths the consciousness, bringing the awareness down into the body. *Supta Virasana* teaches us how to relax the diaphragm and abdomen correctly while cultivating strength and stability in the groin, thighs and pelvis.

Benefits
This posture brings flexibility to the ankles and knees and will help correct weakness in the ankles for those who have a tendency towards flat feet. The tops of the thighs are fully stretched and the lower abdomen is opened fully. The posture has been found to benefit women suffering from period problems and endometriosis (attachment of the womb to surrounding tissue). It may also help tonify the prostate gland in males and help prevent hernias.

ADHO MUKHA SVANASANA AND URDHVA MUKHA SVANASANA (Dog Pose I and II)

Directions
First Stage: Lie face down on the floor, with the feet one foot apart, and place the hands by the side of the chest just below the armpits. Raise the trunk up, stretch the arms

Adho Mukha Svanasana *(Dog Pose I)*   **Urdhva Mukha Svanasana** *(Dog Pose II)*

to lift the spine, and open the chest. Straighten the legs keeping the knees off the floor and tighten the buttocks with the toes pointed back. Do not hunch the shoulders. Move the chest up and through the arms. Stay 30 seconds–one minute.

Second Stage: From the first position lift the pelvis, turn the toes in and push the heels down towards the floor. Stretch the arms and elongate the spine, taking the crown of the head towards the floor (the hands and feet are roughly four feet apart). Stay 30 seconds–2 minutes. A useful variation is to combine the first and second postures moving forwards and backwards between them, keeping the knees raised all the time. Repeat 5–25 times.

Comment

The arms are often a weak part of the body and yet have an important part to play in our self-expression and determination to achieve our goals. Conversely tension and stress is often stored in the upper torso and shoulders and these two postures will work in removing the tightness. Strengthening the arms will also help strengthen the heart and lungs.

Both positions often prove difficult for beginners when both arms, legs and back feel stiff. Movement between the poses will help increase mobility and build up strength and flexibility in the arms and shoulders allowing us eventually to fully extend the spine. The Dog Pose, with the head up, inspires strength and determination. With the head down the pose turns the same determination inwards to master ourselves.

Benefits

The 'head-up' position will relieve back problems both in the lower, mid and upper spine. Stiff shoulders and neck are also helped and one should be careful not to constrict the back of the neck and keep strongly lifting by pushing down on the wrists. The 'face-down' position strengthens the heart and lungs and gives a complete stretch to the back of the body, from the fingers to the toes. Initially, one may just be concerned with weak wrists and aching legs, but regular practice will gradually overcome these problems and the effects will be felt more completely through the whole body.

Movement between the two postures prevents stiffness in the spinal column and hips and is an excellent way to arouse a sluggish body first thing in the morning. Moving rapidly between postures acts to purify the system from stress and tightness be it felt mentally or physically. The two Dog Poses are part of a yoga sequence called 'Salute to the Sun' which is taught in many beginners' yoga classes. (B. K. S. Iyengar's book *Light on Yoga* contains an even more dynamic version of 'Salute to the Sun'.)

PASCHIMOTTANASANA (Forward Bend)

Directions
Sit with the legs outstretched and the heels extended. Pull the buttocks back and first practise tightening the knees and sitting up straight. Try to move the lower spine into the body and lift the rib cage and skin on the chest. Do not hunch the shoulders or constrict the neck. Use the hands to lift the chest by pushing on the floor, or hold a belt around the feet to pull the ribs up. Forward bending should not be done by collapsing the chest and trying to put one's head on one's knee. At first it is recommended to practise holding a belt around the feet and sitting up straight feeling the stretch in the legs and the back. Moving forward should be done gradually, bending from the hips without dropping the chest.

Comment
Eventually, with practice, the ribs will touch the thigh and the chin will rest below the knees, although this may take some considerable time. All benefit of the exercise will be lost if one collapses the chest, and the lower spine may be strained if one does not work correctly. If the pose seems very difficult work in short 'bursts' for 1–2 minutes at a time repeating 4 or 5 times.

Although this posture may present great difficulty and create discouragement, it allows one to build up patience and insight into our mind–body relationships. Whereas backbends push us to our limit of openness and stretch, forward-bending makes us concentrate on the development of our inner space and through continual practice the mind learns discrimination, receptivity and understanding through overcoming the difficulties presented.

Benefits
The pose fully stretches the legs and strengthens the spine. Staying in the pose provides a massage to the abdominal organs, rests the heart, and nourishes the kidneys. The mind learns to stop fighting and calmly accepts the body as a friend. When mastered, the pose confers peace of mind and puts us in touch with our spirit, 'self' or centre.

SARVANGASANA (Shoulder Stand)

Directions
Take a thick blanket and fold into a square approximately 2½ feet square. Lie on the blanket with the back of the head resting on the floor (this is to protect the neck). Raise the legs and pelvis and support the back ribs. Stretch the heels, straighten the legs and lift the chest, aiming to reach as vertical a position as possible. Do not turn the head. Turn the front thighs and knees inwards squeezing the inside legs together. Move the tailbone in and up and keep lifting the chest up from the chin. Stay 1–10 minutes.

Iyengar has said that this posture is like a mother who strives for the harmony and well-being of the human system. For this reason it has been called the Queen of *asanas* (Headstand being the King). For once, the student places the body's needs above those of the head and by looking at the body we give it our full attention. Through the reversal of gravity, the body and brain are refreshed with the reduction of venous pressure. Often the beginner feels fatigued by this pose and may experience some backache as the body adjusts to the new position, but this will pass with practice. The

Sarvangasana *(Shoulder Stand)*

effects of the posture are felt by increasing the stay in the pose and strengthening the legs and back in order to overcome the altered effects on body weight. When coming down, bend the legs and lie with the legs bent for a short period to allow the lower back to relax.

Benefits

The circulatory, digestive and nervous systems are relaxed, toned and rejuvenated by this pose. The endocrine system is re-balanced with the effects being especially concentrated on the pituitary, pineal and thyroid glands. These are situated in the head and neck region and control the body's metabolism and overall functioning.

The posture also relieves weakness and fatigue in the legs and spine (although one does have to work to achieve this!). It is recommended for sufferers of virtually any condition whether the symptoms be physical or psychological. (Those with high blood pressure should practice *Supta Virasana* and the forward bend first before doing this pose.)

Overall, the Shoulder Stand has a highly relaxing effect on the body. This effect is somewhat paradoxical because while doing the pose one has to work the body 100% while the brain and mind are kept in a state of calmness. Any stress accumulated is, therefore, recognised and discharged gradually through the body and nervous system while the brain is not given a chance to interfere with the process. The posture is therefore excellent for those suffering from hypertension, insomnia and feelings of weakness, fear and insecurity.

Although at first the pose may feel 'impossible' and test one's strength of will thoroughly, continued practice and length of stay in the position can act more effectively than any tranquilliser or anti-depressant since the body learns how to overcome stress and tension through its own efforts.

This pose is excellent to practise before *Savasana* or the Relaxation Pose as it will create a complete sense of letting-go in body and mind after all the hard work.

SAVASANA (Corpse Pose)

Directions
Spread out a thick blanket and lie down keeping the head, spine and legs in line. Turn the palms upward, with the arms slightly away from the waist. Tuck the tail bone down and allow the legs and feet to turn out. If the chin is raised and the neck feels tight place a small cushion under the head. Close the eyes and allow the awareness to focus on the breath and body. Stay 5–15 minutes with eyes closed. When getting up, first roll to the side and stay 1 minute before rising.

Comment
Many people are attracted to yoga in the pursuit of mental relaxation. However, more and more western therapies are centring their attention on releasing stress in the body in order to relieve psychological worries and anxieties. Thus, many people are unable to relax even when lying down in bed and sometimes feelings of tiredness may not be sufficient to induce sleep. Most meditation and relaxation courses today encourage the students to do some initial exercises before practising. Patanjali, author of the famous *Yoga Sutras*, advised students that a 'comfortable' posture was an essential prerequisite to meditation. He therefore placed the study of *asanas* (postures) and *pranayama* (breathing), before that of meditation, in his eight steps or 'limbs' of yoga.*

Having spent 10–20 minutes doing a yoga routine, one will find great satisfaction and enjoyment in lying down to take a rest! However, the important difference between rest and relaxation is in the awareness and state of mind. In a state of rest the mind will often jump around, indulge in fantasy and reminiscence and, even if one falls asleep, the unconscious brain will be dreaming and generally active.

Rest and relaxation in a yogic sense implies keeping a disciplined awareness of the whole mental and physical organism. The discipline is not to impose a particular 'state' on the body but rather to minimise distractions originating both in body and mind. One should not repress feelings, physical sensations or thoughts but rather seek to remain non-attached to them and act merely as an observer, patiently waiting for the thoughts or sensations to subside.

In the beginning when practising the Corpse Pose there is a tendency either to fall asleep or become involved with thoughts and images. Sleep may be just what one needs, but if it becomes a habit one should work to overcome it! With the sleep tendency having the eyes half open may help, or concentrating on some soft music may help to keep the consciousness alert.

With the other tendency for the mind to be overactive the above techniques may also be helpful. Another approach is to listen to the sound of your own breath which manifests as a slight hissing noise in the throat. Use the intellect to focus intently on this sound and hold it in the mind. Visualisation on the abdomen and various parts of the body may also help.

Stilling the mind is a slow and gradual process which, like bodily flexibility, improves with practice. This is where a teacher can be of great help. Firstly by working one harder in the postures to take out the resistance of body and mind to letting go; and secondly to act as a guardian to which one can safely surrender in the Corpse Pose. 'Surrender' does not essentially imply giving in to anything or anyone other than your-

---

* The eight limbs are *Yama* (ethical precepts), *Niyama* (personal observances), *Asana* (posture), *Pranayama* (breath control), *Pratyahara* (sense control), *Dharana* (concentration), *Dhyana* (contemplation) and *Samadhi* (contentment/enlightenment). See Iyengar's book *Light on Yoga* for a full discussion of the eight limbs.

self. Relaxation and meditation is primarily a way of allowing mind and body to rest in one's 'inner self', much as we allow our body to rest in a comfortable armchair. Relaxation is the art of creating harmony between mind and body releasing the effects of tension and stress and allowing a spontaneous and creative flow of mental and physical energy.

Conclusion

Yoga postures and meditations are simply techniques to allow us to experience our source, our centre, our wholeness and our connection with the Universe, Nature and each other.

We must create strength if we are to be responsible for our weaknesses, create inner harmony if we are to be responsible for chaos around us. We can learn to constantly enhance our awareness of living, so that being alive provides us with an immeasurable capacity for enjoyment and creativity.

Yoga is not an end but merely a beginning.

CHAPTER 6
OKI YOGA
Barbara Kimbrey & Carl Webster

Forget your images of austerity and a regimented discipline. Oki Yoga is about having fun and laughter, screams and playful struggles. It involves highly mixed groups of people, from tiny children to elderly invalids: people of various physical conditions, mental outlook, and cultural backgrounds. It entails learning, playing, practising together, cooperating to improve each other, and in the very process shedding all kinds of unwanted habits, illnesses and cares so familiar to modern people. Oki Yoga is something everyone can participate in, because everyone is capable of trying, doing their best in all that is asked. It is not about answers, but making an effort, sharing and encouraging each other and through this process discovering oneself.

Practising together . . .

Dr Masahiro Oki

BACKGROUND ON OKI YOGA

Dr Masahiro Oki, the founder of Oki Yoga, has been a well known yoga teacher in Japan for many years, and now his influence is being strongly felt in Europe, America and Australia. Dr Oki certainly defies the usual preconceptions about what it is to be a Yoga Master. He doesn't claim to provide the answers to life, but still people come to his *dojo* in Mishima, Japan, from all over the world to experience the teachings of this remarkable man. Dr Oki shows that what we do through the discipline of Oki Yoga is to discover our own answers. This only comes from the process of taking ourselves to the limit in everything we do, and at that point, the answer begins to reveal itself. From his broad personal experience, Dr Oki has brought together an essential understanding from many disciplines — both ancient and modern, oriental and occidental — and distilled them into a very practical teaching for everyday living.

Born in Korea in 1921, Masahiro Oki now maintains the largest Yoga Institute in Japan. He travelled extensively throughout his life, and studied medicine, religion and philosophy in Japan and China. He spent time in Mongolia and Tibet studying theology with the Lamas, visited Arabia and Iran to study Islam, and also travelled to India, where he studied Hinduism with Mahatma Gandhi and experienced the daily life of a Yoga Ashram. After many years of intensively surveying the philosophy and practice of yoga, he founded the Japan Yoga Association in 1958. In 1967 he opened the Oki Institute in Mishima, which continues to attract people from all over Japan, as well as from many other countries — including Europe, Australia, the United States, Brazil, Korea and India.

OKI YOGA

The training method of Oki Yoga is known as Dynamic Zen. As Exercise, it stresses the importance of the balance between opposite kinds of stimulation: tension and relaxation, heat and cold, stillness and movement. For example, static Zen is practised through seated meditation, while moving Zen takes the form of dynamic exercise. Oki Yoga is a balance of opposites — tensing and relaxing, contracting and stretching, running and jumping, pushing and pulling — embracing a whole range of body movements and non-movement. Oki Yoga includes a blend of traditional Indian yoga, with oriental exercises, martial arts, chanting, Zen meditation, dancing and physical games (or *kyoka-ho*), done in pairs or groups.

Years of study and research have also enabled Dr Oki to develop a unique system for the treatment of many chronic illnesses. Many people not cured by medical science, and those who wish to improve their creative ability or simply to feel more alive, come to Mishima Dojo. Masahiro Oki is also a recognised master of many kinds of martial arts, the Japanese Tea Ceremony, and Japanese Flower Arrangement. He has been appointed as advisor in six hospitals, given special training to members of the Japanese Parachute Regiment, professional baseball players, Olympic Alpine skiers, violinists, pianists, professional dancers, businessmen, religious devotees, doctors and teachers, and has also given special lectures to the Japanese Royal Family. He has written more than 60 books on Yoga and different forms of natural healing and meditation.

THE PHILOSOPHY AND PRACTICE OF OKI YOGA

Oki Yoga philosophy states that everything should exist in its natural state. Health, for example, is the natural state of the body, stability and integration the natural state of mind, happiness the natural feeling of life. Peace exists when all surrounding circumstances exist in their natural state.

'Peace exists when all surrounding circumstances exist in their natural state'.

OKI YOGA

*Workout in the Mishima **dojo***

Naturalness has to do with balance. By achieving a state of balance within the body, and harmony with others, an overall state of well-being can be enjoyed. Dr Oki refers to this as a 'mutually beneficial relationship'. Such a relationship cannot of course exist if one's own condition is good, while those around remain in trouble. Only together with others can we really experience and enjoy life.

At the Oki Yoga Institute in Japan, both students in training and patients seeking to cure diseases pursue a natural life style with a daily schedule of balanced activities. Everyone follows a similar routine, but specific treatments, exercise or techniques are employed in appropriate situations. The activities at the Institute are designed to produce balance and purity in the body, mind and daily life — in accordance with the true Oriental philosophy. The training and cure are highly educational, and are directed in both the physical and spiritual realms.

The Oki Yoga Institute is located in farm country, below wooded hills. An example of the daily schedule is as follows:

5 am — Awake

5.30 am — *Sutra* Chanting

6 am — Running (or walking for the weak and sick) through the mountains, and bathing in cold mountain streams

7.45 am — Breakfast: a bowl of vegetable miso broth

9 am — Purification Exercises designed to promote blood circulation, strengthen the digestive system, and aid elimination

10 am — Meditation or soft exercise to calm the mind and nervous system

11 am — Lecture to stimulate the intellect, educating both student and patient alike

12 noon — *Khoka-ho* strengthening exercise. This is very vigorous and promotes overall bodily strength and stamina. It often includes training in the martial arts of Judo, Aikido and Karate

1 pm — Lunch and rest. All meals are made from natural wholefoods, are skilfully prepared, and beautifully presented

3 pm — Usually a walk in the woods, sometimes with a view to learning about wild medicinal plants, gathering them to be prepared for teas, or included in the evening meal

4 pm — Therapy Class. This can include therapeutic massage, shiatsu, acupuncture or moxibustion

5 pm — Yoga postures, breathing exercises or meditation. Alternatively, a class featuring a cultural activity such as the art of the Japanese tea ceremony, flower arrangement, song or dance

6 pm — Supper

7.30 pm — Lecture or 'Question and Answer' session with Dr Oki

9 pm — Write a daily report of thoughts and feelings, or suggestions concerning the day's activities

11 pm — Sleep

In the morning it is best to first practise the 'soft' forms of warming-up exercise, which loosen the muscles, stimulate the bodily systems and aid the elimination of waste. Oki Yoga refers to these as 'purification exercises'. Later one can progress to the more dynamic forms which use strength and tension to produce power, release energy, and arouse the spirit of challenge. The class featuring the strengthening exercise known as *kyoka-ho* is the prime class of the day at the Oki Yoga *dojo* in Mishima, and is perhaps the most characteristic or unique aspect of Oki Yoga. In fact, anyone who has had the opportunity to participate in such a class is unlikely to forget it. It often involves deliberately unreasonable, fast, difficult and vigorous feats. Because people generally tend to remain within their comfortable ability, the 'unreasonable' approach generally helps one to confront, and go beyond, their limitations and weaknesses. These classes are ingeniously varied. There are group games in which men, women and children contend with each other, creating good humour. There are also activities involving running, jumping, pushing, pulling or carrying partners. While building their strength participants get caught up in laughter, and fear and tension disappear. In this way emotional balance is achieved.

After strengthening and generally revitalising all aspects of the body, the next step is to find special exercises to strengthen weak points, and correct imbalances. Just as no one diet is perfect for everyone, no single system or set of exercises is suitable for everyone.

Dr Oki has gained wide recognition for his system of Corrective Exercises, which, by adjusting the body posture, effectively treats many illnesses. For example, it is often said of people who make mistakes, or who are forgetful, or accident prone, that they 'don't have their heads on straight'. It's not really as silly as it sounds. The improper alignment of the cervical vertebrae (the vertebrae of the neck) in relation to the rest of the spine may result in these and other similar problems. The following is a simple Oki Yoga exercise for correcting the vertebrae of the neck and spine.

YOGA POSES FOR NECK AND SPINE

Bow Pose
Do the Bow Pose and have a friend check to see which way your neck is bent (left or right). Stretch out your neck in the opposite direction and rock backwards and forwards in the Bow pose.

Bow Pose

Now repeat the Bow Pose and have a friend check to see which way the spine is curved. Change your hand to grasp the inside of the ankle on the side around which the spine is curved and rock backwards and forwards.

In classical yoga, *asanas*, or poses, have been practised for thousands of years, and are well known for their effectiveness in promoting a healthy, flexible body. If one's body is perfectly balanced, these exercises can only have a beneficial effect. However, if your body is not perfectly aligned, the yoga poses can actually increase the already existing imbalance.

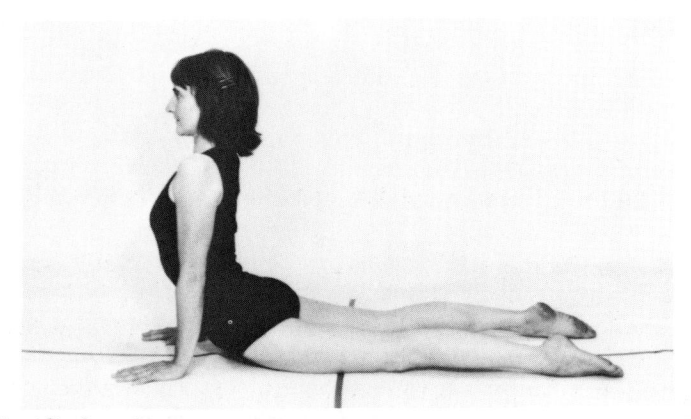

Cobra **asana**. First lie face down with your hands by your shoulders. Exhaling, straighten your arms without lifting your shoulders or pubic bone. This **asana** is very good for the lower back.

For example, the pose of the Cobra *asana* is known to have a strengthening effect on the kidneys. But if the left kidney, and the muscles on the left side of the back are weak compared to those on the right, the right side will naturally take the greater force of the pose. In this way, the stronger right side becomes ever increasingly stronger than the left.

Here are some examples of some simple corrective techniques for yoga *asanas*:

Arch Pose
Do the Arch Pose, and have a friend check to see which hip is lower. Keep the same position, but come up on the toes of the foot on the same side as the lower hip. Next try to raise that foot off the floor.

Arch Pose

Twist Pose
Do a Twist Pose from any upright sitting position. Which side is more difficult? Repeat several times on that side.

Repeating the exercises on the more difficult side is the most obvious form of corrective exercise. This can be applied to all kinds of exercises, as well as in daily life. Can you turn your head more easily to one side than the other? Do you always reach for things with the same hand? Can you stretch one leg further than the other? These kinds of imbalances and many others can be corrected by training the weaker or tighter side. And remember the Oki Yoga dictum: 'Accept nothing as true without proving it so yourself'.

Twist Poses

Through many years of such experience, Dr Oki has also developed a unique and somewhat novel approach to diagnosing and treating internal ailments. It has long been acknowledged in various systems of oriental healing techniques that internal conditions reveal themselves in external appearance. Here are some interesting experiments you can try with a friend:

The Eyes
Check to see which eye is smaller (which eye does not open fully). The kidneys and the eyes are related. The kidney on the same side as the smaller eye needs to be strengthened. Lie face down, and have a friend hold your leg in a position about 45° from the floor. Exhaling, try to force your leg downwards while your friend resists. This will bring power to the kidney area. Repeat a few times using full effort, relax, then check the eyes and see the difference.

The Nostrils
Check to see which nostril is smaller. The nostril relates to the lungs, or organs under the right rib cage. If the right nostril is smaller, the right lung and liver need to be strengthened. If the left nostril is smaller, the left lung, heart and stomach need strengthening. Kneel down and have your partner press down firmly on your shoulder on the same side as the smaller nostril. Try to raise your shoulder against your partner's force. This will strengthen the weaker side.

The Quality of 'No-Mind'
You will enjoy these exercises if you can do them with an empty mind. That's what the Japanese call *mu-shin* or 'no-mind'. This quality of 'no-mind' doesn't imply any kind of foolishness or absent-mindedness. On the contrary, it is said that to exercise (or act) properly, the mind must be silenced. In this way the body can function as a unit. When the mind speaks, we think, 'I must do', 'I will do', 'This is difficult' and so on, and in so doing we are actually inhibiting the naturally harmonious movement of the body. Hunting-dogs on a chase never stop to consider what to do or how fast to run. Their movements are quick are sure, their decisions instantaneous. This is the result of a co-ordinated brain and body function uninhibited by excess thinking. Children at play, as well as the movements of many highly skilled athletes, also exemplify

this phenomenon of free movement flowing from an unfettered mind. For this reason Oki Yoga teaches the techniques of Zen meditation for its effectiveness in quietening and calming the mind.

In life, everything changes as naturally as day into night, summer into winter, seed to fruit to seed. This is a quality of life itself, and our health and well-being depend on our maintaining flexibility to deal with daily life, as well as stamina to keep going. Becoming unhealthy is a product of violating that cycle of change — becoming too rigid to change, or getting trapped into bad habits.

Oki Yoga challenges our pattern of behaviour and creates an understanding of health and balance through the practice of highly varied activities for the body, mind and spirit. Dr Oki advises each person to listen to the innate wisdom of the body, rather than to rely on external authorities for 'answers'. Dr Oki states emphatically, 'Don't rely on people or things. Don't rely on external factors. Try to build your truth by your own actions and efforts. In this way you will be able to master your own life'.

Typical forward bending postures

To enhance the stretch of the legs and movement from the hips stand on some elevated surface, such as a chair. Bend forward, allowing the movement to come from the hips as much as possible.

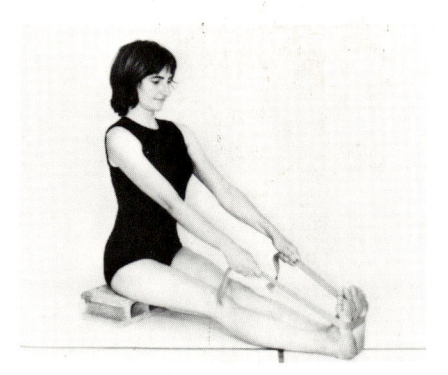

For beginners, or where there is stiffness in the lower back, it is useful to begin forward bends from the floor, first elevating the hips. This allows the weight of the body to be taken on the buttock bones, rather than on the base of the spine.

CHAPTER 7
SHIATSU
Daniel Weber

The word *Shiatsu* comes from the Japanese — *shi* meaning 'finger', *atsu* meaning 'pressure'. There are a number of traditional massage techniques. These include *anma*, which is similar to remedial massage in the West; acupressure — a form of Shiatsu which manipulates the *tsubo*, or points associated with energy — and several forms of joint manipulation similar to osteopathy.

BACKGROUND

Shiatsu is of rather recent origin and was finally officially recognised by the Japanese Government just after the Second World War. Shiatsu was established in the late 1920s as a reaction against the degeneration of *anma* from a medical therapy into a purely pleasure-oriented massage technique. Shiatsu itself, contrary to its name, is more than just the use of finger pressure. In Shiatsu the fingers, or digits, are used for a specific stimulation of the *tsubo*, or acupressure points. Also, there is quite a lot of stimulation done with other parts of the body — the knees, elbows, toes, the heel of the hand, heel of the foot and the pad of the foot. These particular techniques are used more for stimulation of the meridians, or channels of energy, which circulate through the body. The intention of all Oriental therapies, as distinct from Western massage therapy, is to stimulate the circulation of *ki* (or in China *chi*), which is the circulation of energy through the body. The stimulation of the points along the meridian helps move the energy, re-balancing the person and thereby helping him to regain health. Shiatsu uses no technique other than that involving the body, and is relatively safe for beginners.

Shiatsu is much more of a healing art than a medical technique and is therefore best approached with a calm, even mind and a loving, warm attitude. The technical part can be learnt in time but emphasis is placed on the support, love and openness of the individual practitioner. Shiatsu, *anma* and other forms of acupressure have their origin and development within the context of Oriental therapy. The Oriental healing arts, including acupuncture, Chinese herbalism and manipulative therapy, basically follow one line of thought, namely that disease is an imbalance of *yin* and *yang* energy within the body and the meridians, and the way to maintain health or to regain health is to re-balance the energy within the body. Correspondingly, Western medicine is more concerned with the biochemical imbalance in the body and achieves its results by changing the cellular biochemistry or by surgical intervention. All therapies, Eastern or Western, are ultimately only useful if they serve the client and restore health.

Shiatsu is of particular use because it can be approached and used by a person with little experience, and secondly, because it emphasises human contact. The Shiatsu therapist must maintain continual and real contact with the client in order to understand the nature of the condition and the changes that may occur. The diagnosis is through palpation pressure. Oriental medical theory holds that the energy of the body *ki* — circulates from the internal organs to the periphery of the body and returns again through channels called meridians. There are six channels of *yin* energy and six channels of *yang* energy. In Oriental medicine the quality of *yin* and *yang* energies are distinguished as follows: *Yin* energy is quiet, deep, passive and nourishing. *Yang* energy is active, purposeful, aggressive and functionally protective of the body. By a sense of correspondence between the internal and the external, we determine the imbalance between the *yin* and *yang* energy, and treat appropriately along the channels of energy. The six internal organs and meridians associated with *yin* energy are called *tsang*, and the six organs and meridians associated with *yang* are called *fu*. All symptoms of illness belong to a *yin* or a *yang* quality. Therefore, unlike Western medicine which immediately attaches names to the symptoms and treats them accordingly, Oriental medicine focuses on the nature of change, or the cycle of change from *yin* to *yang*. For example the common flu or head cold starts with very *yang*, hot, painful conditions — stiff neck, high fever, red face, restlessness, thirst. Given correct therapy, or with time itself, the fever breaks, sweating occurs, the muscle tension relaxes and the person rests. However, after several days the condition may become *yin*. The person will then be very tired, pale, chilled and needs support and energy, so the condition that we call a cold is really a continual cycle of *yang*, not-so-*yang*, small-*yin* and so forth. The appropriate treatment is used at the correct time by the therapist.

DIAGNOSIS: THE ART OF BALANCE

In the assessment of Oriental healing techniques we find that they are much more of an art than a science. The objective science of Western medicine, while having a major impact upon the health and well-being of the people, has difficulty in giving treatment to those conditions which have not yet been assigned to a category or which have no organic cause. Oriental medicine, without having to rely on categories and names, treats according to the condition or the confirmation that the person exhibits. This develops from common sense and its art is a highly refined one, depending upon the sensitivity of the practitioner. It is best used for those long term chronic conditions which really have no diagnosed name. For example, the patient exhibiting symptoms of lassitude, poor muscle tone, frequent urination, a very pale colour, little appetite, and a depressed or defeated emotional condition, would be referred to as *yin*. In that case the quality of treatment would need to stimulate the opposite, or active energy, *yang*. On the other hand, a client or patient who exhibits excessive tension along the shoulders and neck, redness in the face, irritation and anger as an emotional state and a tendency to over-eat and over-drink, is said to have a *yang* confirmation, and in this case the therapist gives a *yin* or sedating treatment. The concept in Shiatsu is thus to balance the *yin* and *yang* energy in the person according to their condition.

A very fast, somewhat painful, deep stimulation with the thumb or elbows sedates or relieves tension in the body. It is usually accompanied with fast, deep breathing or panting. Another form of therapy consists of very firm but even pressure on a point or meridian, involves very little movement, and encourages the breathing to be very calm and relaxing. These are the technical aspects of Shiatsu. The other part of Shiatsu involves the simple role of touch, and this is one of the reasons why the therapy has gained so much popularity in the West. Living as we do in a world characterised by electronic communication, automobiles, aeroplanes, high pressure work and large cities, there is very little opportunity for us to be touched, either physically or in our hearts. Shiatsu is an opportunity for the therapist to work deeply with the person's spirit, heart and body, re-balancing them within, and also in relation to the external world. The great stress that we live under is admirably treated with Shiatsu, although the sense of touch is really an art, and is difficult to teach.

There is a story which the Orientals tell to demonstrate the quality of touch. A daughter-in-law went to a Chinese herbalist to buy some poison to kill her mother-in-law. She had said that she was deeply disturbed that the mother-in-law treated her cruelly, did not give her any affection and came between her and her husband. The doctor told her that she must give her mother-in-law this potion and at the same time do Shiatsu on a daily basis. The potion or poison would not be effective unless the mother-in-law was massaged every day for a duration of three months and after that period of time the mother-in-law would die, apparently of natural causes. The daughter-in-law did as she was instructed. She administered the poison in the food daily and manipulated her mother-in-law with Shiatsu. However, after a period of several months, the daughter-in-law began to regret what she was doing and felt very badly about her desire to kill her mother-in-law. At the same time the mother-in-law began to treat her very well and was supportive and kind. Finally the daughter-in-law ran back to the herbalist and asked for an antidote, declaring, 'I am very sorry, I did not want to harm my mother-in-law.' The herbalist responded by saying that really there was no poison, only water collected from flowers. The story goes to show how touching the body changes our physical, mental and emotional state.

Shiatsu is not a difficult manipulation, but it does treat very deeply the nature of energy in the body. We can distinguish the energy of heaven, and the energy of the earth, both of which nourish all human beings. We emerge from mother earth and grow towards our heavenly father — two archetypes in the West which correspond to the *yang* and *yin* energy. As we grow between the two, this energy flows through us from earth to heaven and from heaven to earth. As long as the flow is uninterrupted, our health is maintained. However, should it begin to block we then start to show symptoms — whether physical, emotional or spiritual. Shiatsu, in a very gentle and supportive way, releases these blockages and restores the harmony so that the body may heal itself. In this sense Shiatsu is not just a medicine, but one of the highest forms of healing.

In Shiatsu, diagnoses and treatment are one. When we observe the body of a person who is healthy, the skin-tone and temperature are even and warm, and the skin resilient and dry. The Shiatsu therapist uses only the fingers, hands, elbows, knees and feet, and those too must be sensitive and warm. There are no side effects, since the points are treated according to the condition.

We only have to rely on common sense to see the most appropriate way to treat. For example, a strong client — an athlete with good muscle tone, excessive tension in the shoulders, neck and back muscles, and an impatient manner — would be given a very different treatment to someone much older, whose muscle tone was much softer, who lacked tension in the body and who had a quieter, more resigned attitude to life. The amount of pressure used on a larger person would also be much greater than that used on a smaller person.

These kinds of common-sense approaches make Shiatsu a very viable therapy for the beginner. For example, when the subject exhibits an acute symptom — that is, when there is pain without palpation, an accelerated pulse rate and thoracic breathing, and the person speaks of sharp and throbbing pain — the treatment should not be given locally. Instead it is applied at a distance, along the meridians at a distant *tsubo* point, in order to relieve and sedate the inflamed condition. On the other hand, pain which is dull, quite deep on palpation and associated with lassitude and fatigue, indicates a chronic condition and can be treated locally. In practice we often use both forms of treatment because a person can exhibit an acute condition in one part of the body and a chronic condition in another.

Shiatsu can also be used by all ages, from young children through to the elderly. In fact, in Japan, the young are taught to give Shiatsu to their grandparents. Regular Shiatsu is also a preventive therapy and a barometer of one's condition. It also shows very quickly if there is an imbalance arising, and can be used as a way of determining the likely consequences — for this reason Shiatsu therapists recommend early diagnosis. Also the continuing relationship between the practitioner and the patient creates a sense of security and trust which affects other aspects of life. Shiatsu is effective for the physical body, but its benefits also flow through to the mind and spirit, for it operates on each of these levels.

SHIATSU TREATMENTS FOR TENSION

One of the most common areas of tension in the body lies across the trapezius. Certain aspects of our modern lifestyle — especially the practice of sitting for long periods in chairs or cars — weaken the lower part of the body, particularly the legs. In Japanese the area just below the navel is called the *tandin* or *hara*.* It stores the energy, and is referred to as the 'storehouse' or 'vital centre' of energy. When a person is weak in the lower part of the body, there is a tendency for him to pull up and tense the shoulders and neck. The resultant experience is often referred to as 'tension'. In fact, the condition arises from a deficiency of energy in the lower part of the body. The Shiatsu approach to this problem is to tonify the lower part of the body — especially the abdominal area, called *ampaku* — and later sedate the neck and shoulders to re-balance the energy between the upper and lower body.

LOWER BODY TENSION

Ask your client to lie on his back and place a pillow or folded blanket underneath the calves so that the knees are slightly bent, taking tension away from the abdominal muscle. Sitting *Seiza*,** Japanese style, on the right side, begin to move very gently with the fingers, in a clockwise direction as illustrated. Starting in the lower right-hand quadrant, work slowly and deeply in harmony with your breathing. Release, and continue in the next position three inches up. Repeat this action until you reach the region just below the rib-cage. Proceed across the body in a straight line until you reach the costal border on the left side. At this point change from a sitting position to a kneeling position but keeping your shoulders relaxed and your weight directly over your client's abdomen. Now begin to work downwards, in the same fashion, using four fingers of one hand while placing the other hand on top in order to maintain the pressure. Once again the action is co-ordinated with the breath. Move down to the iliac region of the spine, and twist slightly into the pubic synthesis. We have now traced the entire length of the colon.

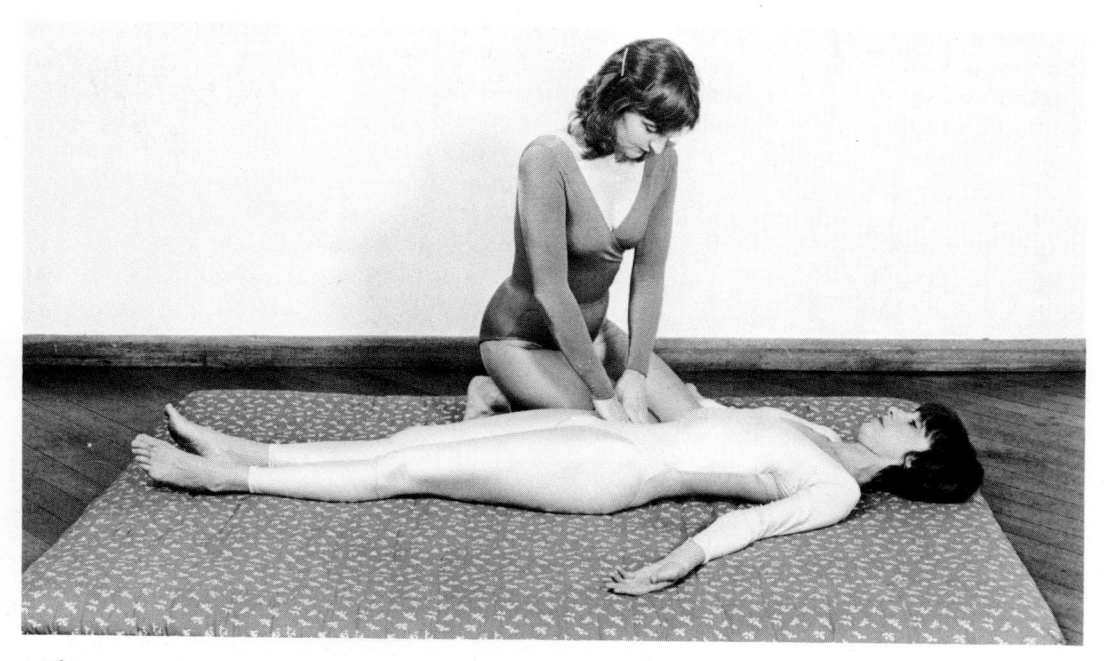

* This energy centre is said to be located two finger widths below the navel and its exact position varies from person to person.

** A position in which one sits with the back straight, and legs folded under.

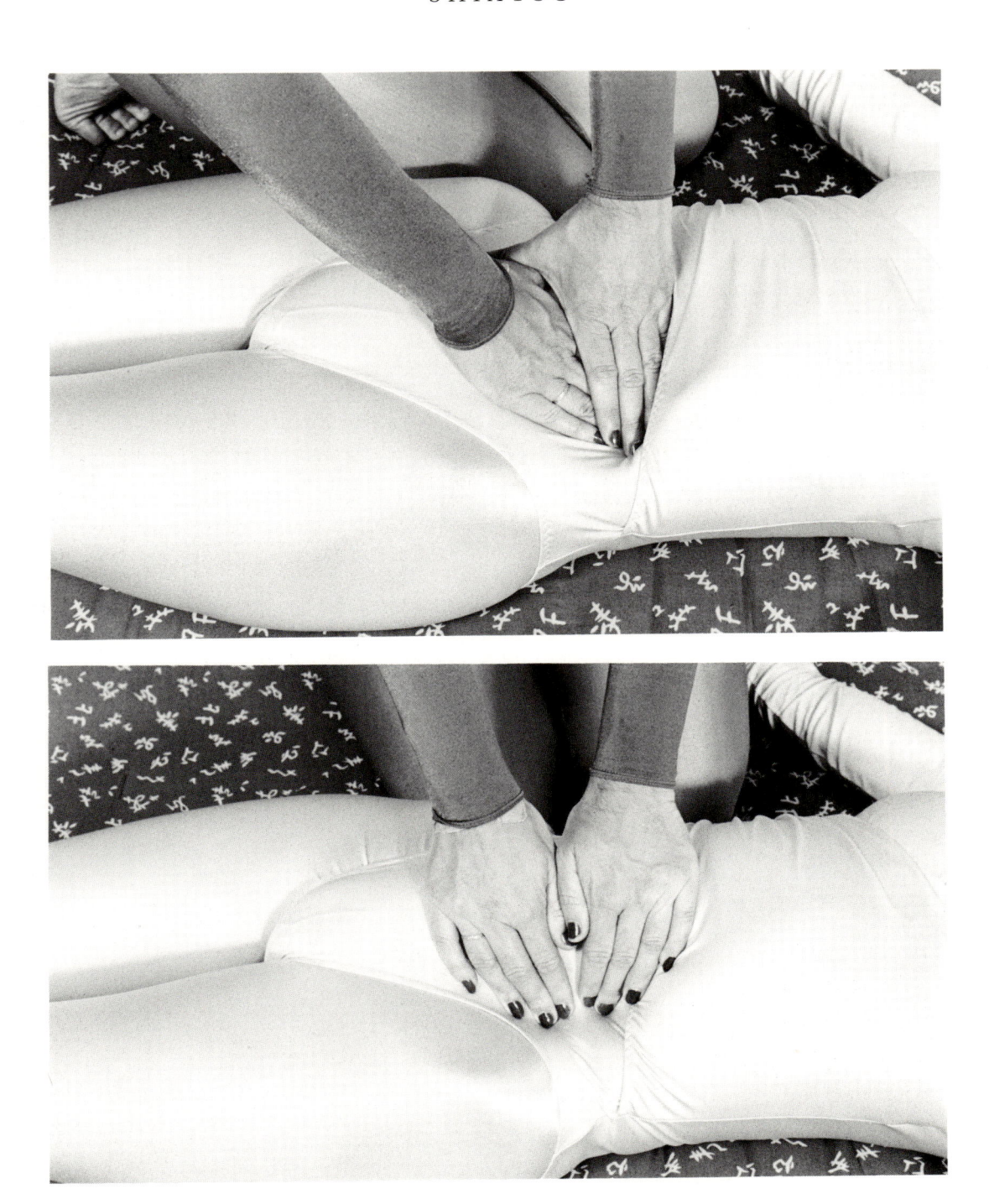

Next, place the hands in the same way, this time to the left of the navel, and press deeply. Repeat above the navel at a distance of two inches, to the left of the navel: two inches, and then just below the navel: two inches. We have now worked that central small intestine area which is associated in Chinese medicine with the element Earth and specifically with the pancreas and the stomach.

Placing one hand, palm down, on the navel, and using four fingers of the other hand, work down a central line, from the navel to the pubic synthesis. There should be firm tension along this line, like the head of a drum. If there is weakness it indicates that the *hara* is empty of energy. As we have indicated earlier, when an area lacks energy we tonify, that is, we hold without much movement. Place the right hand, palm down, on that point two to two and a half inches below the navel, and re-trace with the left hand those points which had an obstruction, or which were quite tender, either around the navel or along the line of the colon. Work slowly and deeply with the breath to disperse the blockage. Move in and out, maintaining energy in the right hand and applying a deep, satisfying pressure across the entire palm. Ensure during this process that your breathing corresponds to that of your client. Inhalation and exhalation must be the same.

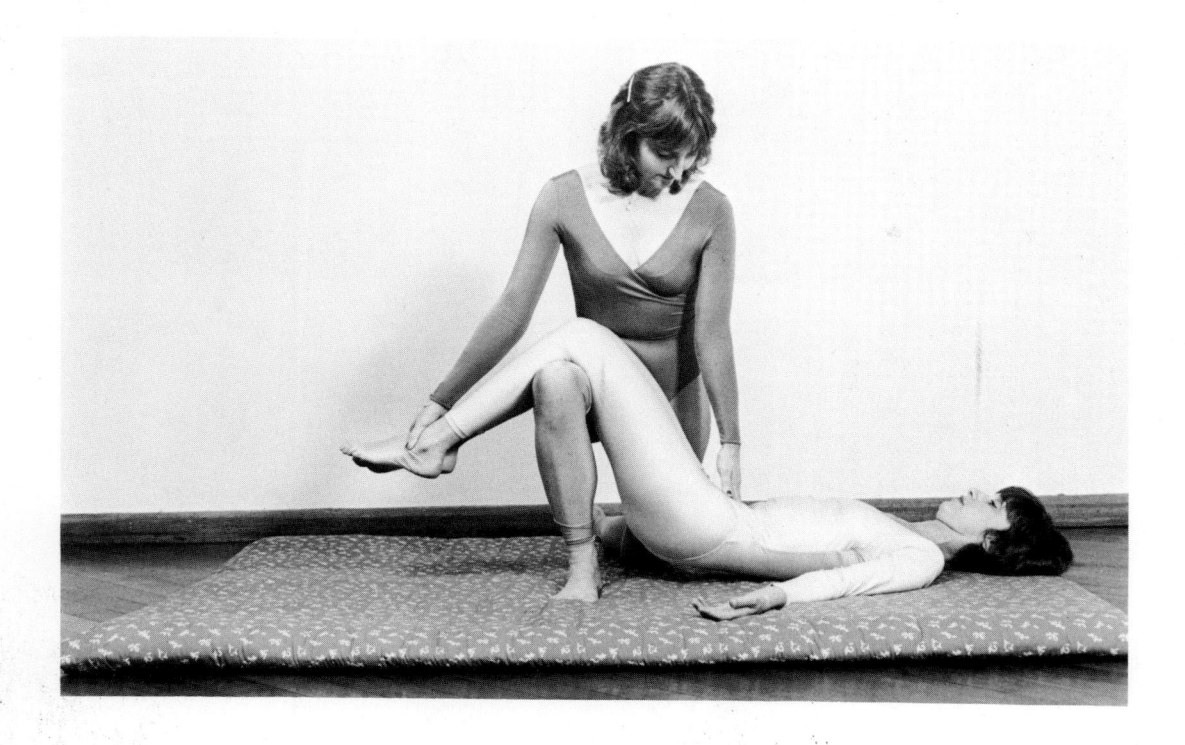

Pick up your client's legs, allowing them to bend at the knees and place them across your own knee — so that one knee is up and the other down. Maintaining this position, apply the left hand to the *hara* just below the navel, and exert gentle pressure. Place the right arm across the ankles and apply pressure downwards on the ankles, creating tension across the hips and lifting the hips gently off the floor. The continual pressure of the left hand stimulates energy production — and release. Keep the left hand on the lower abdomen, pick up one leg at a time and firmly press the client's leg against his own abdomen using the weight of your own body. At the same time, push your left hand more deeply into the *hara*. This action is first performed with the right leg and then again with the left leg. Watching your own posture and maintaining the breathing pattern, lower each leg back to the pillow on the floor. Finally, holding the knee with your right hand, and with your left hand deep and flat on the *hara*, use a circular motion to stretch left, right and down, while turning the hip and moving the leg. Continue the stimulation in the *hara*, release and repeat with the left leg. To finish, return to the *Seiza* position, place one hand above the navel, the right hand on the *hara*, and match your breathing with that of your client, holding this position for five minutes. The entire process should take from 15 to 20 minutes.

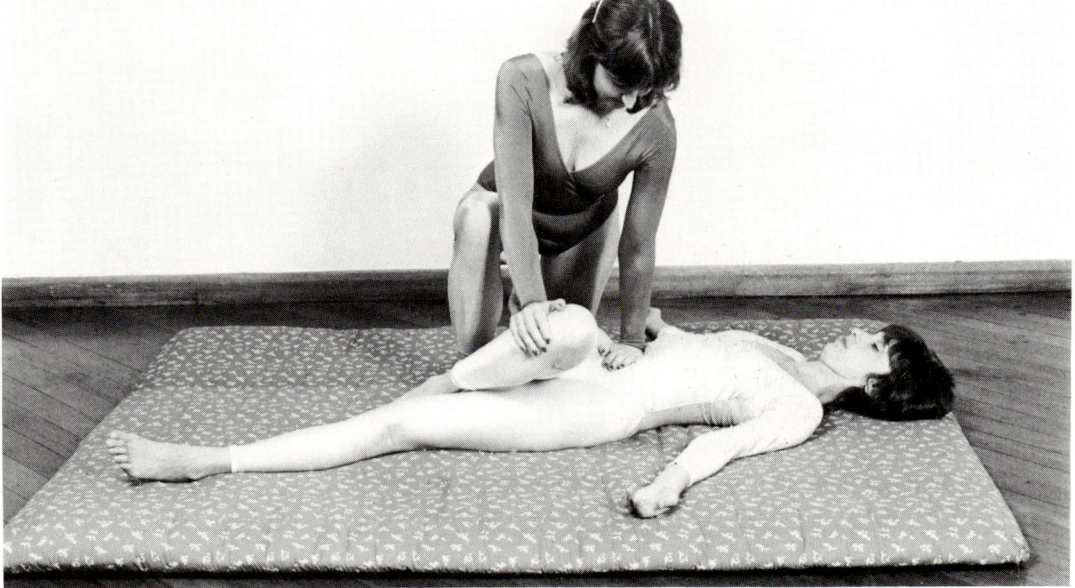

TENSION ACROSS THE SHOULDERS

Ask your client to sit *Seiza* or, if that is not possible, have him sit on a folded blanket or a very firm pillow. The key is to keep his lower back flat, so that when pressure is applied to the trapezius he does not round his lower back and collapse into his abdomen.

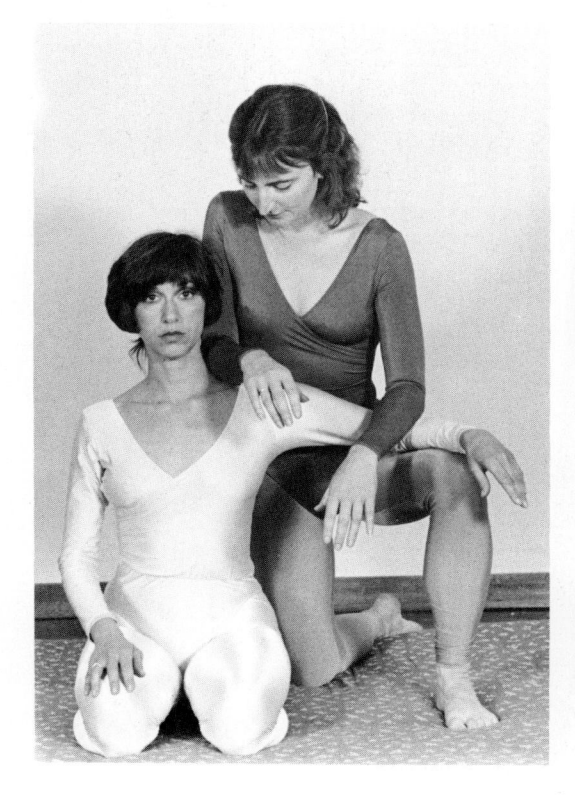

Starting behind your client, kneel on your right knee directly behind his left shoulder. With your left knee bent and your foot squarely on the floor place the client's left arm on your knee as if on the arm of a sofa or chair. Place pressure upon the trapezius or the top of the shoulder of the right arm, and also upon the crook of the same arm. This pressure should first of all be directed downwards, using the breath, and then each hand should press outwards — the right arm pushing further to the right and into the base of the neck, the left arm outward across the forearm. Ensure that the amount of pressure is appropriate to the person's condition. For larger and more heavily muscled people, the pressure should be deeper while older or smaller people require less pressure. The amount of movement, whether slow or rapid, again depends upon the musculature of the person. A faster movement, for example a cycle of 20 per minute at almost a panting rate, is much more dispersing than a rate which is four to six times per minute. Again, the rate of pressure should be appropriate to the person's size, age and physique. The stronger the dispersal, the more effective for the client.

Now move closer to the client, so that your left thigh is underneath the axilla, or armpit and the client's left arm hangs over the edge of your thigh. Apply pressure to the mastoid bone behind his ear by bringing your forearm across the top of his head. Pull his head to the right, as you pull his left arm down.

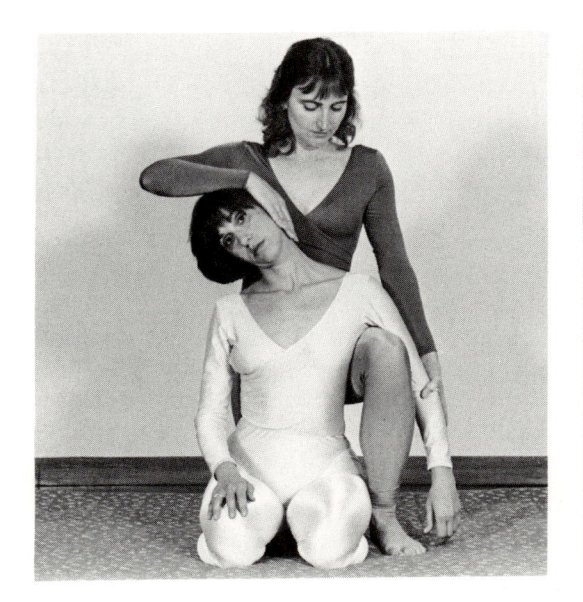

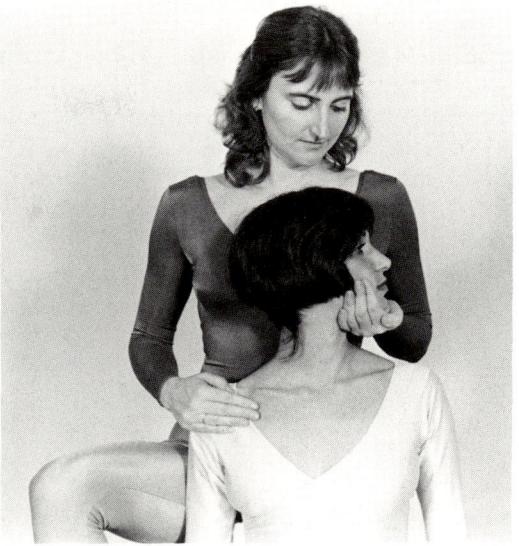

The total amount of time for this cycle of pressure points is approximately four minutes. The technique may then be repeated on the other side. After you have done this, kneel behind your patient and turn his head to the right so that he is facing his right shoulder. Position your hand across his jaw line, with the fingertips just at the edge of the mandible, and place your left hand on his left shoulder, pulling it back. This turn is designed to lift the head 90 degrees to the front. The amount of pressure applied should once again be appropriate to the stiffness of the person and his age. Release the pressure slowly and perform a similar stretch to the left. Finally, place both the forearms on the trapezius and roll the hands both inwards and outwards, so that the bone of the forearm — the alma — passes across the muscle. This technique should take about 10 to 20 minutes.

NECK AND UPPER SHOULDER TENSION

Ask your client to lie on his abdomen and, if he has a particularly stiff neck, place a pillow beneath his chest so that his head hangs over the edge. Turn his head to the right, placing his right arm up, and his left arm back. Both elbows should be bent at 90 degrees. Kneel to the patient's left, placing your left hand on the lumbar, palm down, your right hand on his left elbow. Your left knee should be placed on the spinus erectus muscle taking care to avoid the fifth thoracic vertebra. From this position apply pressure by moving your hips over the client's body, ensuring that the pressure is appropriate to his size and build. Then release, and bring your knee two or three inches closer to the shoulder. Apply pressure again. With people who are very strong, pressure can be applied and released approximately eight to twelve times per minute in unison with the breath. With people of a medium build, the pressure cycle is four times per minute and for people who are weak or older, mild pressure is applied and held for approximately one minute. This procedure should be repeated three to nine times, moving slowly up the spinus erectus muscle to the trapezius. Apply pressure from the toe, straight into the knee and work down the arm with the palm and heel of the right hand. Pressure can now be applied to the tricep, carefully around the elbow, and on the forearm.

Change your position by approximately 90 degrees, so that you are now sitting *Seiza* on the left side of your client. Maintaining this position, lift the client's shoulder, placing it on your left knee. At this point his elbow is down, and as a consequence his scapula raised up. Place your fingers underneath the scapula and pull, gently lifting the scapula away from the thoracic region of the body. Slide your hand underneath the scapula with the other hand pressing down onto the shoulder. Tension is released.

Repeat the entire sequence above on the other side. Finally, position the client face down on your thighs and work with thumb pressure across the upper back and trapezius.

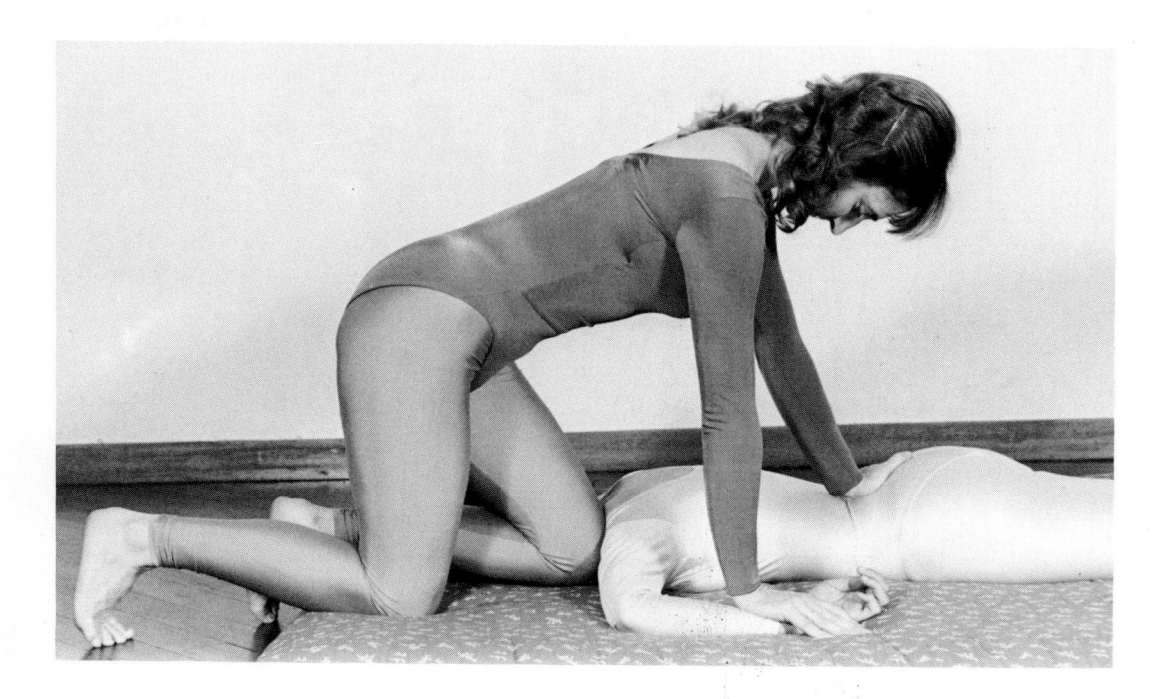

SHIATSU

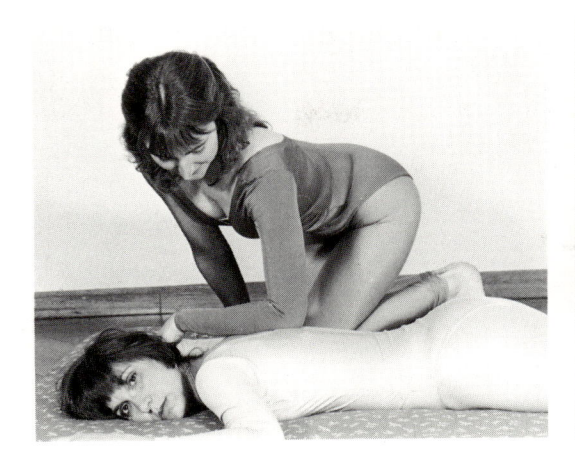

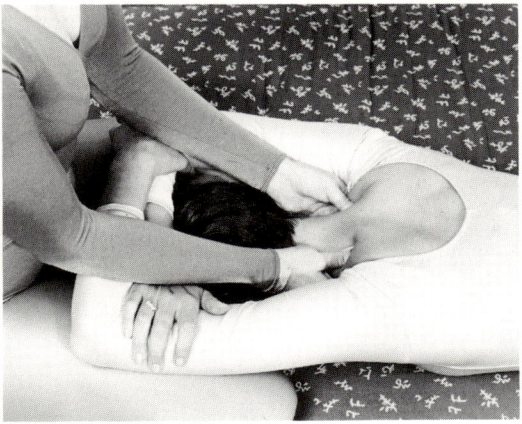

THE VALUE OF OBSERVATION

The origins of Shiatsu, like the origins of all bodywork, really come from caring for one another. Although there are many systems and schools of Shiatsu and a wide variety of bodywork techniques, the ability to transcend these and to work intuitively, responding always to a person's condition, is ultimately the hallmark of a successful practitioner. For example, when you are working on someone's abdomen, you will notice a great deal about the person's internal condition. If an individual is well muscled, has a firm yet resilient abdomen, exhibits a good temperament and shows no swelling, we recognise this as a healthy condition. On the other hand, if the musculature is thin and weak and there is swelling and resistance when pressure is applied deeply, this indicates a less satisfactory condition. Specific areas to look for in the abdomen form a line from the navel to the pubic synthesis. If the muscles appear to have spread and there is an area which lacks tone or is very cold, the Orientals acknowledge this to be a deficiency of kidney energy. For example, the area around the navel relates to the spleen and pancreas and if it is very tender and guarded there is a deficiency in that area. Similarly, the line between the navel and the zyphoid process, or the bottom of the sternum, represents the area relating to the stomach. If this area is weak or swollen then the stomach is affected. Just underneath the zyphoid process is the diagnostic area for the heart, while tension under the ribs, both on the left and right, relates to the liver. If it is particularly guarded or excessively tender than we look to an imbalance of liver energy or liver *ki*.

A practitioner, or any sensitive individual, can begin to respond to the client by looking directly at his body and feeling it. In Shiatsu, all the joints have internal relationships to the organs: the ankles are said to relate to the sexual organs; the knees to the kidneys; the hips and pelvis to the spleen and pancreas; the vertebrae to the liver; the shoulders to the lungs; the wrists to the intestines and the elbows to the musculature of the body. Traditionally the Shiatsu therapist does not treat only over the afflicted organ, but also at a distance — either through the channels or the corresponding area of the body. It is also important to rectify the differential energy between the upper and lower body, and there should be an equal amount of energy between the front and the back as well. When there is an over-charge, or excessive energy, correspondingly there will be a deficiency or weakness in another area. It makes common sense, of course, to balance the energy, to sedate or disperse the excess, and to tonify and build up the deficiency.

OUR ATTITUDE

The last thing to remember when performing Shiatsu is to be in a state of grace. The most effective therapist leaves his worry and rational mind behind and approaches his client with a sense of wonder and awe. It is important to be open: to look, to experience, to be aware of, the relationship between one's own body and that of the client. A practitioner is not effective if his own body is out of balance and in a twisted, uncomfortable position. Always take a few minutes before beginning work on another human being by centring yourself, sitting on your feet Japanese style, placing your hand gently on the abdomen and connecting to the breath. You can then respond to the tension in the client. By being aware and sensitive to the processes occurring in both his body and your own you will ensure success. Your client will be refreshed and energised by the experience, and you will be strengthened and alert from giving Shiatsu.

In the Universe it is important to share, to be open and to express the energy that heals. This energy flows through each of us with our breath and movement, and you will be able to feel it pass through your hands to the person who is with you. In this way Shiatsu enables each of us to create, to share and to love.

CHAPTER 8
TOUCH FOR BEAUTY
Susan Roche & Helen Smith

BACKGROUND

To look your best you must first be healthy. Simple 'touch' techniques can help eliminate minor ailments and form the basis of preventive health care.

The 'touch' therapies first began to gain widespread respect and acceptance during the 1970s. The extensive modern knowledge of the musculo-skeletal system, combined with ancient Chinese principles of the energy pathways of the body, have inspired the growth in the West of healing therapies such as Applied Kinesiology, Polarity Balancing, Zone Therapy and Foot Reflexology.

All of these therapies have one common feature — they acknowledge and make use of the energy circuits of the body and maintain that when these 'life forces' are flowing unimpeded in the pathways defined by ancient Chinese physiologists five thousand years ago, there is optimum function of mind, body and emotions.

When a blockage occurs — from either internal or external factors, both past or present — there is a potential problem area. This can manifest immediately, the following week, or in twenty years' time. The fail-safe system of the human body is so efficient that it may take years before a problem moves from the energy circuit and invades the associated organ.

The ancient acupuncturist believed in living as close to the laws of Nature as possible. He observed the change of seasons and adjusted his food, clothing and lifestyle accordingly. This is as valid today as it ever was. If a person lives in harmony with his surroundings, disease and many of the effects of ageing may be prevented. The traditional Chinese physician's diagnosis, under close observation of the face colour, lines, areas of heat and cold, and palpation of the pulses, all serve to indicate a pre-disease condition. His treatment, using needles, pressure, herbs and exercise, restores the energy balance which allows 're-irrigation' of a blocked area. Disease occurs in areas of stagnation of blood and 'life force', or energy.

So often an individual knows he is not functioning well. Medical diagnosis may show nothing clinically wrong. Sometimes a patient will come to an acupuncturist describing a symptom in perfect acupuncture terms: 'I know it sounds ridiculous, but my kidneys feel hot', or 'I have a pain in my right shoulder, waist and ankle', deftly tracing the path of the gall bladder meridian or energy line which actually covers the function of the muscles and tendons of the body.

The Touch for Beauty programme has selected simple, effective and quick techniques to locate tender areas on the body and to restore circulation through them. (See suggested morning programme).

Usually a natural therapy diagnosis is complicated by the fact that symptoms have been suppressed by years of drug medication. Often a drug is administered to treat the side-effects or aftermath of a previously administered medication. The actual cause of the condition has been masked by the suppression of symptoms.

In treating with natural therapies, the original blockage and body toxins must first be removed. There may be strong reactions as waste matter and poisons are released back into the system for elimination through bladder, bowel and skin. To cleanse the body there may be discharge from the eyes, ears, nose or stomach, headaches, nausea and bowel cramps. Ideally, the release should be gradual so that no discomfort occurs, but this process may take longer, and the patient must be told what to expect. If not, he may hurry to the doctor for a quick suppressant.

The alternatives, therefore, provide excellent preventive care. They are also helpful in many cases where a drug would have been taken permanently (high blood pressure, asthma) or where a patient has been told to cope with such problems as chronic pain, allergies, menstrual discomfort.

Scars caused by both surgery and accidents may also be the cause of severe energic disturbances and often treatment is not successful until the area is repolarised. This can be done by touch techniques as well as acupuncture needles.

If there is a block in the energy circuitry, it is like a river system which has become dammed; there will be an accumulation above the blockage and a 'drought' below. It is therefore important that an area or point of 'no energy' flow should be located and cleared as soon as possible. An area of tenderness on the body indicates a block of energy. The tender area can be massaged or pressed until it is relieved. A distant point along the same pathway is used to stimulate and transfer the healing energy, and is often more effective than a local point.

If there is a deep-seated problem, acupuncture with needles is quicker and less painful than massage. Also, a full acupuncture diagnosis provides a clearer understanding of the root cause of the problem. However, if a person is trained to be aware of the body's imbalances by simple, daily exercises and pressure point checks, he will be able to prevent a problem developing or know where to seek help in the very earliest stage.

GENERAL ENERGY BALANCING AND STRESS RELEASE TECHNIQUES

Stress in one of its many forms may well be the root cause of 90% of our problems. This is not to say that we must eliminate stress altogether, for a period of 'stress' may be necessary to achieve emotional or artistic growth, or to cleanse the body and restore health. It is not necessarily the stress itself which is important so much as the effectiveness of our defences. One person may have a nervous breakdown in a situation where another would not feel that there was a problem.

Environmental Stress includes: smog, exhaust fumes, cigarettes and side-stream smoke, fluorescent lights, air-conditioning, synthetic fibres, pain, or lack of sleep.

Biochemical Stress includes: nutritional deficiencies, excess or deficient food intake, chemical additives and food processing, allergies, lack of oxygen, too little exercise or excess amounts of stimulants such as drugs and alcohol.

Emotional Stress shows as difficulty in concentrating, anxiety, fears, phobias, chronic fatigue, muscle tension, indigestion, irritability, insomnia. Another cause of stress in Western society may be the emphasis on material security and stability whereas the

Buddhist, for example, is taught that the only constant that he may expect in life is change!

LETTING GO

The following suggestions are simple enough to be used anywhere, anytime, as and when required. To release stress frequently during the day is to boost energy. At least once a week you should check your posture, shoes and feet. Is there undue pressure being caused by the way you hold yourself or walk?

Posture
Stand with your back to the wall and heels ½" away. Place your hands on the wall at the waistline and notice whether the fingertips touch each other. If they do, there is an excessive curve to the spine (lordosis). This may be corrected with simple back exercises (see Chapter 4). In the meantime, curl the base of the spine forward, expand the rib cage and stretch the spine as if an elastic was pulling from the *crown* of the head to the ceiling. Standing tall helps to realign the spine and create space between the vertebrae which are usually so hard pressed together. It will also free the lungs *and* whittle one inch off the waistline. Try it and see!

Stretch for Life
At any time during the day and especially before getting out of bed in the morning S-T-R-E-T-C-H. Think of a cat and the luxurious way it stretches every limb before getting up. This tones every nerve and muscle in the body. If you hold your breath as you hold the stretch, oxygen has time to circulate to the brain and extremities and allow for a complete exchange with carbon dioxide and other gases in the lungs.

Clasp the hands above the head and turn them palms out. Breathe in, and lift your ribs from your hips. Bend *slowly* from side to side. If in bed, arch the back into a crescent, lying on one side and then the other. While sitting: place your hands on your thighs, breathe deeply, squeeze your shoulders to your ears while pressing down with your hands. Squeeze your face and eyes. Hold as long as the breath. Repeat often during the day. Stretch your arms behind a chair, palms clasped. Raise towards your shoulders.

Stretch . . .

TOUCH FOR BEAUTY

Think of a cat

Release shoulders, neck and face

TOUCH FOR BEAUTY

Exercise
This takes many forms. If you have a dynamic exercise programme, you may need a passive *yin*-type exercise to balance and involve the mind and breath with the body action. Take up *Tai-chi* and learn to flow with Nature. Even if you are 70 there is still time to start. Yoga, too, is wonderful for all age groups if it is learnt slowly. Remember, both of these were designed for men originally so don't underestimate their benefits for muscle tone and coordination as well as for the mind and emotions. They work the cardio-vascular system without over-straining the skeletal system.

Walking is also an excellent form of exercise. Be sure to swing the arms free and walk tall like a South Sea Islander. If you can't get outdoors, dance to music and flow freely. If you have a mini-trampoline or rebounder, dance on that several times a day, even for just a few minutes. It is likely to prove the most efficient form of exercise yet devised for both cardiovascular and skeletal health.

Breathing
Breathing with a sense of rhythm can control pain, calm the mind and emotions and thus life itself. Be aware of your lung capacity and the oxygen supply to the brain.

Massage
Ask a friend to massage the reflex areas of your body and also your neck and shoulders. Wring your hands, squeezing the knuckles. The *yin* and *yang* (negative and positive) energies polarise at the fingertips so this natural action has a real harmonising effect.

Eye Palming
The eyes need more care when we are exposed to stresses, medications, chemicals, artificial light, ageing and everyday pollution. Palming allows the muscles of the eyes to relax, bringing a fresh, healthy supply of blood and energy to help improve vision

Palming the eyes

and revitalise the optic nerve. Rub the hands together to warm them. While sitting, place your elbows on your knees, or preferably on a table, and rest your head on your hands. The 'heel' of your hands should lie along the upper cheek bone with your little fingers crossed over the bridge of the nose and over each other. Cup your palms so there is no pressure on the eyes. Move your fingers until all light is excluded. Now gaze into total darkness with your eyes open and imagine a black room hung with black velvet curtains. After some minutes there is a sensation of tension literally draining from the eyes.

Do this for 5 to 20 minutes as required, especially during study or close eye-work. Everything looks clearer and brighter after palming.

Energy Boosters
To release stress is, obviously, to boost and channel your available energy. Here are some discreet hints to aid your routine: Hug someone for a harmonising exchange of energies. It can resolve a conflict. Think and say 'I love you' — especially to your children. Be open-handed and watch your body-language. Do you cross your arms and legs and close off when talking to people?

Smiling is also a quick energiser. It relates directly to the thymus gland which is tucked behind the sternum or breastbone. We are learning more about the potential of this gland which used to be considered redundant after puberty. It stimulates the body's immune response, making the T-cell lymphocytes active against viruses, fungi and chronic bacterial infections.

When you need a quick burst of energy or are exposed to physical or emotional stress, tap the breast bone (upper third) ten times lightly. Galen, the second century philosopher/doctor, called it the 'sea of life energy' or 'bunch of thyme'. Thyme is in fact the herb traditionally used by those who are sensitive to moulds in their diet.

The thymus is the first organ to be affected by stress and negative mental attitudes as it monitors and regulates the energy flow like a reservoir. So like Tarzan and the apes, *tap the thymus* — but lightly please.

Thyroid Regulator
The thyroid is a major endocrine gland and is responsible for maintaining growth and metabolism as well as storage of iodine. It increases in size and activity during stress, puberty and pregnancy, and the hormones affect almost all tissues of the body and influence weight distribution. Ancient Indian courtesans found that applying daily pressure on the thyroid helped to give them a smooth skin and prolong their youth and beauty.

For a daily boost, find the centre of the windpipe or trachea in the neck and slide the four fingers of one hand beside it (on one side at a time only) the length of the neck. Press *gently* three times for three seconds each time. Repeat on the other side. Once a day is sufficient (see 'sixty-second energy boost' below).

Positive Thoughts and Words
With Kinesiology (or muscle testing) methods, it can be shown instantly that negative words as well as emotions have an immediate weakening effect on the body. Even a simple 'no' affects us in a negative way since we have been so programmed from earliest childhood. So it is important to monitor our thoughts and words and replace, immediately, a negative with a positive.

Peace of mind may be our greatest ambition and achievement. For this it is important to have a gentle philosophy to help us through life's ups and downs. Here too the Eastern acceptance of the inevitability of change is helpful.

Sixty-Second Energy Boost
This quick harmoniser has been put together in an active/passive sequence which covers all the acupuncture meridians and some vital pressure points. It is described below, and is one of the most popular ideas in our course.

1   Rub hands briskly together   *3 seconds*
2   Rub cheeks upwards lightly   *5 times*
3   With cupped hand, tap from wrist to neck and back vigorously inside, then outside, each arm   *3 times each*
4   Press thyroid area gently one side of windpipe at a time, three times in total. *3 seconds each*
5   With finger tips pitter-pat all over the scalp   *3 seconds*
6   With thumbs (or second and third fingers) press base of skull firmly up against the bone from behind the ears to centre   *5 seconds*
7   Tap breast bone (thymus area) lightly with finger tips   *3 seconds*
8   Pinch and squeeze big toe all over   *3 seconds*
Pinch and squeeze behind ankles   *3 seconds*
9   Rub top of foot briskly with instep of other foot   *3 seconds*
10   With palms of hands, slap legs from feet to groin, front, back and sides (avoiding varicosities)   *5 seconds*

REFLEX THERAPIES

Acupressure and the general reflex therapies are among the most effective means of using Nature's healing methods for maintaining the body function in optimum condition. They are probably also the least familiar methods. They do not require pills, drugs, tranquillisers or surgery and can be administered with safety anywhere or anytime by anyone on yourself or on others. The elderly, the active and even babies can benefit.

By daily checking for tender areas on the body and gently easing away the blockage of energy which has caused them, future problems can be prevented. When a sprain or injury occurs, the reflex areas provide instant means of relief of pain and swelling. This can be most effective on the sports field.

To understand how this is possible, it is useful to study the pathways of the body's energy lines (see diagram). These are allied to the nervous system, but separate and distinct from it. One can then appreciate why a headache can be treated from the feet. The approach developed from the five basic bilateral zones of traditional Indian medicine through to the highly sophisticated Chinese system describing twelve major bilateral pathways and a subsidiary network numbering seventy-six functional energy paths. It is the trigger points located along these lines which may register blockages by feelings of heat, cold and tenderness and may be manipulated by the finger, or other pressure which we describe.

When the reflex centres are massaged, a surge of energy is generated along the neural and meridian lines to the related part of the body and eventually to the associated organ. This primary flow of energy strengthens the body's own healing and defence mechanisms instantly.

Method
Press firmly and deeply with the tip of one or more fingers or a fingernail held at right angles to the flesh. As well as pressure, use a slightly vibrating or circular movement

for 3 to 7 seconds only before moving on to another area. You can return to a problem spot later.

Use only the amount of pressure which can be tolerated at the time, otherwise the release of acids and toxins into the body may be too fast for the system to handle comfortably. There is no need for acute pain. An exception may be in the case of recent injury when a corresponding pinpoint area in the ear will be excruciatingly painful to touch. It is best here to persevere with pressure from a fingernail until the pain is relieved. Healing of the affected part is thus speeded up.

Firm pressure dissipates energy (recent problem or acute pain) while feather-light stimulation will tonify (long term or chronic problem). An acute problem can be treated at frequent intervals during the day for a few seconds. Otherwise, treat daily for the first week, then two or three times a week and finally once a week. When the tenderness has gone, the condition and congestion have been relieved. The general foot massage should however be maintained daily, for example, after bathing, if only for a matter of seconds, for preventive care. It is also appropriate during massage sessions to use your mental powers. Focus on a clear picture of the desired result as if it were already achieved. If possible, visualise a 'laser' beam of light suffusing the affected area.

Remember, treat gently the first time. Do not treat people who are pregnant, over-tired or who have serious or contagious diseases. Do not treat after a heavy meal. Always avoid pressure on a bruise, oedema (swelling), fracture, infection, varicose vein or other problem area.

The Five Body Zones
Before the Chinese developed the meridian system of energy pathways over 5,000 years ago, Indian sages described five bilateral zones of the body. These are said to run vertically from the top of the head to the bottom of the feet and fingers, and also extend from the front of the body to the back.

Every part of the body is covered by one of these zones. Each line runs through the centre of its zone, e.g. Zone 1 from the big toe up the medial aspect of the leg and body and head and also from the thumb and on up to the centre of the head. Problems in one area can be treated at a distant point along the zone thus bringing fresh energy to a congested area. Each zone has a *reflex area* on both hands and feet which stimulates nerves, blood supply, lymphatic system and organs of that zone. For example, toothache can be treated by using corresponding fingers or toes.

Method
Massage or squeeze the toes and fingers. Be generous to be sure to cover the area and use two or three fingers. A rubber band or peg may be applied, but be careful not to leave it on too long: 15 minutes is the maximum. For general pain use the teeth (if you have a good bite) or bite on an eraser. (Remember seeing in films how they used to bite the bullet for an amputation or bite onto a piece of wood for childbirth?) A pad of cottonwool clamped between the upper and lower wisdom teeth will help an earache.

Ear Acupressure and Reflex Zones
The ear has over 200 acupuncture points relating to the organs, limbs and functions of the body. Some acupuncturists use only ear points to treat the whole body.

As a general tune-up, pull the ears upwards, downwards by holding the lobes, and outwards uncurling the helix or outer rim. The ear will feel hot and turn a healthy pink. Any tender spots should be worked out of the ear.

In the case of injury to a limb, press the corresponding area of the ear with a fingernail or finger while moving the painful part if possible. There may be a slight depression, raised area, lump or redness, the size of a pinhead visible on the ear. Pressure can be extremely painful, but it is worth persevering with intermittent pressure until the pain lessens. It is interesting to note that the ear lobe includes the region identified as the 'tooth extraction point' for pain and anaesthesia.

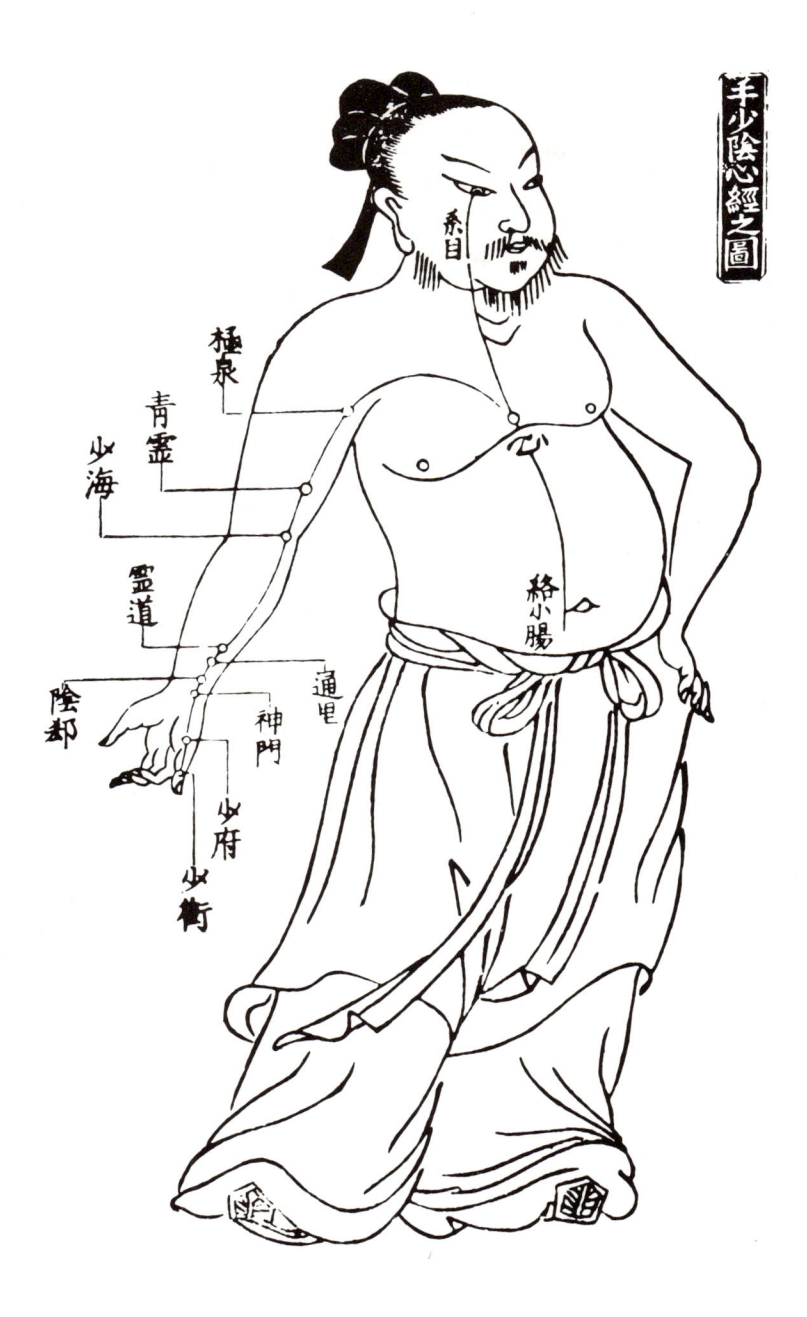

Foot Acupressure and Reflex Zones
The idea of using the zones of the foot as reflex areas of the body was first introduced to the United States in 1913 by Dr William Fitzgerald. Some therapists use only foot massage for healing. The hands and feet are the parts of the body with the least depth so the nerves and energy circuits are more accessible for massage. Feet in their natural state have developed to enable us to walk over rough ground — an action which serves

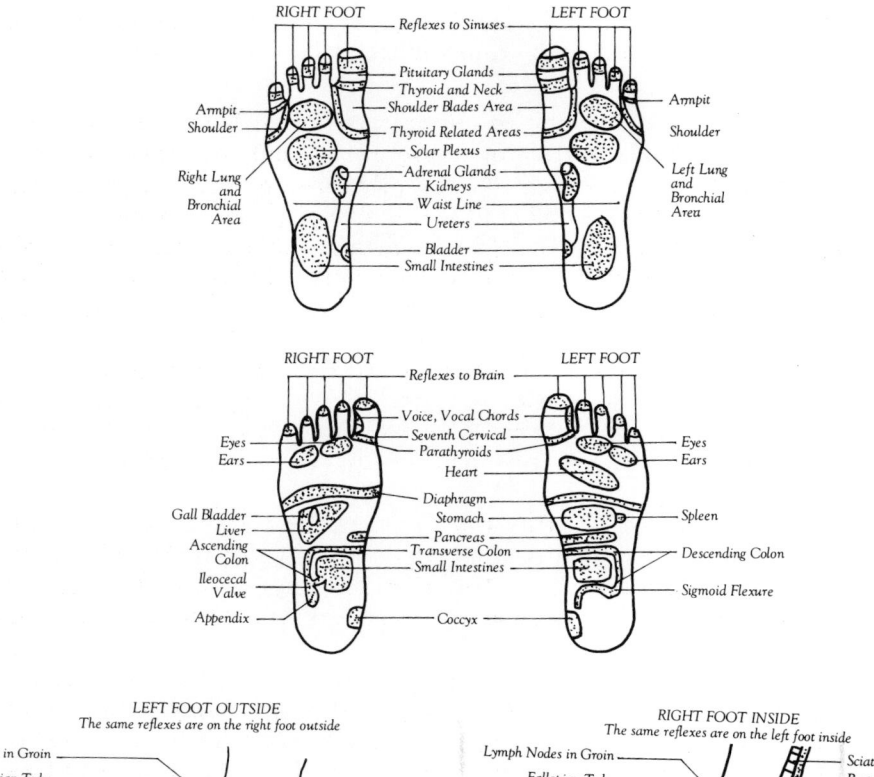

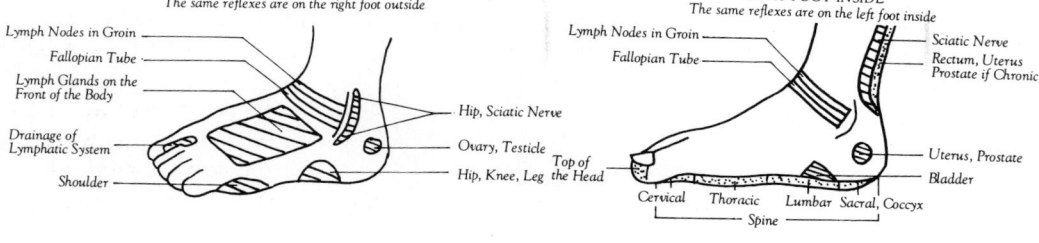

as a continual 'massage', breaking down the accumulation of toxins and acid crystals on nerve endings. In ill-health the feet become very sensitive.

You may find that diagrams for foot acupressure vary in the exact location of points. Some points are the size of pinheads, others relate to general areas. Each person is individual and the massage area will vary according to the circumstances. In general, the organs on the right side of the body are found in the right foot (and hand). The liver and gall bladder pressure points, for example, are located on the right foot, whilst the heart and spleen are on the left. The ascending colon travels up the sole of the right foot, across the insteps of both feet, and the descending colon moves down towards the heel of the left foot following the pattern of the body. The colon should be massaged according to its flow.

If you refer back to the 'Sixty-second energy boost' you can now appreciate the value of briskly rubbing the sole of one foot over the top of the other for a general, overall toning. This is excellent for long trips by car, plane or train. The initial pressure on the ball of the big toe boosts the function of the pituitary or master gland of the body, and is helpful for headaches as well. The point is deep within the toe and heavy pressure should be applied, even to the point of using the blunt end of a ball pen. Initially the feeling is that there is a piece of glass within the toe and it is important to gradually break down the crystalline deposits around the reflex.

Method

Always treat both feet, even if working on a specific problem. First relax the whole foot by grasping all the toes and moving them backwards and forwards, circling them together and individually. The toes, fingers and all joints should be kept mobile at all times. Then place four fingers of each hand — knuckles together — under the sole with the thumbs on top of the foot. Work the thumbs from the centre of the foot to the outer toes whilst kneading the sole with the tips of the fingers. This is very soothing to tired feet and in fact serves to release tension throughout the body. Rotate the foot at the ankle in both directions.

Next assess the condition of the glands using the thumb and, starting at the pituitary gland, move along the big toe joint for the thyroid area, to the centre of the foot for the solar plexus and adrenals and pancreas. The back of the heel on the Achilles tendon is linked to the reproductive organs, with the sex glands on the heel bone under the ankle bones.

Go back to the tip of the toes for the sinus reflexes and the base of the toes for the eyes and ears. These are more easily worked with four fingertips. One of our students was able to relieve overnight her son's red, painful ear. Later, by working on the lung area of her father-in-law who had suffered from emphysema for years, she gave him an unaccustomed good night's sleep.

The spinal area extends from the base of the big toe, along the instep, up against the bone of the first metatarsal. Firm pressure is required here, usually with the thumb. The thumb and fingers will strengthen as you learn these massage techniques! At first they may ache and not give sufficient pressure. You can diagnose the area of a spinal problem quite easily from the reflex points along the instep.

A quick booster can be given with the knuckles of one hand — move briskly up and down the sole of the foot. At first it may be tender or 'ticklish' but it is worth persevering once you know the benefits. As we have said, it is better to return to tender spots and work 3–7 seconds than to overlook any particular area and risk a strong reaction.

You can also roll the foot over a golf ball or stand for some part of the day on a pressure mat or sandals which have raised rubber nodules designed to stimulate. Start by allocating 10 minutes or so a day. You will feel improvement with each treatment, so there is no need to overwork.

Hand Acupressure and Reflex Zones

These general reflex areas correspond to the feet and are used in the same way. However, they are useful during the day as they are more readily accessible. The areas will not be as tender as the corresponding part of the foot because the hand normally receives much more use. Again, you may find it effective to use a ball, a smooth stone, a 'worry bead' or perhaps some similar object, to apply pressure.

The heart area under the little finger of the left hand may be massaged here for circulatory problems. The heart meridian ends at the little finger tips and if there is tenderness in this region you may have an incipient heart condition. For a heart attack emergency, the advice of reflexologist Dr Cerney is to 'grab both little fingers at this point (either side of the little fingernail), and twirl them vigorously as you squeeze. You may very handily save a life!'

If you pinch and squeeze the fingers on either side of the nail and the toes as well, and rotate each one, you can stimulate the whole meridian system. All the energies start, or finish, at the fingertips or toes, so this is where the *yin* and *yang* energies polarise. Kirlian photography actually shows energy flares at these points.

Special Acupressure Points on the Hand
In addition to the reflex areas of the hand, there are specific points used by acupuncturists to treat a number of conditions. We find many of these are remarkably effective. There are points on the palm for heart palpitations and oral ulcers. Below, on the edge of the lung reflex, are points for cough and bronchitis, while at the base of the thumb, the point for a common cold, and especially rhinitis or runny nose, works quickly. The heel and sprained ankle point on the centre of the wrist is also useful and on the little finger side of the wrist/arm you can rub briskly up and down for nervousness and insomnia.

On the back of the hand between the knuckles, relief can be obtained for a stiff neck (also while driving), sore throat and sciatic pain. Five or ten minutes pressure on the constipation point daily has cleared a problem of many years' standing. Below it, the shoulder point may be pressed or bitten with the teeth, and on the inner side of the thumb, the eye point helps to clear gritty, runny, itchy or dry eyes.

Method
Your best tool is the fingernail! You can also use your fingers or knuckles, the end of a ball pen, rubber bands or your teeth. Treat often in acute cases, if the treatment is bringing relief. Treat once or twice a day in chronic cases. Treatment time and amount of pressure depend on the severity of the symptoms.

LET'S FACE IT

The face is a major stress centre of emotional energy, especially in western people. Adelle Davis, the nutritionist, suggested that ageing may be due to multiple deficiency states. This makes good sense when you consider how artificial our foods have become. The longest living people in the world are still actively working in the fields at ages well over 100 years. They live in pollution-free altitudes on the simplest diets harvested with their own labour, and they never 'retire' from work.

The skin is only as firm as the muscle flesh structure beneath it. Involuntary grimacing forms uneven pull, causing creases and crinkles, but does not exercise or work the muscles. Emotional stress, as well as smoking, harsh climates and nutritional deficiencies, play havoc with our appearance.

The acupuncture meridians, or energy circuits, travel in well-defined lines all over the body but they all, either directly, or indirectly via linked partners, reach the face. Each of these meridians is associated with a major organ of the body. For this reason the vitality or collapse of an area of the face depends not only on circulation, muscle tone and surface skin care, but also on the health of the body itself.

In Chinese physiology, the face is an important area of external diagnosis for internal problems. Lines tend to occur at areas where there is a blockage of energy. Thus by taking care of the muscle tone and lines of the face, we can help the body in general. People may spend a great deal of time in the gym or doing regular exercise but, for some reason, they stop exercising above the neck!

There are 14 major muscle groups in the face. By learning to isolate these and apply isotonic challenge (muscle against muscle), we can increase the blood circulation to the face and restore energy and balance. The body benefits as well. In cosmetic acupuncture, the effect of the needle is to tighten skin and muscle. Exercise reinforces it — together with normal or improved skin care. Men shaving use these muscle-toning techniques naturally and, with the daily scraping of surface cells from the skin, have a distinct advantage over women. However, they should observe carefully that while 'exercising' the lower face they do not over-use the forehead and eye area.

Points to Remember:
1 The quality of your skin depends upon:
muscle tone
nutritional content
handling (don't stretch it unnecessarily)
moisture and elasticity
2 Frequent deep breathing increases the flow of oxygen to the body, face and brain, and releases tension and toxins. Remember to apply daily pressure to the thyroids and around the base of the skull for circulation to the face.
3 Lie with your feet positioned higher than your head when possible — on cushions, or on a slant board (you may wish to use the ironing board). The yoga 'shoulder stand' is excellent too, but be sure to learn this initially with a good yoga teacher or you may strain your neck. The yoga 'Lion Pose' makes a good all-round face-toner as well as clearing throat problems.
4 Research shows that the skin of smokers can look 10–15 years older than that of non-smokers. The damage caused, like that caused by ultra-violet light, is cumulative. However, regular breathing exercises do help to counteract the habit together with acupuncture treatment and daily acupressure therapy.
   If you do not want to give up smoking, alter your diet to include more alkaline foods and restore the 4:1 alkaline/acid balance of the body. Munch those sunflower and pumpkin seeds!
5 Finally, *chew*. The action is good for the jaw muscles and the stomach will be delighted and much relieved. Ideally, food should be chewed almost to a liquid state before swallowing, because the first process of digestion takes place with the saliva enzyme ptyalin.

BEAUTY THERAPY

Your face requires attention, if only minimal, at least twice a day. Use this time as a mini-meditation. Look in the mirror and get in touch with yourself. You are changing. Be aware. Use your face as an indicator of your general well-being. Your inner harmony and emotional state are showing.

Check your posture frequently in a long mirror. Slumping can add at least one inch to your waistline, as we have said, and also give you a double chin as well as putting too much weight on the back of the feet. Sitting badly and lying in bed reading with your chin on your chest strains the face muscles unnecessarily, too.

Before you exercise your face, cleanse and lubricate it well. Avoid mineral oil-based products which deplete the body of the oil-soluble vitamins, A, D, E and K — all of which are necessary for an attractive, healthy skin. There are many good natural products on the market based on seeds, nuts and fruit. Or, blend your own cosmetics from cold-pressed oils: avocado, apricot, sunflower, sesame seed and coconut oil in equal quantities.

When you need to watch your purse, look to the kitchen for your 'cosmetics'. Butter will cleanse. Try 'tapping' honey (you can soften it with milk) under the chin, neck and face (but don't tap around the eyes). It is invigorating and anti-bacterial.

Yoghurt, blended with brewer's yeast powder, makes a good mask. You can add honey — or use the yoghurt alone. As the soft fruits come into season, rest with the pulp on your face. Again avoid the eye area which you can pat with oil.

Oatmeal softens the water (hang it in the bath in the toe of a stocking). Massage the damp oatmeal into the skin for a thorough cleanse. Barbara Cartland advises patting milk on to the eyelids daily to avoid a crepey skin. Remember, you may get broken veins from ice, heat, coffee, tea or alcohol and you may get brown or yellow patches on the skin from the Pill or from scent.

After exercise, splash your face with cold water at least 10 times. Always remember to splash cold water on your breasts and feet as well as the face after bathing. It will keep the skin toned and the inner organs stimulated. One student who came from Chile, told us that her grandmother made a habit of splashing her breasts with cold water all her life. About 84 years of age, she complained to the family that they had begun to get slack!

Massage
The following massage can be used for cleansing, moisturising or nourishing, and ensures an upward flow of energy. When using strokes **1**, **2** and **3** below, the face should be taut, the mouth forming a square 'O' (see also facial isotonics). When stroking the neck (upwards only), the chin should be tilted back. Frequent deep breathing increases oxygen to the face and assists your massage.

Cream the face liberally:

1 Using both hands for a bilateral movement, place the third and fourth fingers at the chin, elbows out, and sweep along the jawline to the front of the ears.

2 With your elbows down sweep the third and fourth fingers from the centre of your jawline, up in a curve to the base of the nose (smile line). From here onwards, the fingers don't leave the face.

3 Continue the sweep from the corner of the nose along under the cheekbone to the front of the ears.

4 Sweep lightly back to the orbit of the eye and circle along the upper edge of the cheekbone to the nose, up to the eyebrow, and under it to the outer eye. Be sure not to pull the skin here. Unless the skin is well lubricated, it is advisable to use a patting or tapping movement. Circle several times and take the opportunity to press firmly all around the bony orbit of the eye without moving the skin.

5 From the inner end of the eyebrows take fingers 3, 4 and 5 up and out to the temple hair line. The pressure should be firm but not dragging. Keep the flow in a regular pattern and always upwards. Think 'up and out'.

To complete this massage, pinch along the jawline and eyebrows using the thumb and forefinger. This is a firm pressure against the bone in the case of the chin. You will be covering acupressure stomach points which may be tender but which will nevertheless benefit. The eyebrow pinch looks after kidneys and spleen and the pressure around the eye socket covers seven major acupuncture points. The most important of these is either side of the bridge of the nose, above the tear duct and under the bone. Apply three seconds' pressure here several times a day.

TOUCH FOR BEAUTY

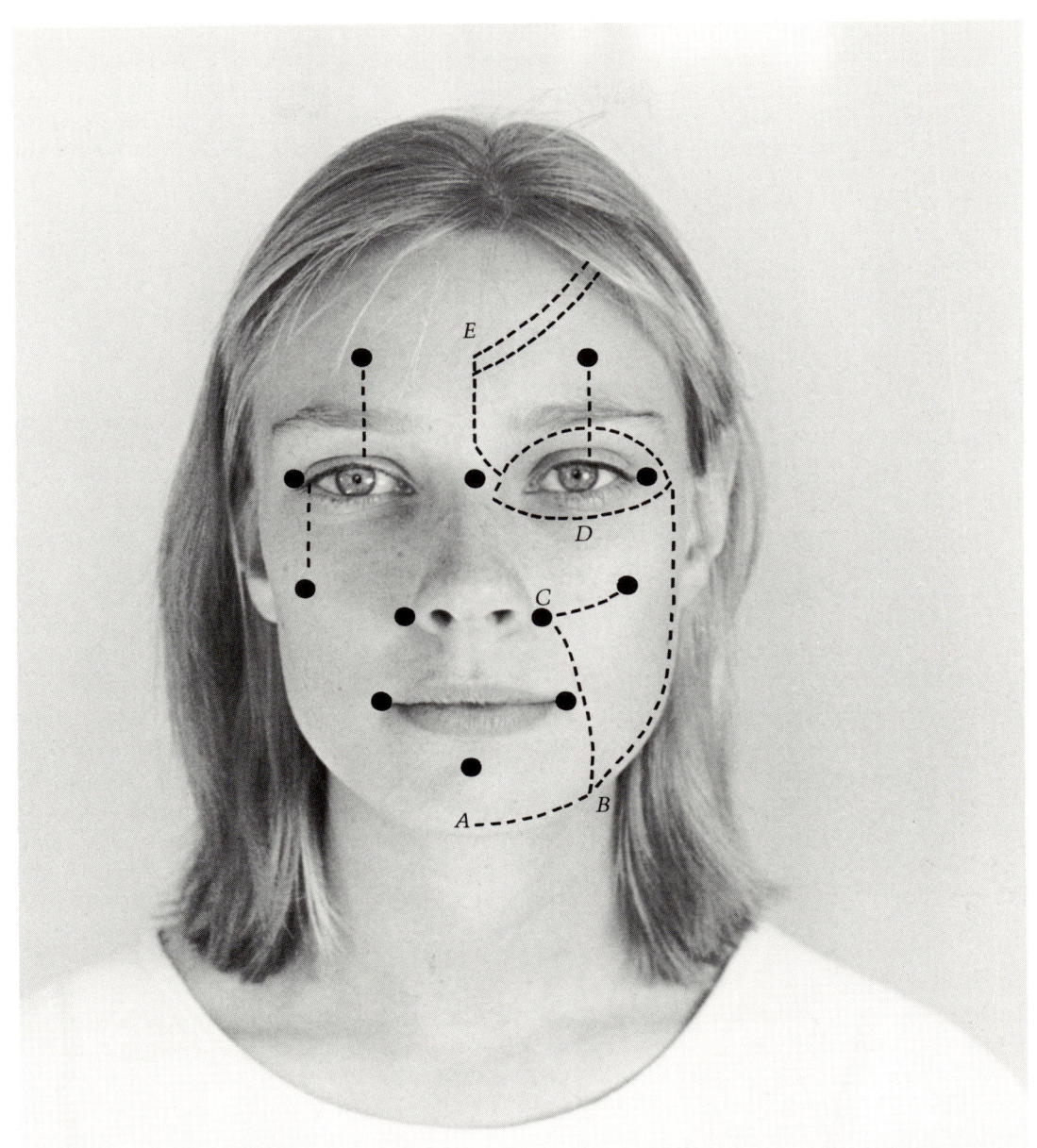

Seven important facial points (use bilaterally). With the thumbs under the chin and using fingers 2 and 5 move:
— *from the chin (A) up to the hair line*
— *from the angle of the jaw (B) to the nose (C)*
— *from the nose (C) under the cheek bone to the ear*
— *tap around the eye several times on bone (D)*
Using four fingers move from the centre of the brow (E) to the hair line then tap each point twice a second for 30 seconds and circle point C

Acupressure points on the head

Tapping and Pressing

Notice the two central and five bilateral points for tapping and pressing. A tense muscle responds well to this action and circulation of the energy and blood connected with that point is stimulated, helping to remove blockages from that meridian. Each cell has a 'memory' so you are helping to re-programme the surrounding structure to a new pattern.

Method

Lubricate your fingers well and press all the points, holding for a count of 10 seconds. Use the third and fourth fingers of each hand. If you have time, go back along the massage lines and press.

Once a week at least do the following: Lightly tap each of the points on the diagram in the following pattern: *two taps per second for five seconds, hold for five seconds.* Repeat three times — this makes a total of 30 seconds' tapping on each point. You will need to use a clock or metronome at first to establish the rhythm. Note that all the points are tapped except the ones beside the nose. These are circled gently but firmly up against the nose cartilage. One student tells us that she can reverse a potential headache by using this gentle tapping routine on her face.

Try 'tapping' on your blusher, make-up etc. for extra therapeutic effect and remember to use this time to get in touch with yourself and switch off the world around you. In the hurly-burly of family life many women don't allow time for themselves. Quite often, when we ask a patient how long they have had a backache, headache or menstrual problem, etc. they reply: 'Twenty years, since the last baby.'

'Feather' Your Face

If you have only five seconds to spare, try this old Chinese secret: With gossamer light movements over the face in an upward movement barely touching the skin brush your fingers towards the hairline. Or follow the massage lines on the chart seven times each: chin to ears, corners of mouth to cheeks, nose to cheeks, outer eye to temples, between eyebrows to forehead.

These five upwards movements may be used whenever the face is handled for cleansing, moisturising, toning, putting on make-up or, for a wonderfully soothing uplift, at any time of the day.

Facial Isotonics

The process of ageing starts at the end of the 'teens, but begins to show according to the lifestyle, thought patterns and nutrition of the person. Equally important are the involuntary facial expressions which so easily become a habit without our noticing. It is sad to see a fresh, beautiful 16-year-old making facial contortions as she speaks. It is a delicate subject to broach, but if it is *your* teenager, perhaps you could ask her to let you know when she sees you raising your eyebrows as you speak, which leaves you free to do the same for her. It is not that you refrain from smiling or laughing or looking animated, but excessive face movements are distracting and indicate inner stress. Underlying muscle is losing tone and sagging as we grow older and the skin has to stretch to follow it. The less we assist it the better.

Frown Lines Avoid scowling. A piece of sticky-tape from hairline to nose will help remind you. (It is advisable to remove it when you answer the door!) The frontalis muscle on the forehead opposes the corrugator. To relax the tension, grasp a handful of hair at the centre of the forehead. Pull up and at the same time let go the tension in the eyebrows, eyeballs and forehead. Hold for a count of five and repeat five times. You can also grasp the hair with both hands to cover the width of the forehead.

Nose to Lips To strengthen the orbicularis oris muscle around the mouth and the tiny canius muscle, 'roll' a ball of air from cheek to cheek around the mouth frequently during the day or:
— 'mouth' silently and with exaggeration the letters of the alphabet. But be sure not to use the upper cheek or eye muscles, or:
— with lips together, smile upwards at the corners of the mouth as hard as you can but don't involve the eye muscles. Hold the smile and at the same time attempt to draw the mouth forward to a square 'O'. Keep the platysma muscle of the neck taut and watch that no wrinkles appear around the mouth. Hold for a count of five and repeat five times, once a day.

Jaw/Chin/Neck The following exercises are designed to tighten and firm the pterygoids at the side of the jaw, and to strengthen the platysma which covers the neck from the jaw to the chest. If the latter is in good condition, it will help prevent a crepey neck. When you work on the platysma you are also using the pectoral muscles which hold up the breasts. So think of your bust line starting at the neck! Draw your lips back slightly into a smile, lift your chin slightly and tighten the muscles from your chin to your chest. Hold for a count of five and then release. Repeat five times and then frequently during the day. Learn to tighten until the muscles tremble — and do watch carefully that the upper face muscles do not get involved.

An alternative procedure is to tilt the chin upwards, then drop the lower jaw. With the chin still in the air, close the lower jaw against resistance as if something were pushing it down as you try to close it. Repeat five times. This is a good time to massage cream into the neck.

If your neck feels strained in this position, you can lie on your back across the bed with your head over the edge. Again, drop the jaw and close against resistance. A good time to do this is after your morning stretch and before getting up.

EXERCISE MADE SIMPLE

Like any machine, the body requires lubrication, fuel and rest. An engine is not expected to run continually without maintenance. Yet often we allow our health to run down until there is a crisis situation where surgery or potent suppressive drugs are required.

Exercise patterns, too, need to be balanced. If you are following an active, Western *yang*-type programme (tennis, jogging, swimming, cycling, squash, gym), you will need to consider a harmonising, *yin*-type activity such as Tai-chi, yoga, breathing and meditation. These 'static' movements may appear non-productive, but they have deep-reaching effects on the muscles, glands and emotions as well as the autonomic nervous system as a whole. They were initially evolved and used for men. When you see a slow, controlled Tai-chi movement speeded up, you can appreciate the lethal potential of the martial art.

A principle we often forget in our *yang*-oriented culture is that to master an exercise, very, very slowly in order to involve the mind and breath as well as movement, gives one the control to do it at speed. Whereas to use a repetitive movement at speed, perhaps to the rhythm of music, tones the skeletal and vascular systems wonderfully but does little for the integration of mind, body and spirit. A fusion of the knowledge of the two great cultures is what we need to bear in mind.

Stretching
We have spoken of the value of S-T-R-E-T-C-H-I-N-G at frequent intervals during the day as a general energy boost and tension release. You can also circle the shoulders

backwards and forwards and roll the head slowly. The aim is to make the muscles elastic.

Stretch the neck up from the shoulders, as if you were being pulled from the crown of the head. Using the top of the neck as a pivot (and not the collar bone), nod the head chin-to-neck in a forward direction and then sideways to each shoulder. Be very careful not to raise the shoulder or bend the head from side to side. It remains on the same plane. The aim is to achieve an effortless 180° turn and the ability at any age to line up the nose with the shoulder.

The Stomach Lift

The 'ultimate' exercise we should choose, if we had to, is the stomach lift or *uddiyana bandha* of the yogis. It looks after the two main body functions of digestion and elimination, as well as keeping a trim waistline by exercising the vertical rectus abdominis muscles and the transverse and the oblique abdominals.

This must be done on an empty stomach so the morning shower before breakfast is a good time to remember it. You can have the added benefit of warm water on your neck and back.

Stand with your feet 18" apart. Bend slightly forward, round the back, bend the knees and place your palms on your thighs with the fingers pointing inwards. Exhale completely, emptying the lungs, then pull the abdomen upward and backward making the midsection as concave as possible. Remember to leave the lungs empty while you do this and resist the instinct to breathe in when you draw the tummy in. Hold the stomach in with the breath out as long as comfortable (at least to a count of five to begin with), then slowly release and breathe in. At first, to isolate the muscles you are using, place one fist under the rib cage to encourage the tummy to tuck right up and under. Repeat at least ten times.

In the beginning, it may be easier to lift and drop the stomach 5-10 times on each exhalation to gain strength in the muscles. If at the same time you lock the chin against the chest and press the hands on the thighs, the blood circulation is concentrated in the navel region, or solar plexus, giving a great toning and energy boost for the whole body. Watch carefully that you don't tense the shoulders. The back is rounded but the shoulders are relaxed.

In addition to keeping the waistline trim, the entire genito-urinary and gastro-intestinal tracts are contracted and all abdominal and stomach ailments are helped: constipation, indigestion, worms, diabetes, prolapse of the uterus and weak stomach muscles. The liver, pancreas, kidneys and spleen are all massaged and toned. The 'digestive fire' is stimulated, thus helping with weight loss and giving both vitality to a lethargic person and peace to an anxious person.

It is also most beneficial to learn to isolate and contract the sphincter muscles of the pelvic floor or peri-anal region on which we sit. Draw the buttocks together tightly and pull the perineum up towards the navel as if you were stopping urination. Hold for five seconds at least and then relax. For the health of the genito-urinary systems, some gynaecologists advise 100 contractions a day! These can, and should, be done during pregnancy when it would be inadvisable to use the *uddiyana bandha* abdominal lift.

The Lion Pose

For ear, nose and throat energy try the Lion Pose known in yoga as *simhasana*. It also serves as a face and chin-line toning when you haven't time for the individual isotonic face exercises. The voice will improve and it is useful for those who stutter. To maintain general health and muscle tone of the face do it ten times a day. For throat ailments and tonsilitis, do at least five per hour. If you can start at the first sign of a

The Lion Pose for throat and face

cold, or tickle in the throat, you can prevent the cold developing. We have both reversed chronic tonsilitis in both ourselves and our children, and it is one exercise which will capture the imagination of children and give you a face-lift while you do it with them.

Again, the muscle contraction is held on an exhalation. Kneel down and sit on your heels. If you can, curl your toes under and persevere with the discomfort. The tendons will stretch. Huff the breath out of your mouth and at the same time contract every muscle you can think of, from your toes through to your calves, buttocks, stomach and arms. Spread your fingers, open your eyes and mouth wide, and push your tongue out in an attempt to touch your chin. You can feel the throat being massaged at the back of the tongue.

The muscles are squeezed dry like a dirty sponge so that when you release the contraction, freshly oxygenated blood flows back through them clearing and cleansing the toxic waste material which the lymphatic system has been unable to deal with. A sore throat is an indication that the garbage disposal system is blocked.

The Moon Pose
From the Lion Pose you can move to the 'great tranquilliser' or Moon Pose, *shashankasana*. Sitting on the feet, curl the toes towards each other and sit back on the heels. It may take time to get used to this pressure on the instep but you will realise that the stretching involved is beneficial when you consider the reflexes of the feet.

Stretch the arms above the head, and then slowly lower them to the ground into a prostrate prayer position. Relax for ten to fifteen minutes. You can also lay the arms

The Moon Pose for tranquillity

beside the body with the hands beside the feet. If you suffer from high blood pressure, place one fist on the other and rest the forehead on the upper fist. This is also an ideal time to do your eye palming exercise in a position that brings extra blood to the head. For this, rub the hands briskly together before bending forward, tuck the elbows to the sides of the body, cup the palms over the eyes, and rest the forehead on the floor.

If the moon posture is practised at the first signs of chest congestion, the heaviness passes and an asthmatic attack may be avoided. The adrenal glands above the kidneys are stimulated. Deepen the breathing to the abdomen so that your pelvic muscles are toned — this helps general sexual disorders. The sciatic nerve also relaxes, benefiting back problems.

You will find, while in this position, that your emotions are calmed and it is very difficult to remain angry or moody. A psychiatric nurse told us once that in cases of drug dependency, 20 minutes a day spent in this foetal position is of great benefit to reintegrate body and mind.

Chest Improvement — Energy Boost
To stimulate the digestive and endocrine systems and help balance the metabolism, this exercise should be done each day. To achieve the energy boost, you should cover the acupuncture 'alarm' points of the stomach, liver, spleen, gall bladder, heart and lungs. These are points which feel tender under pressure when there is a blockage in the energy circuit.

Stand with your feet apart and lean forward. With the outer (little finger) edge of the palms — preferably skin to skin — rub each of the sections ten times with firm, sweeping movements. The shoulders must be held right back to begin the sweep.

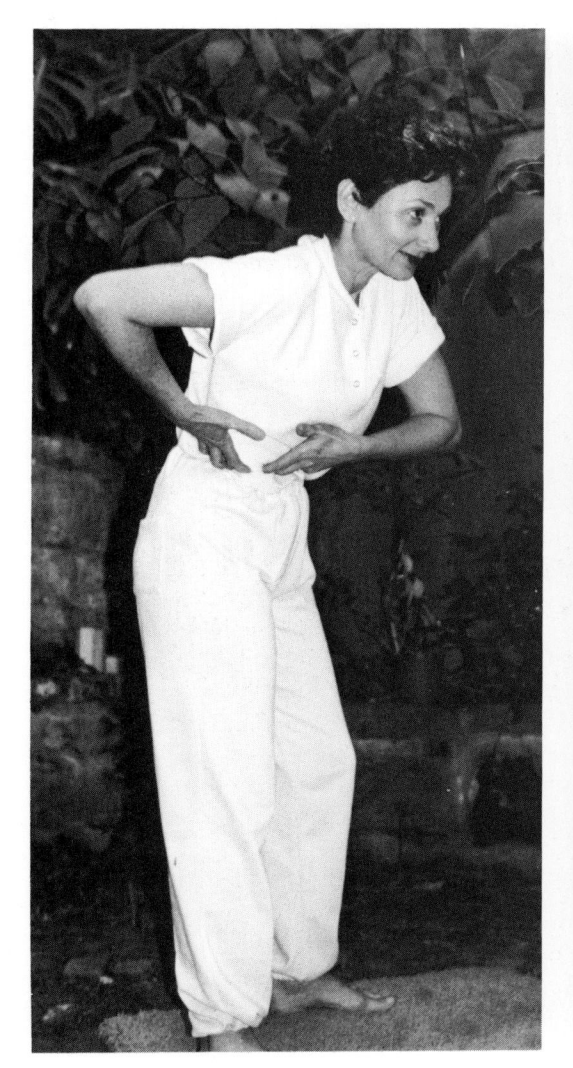

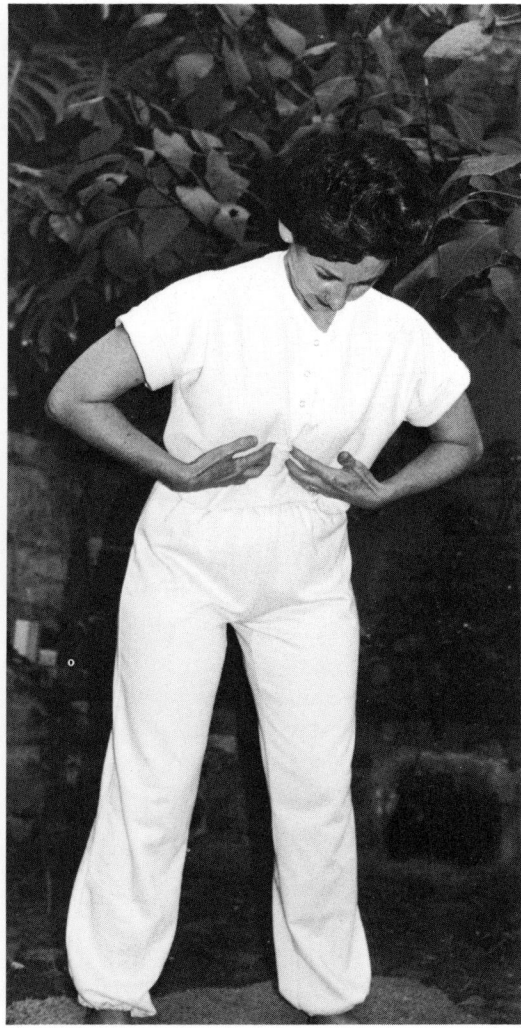

Rib Roll

The Rib Roll
This will complete your morning tune-up: leaning forward, spread the fingers of both hands and tuck them under the length of one side of the rib cage. On an exhalation press the fingers up under the ribs. Hold for three seconds. Move to the other side and repeat. Finally, placing both forefingers underneath, exhale, lean forward, and press inwards for three seconds. Some areas may be tender from time to time but the pressure helps to clear energy blockages. This daily check also keeps you in touch with the amount of flesh you are carrying over your ribs and midriff!

CELLULITE
The exercises described above will ensure a neat waistline forever. However, there is another type of category of bumps and bulges called cellulite, which is more difficult to shift. It is composed of fat, waste material and water trapped in gel-like, lumpy,

immovable pockets just beneath the skin. It is always local and is found in areas of slow or sluggish circulation such as the thighs, upper arms, hips and calves.

These pockets of 'fat gone wrong' act like sponges which can absorb amounts of water and then blow up and bulge out, resulting in the 'orange skin' ripples and flabbiness which is so distressing. Women of all shapes and build, of all weights and ages, suffer from this problem.

The way we live is really the ultimate cause of cellulite. Waste matter and toxins accumulate in the body through poor absorption and elimination as well as excessive drug-taking and medication. Other contributing factors are:

Tension

Irregular eating habits and lack of balance in the fibre/fat/protein and carbohydrate foods

Insufficient water and fluid intake

Lack of proper exercise, resulting in sluggish digestion, constipation and poor circulation of blood and lymph (the waste disposal system)

Hormonal cycle, especially at puberty, pre-menstrually, at menopause, during pregnancy, or when taking the Pill. Also at times of mental or physical trauma which can upset the delicate machinery of the endocrine system

Fatigue

When these occur, the normal process of elimination cannot flush out waste material from the body through the normal channels. Circulation problems and cellulite seem to go hand in hand and, once formed, cellulite obviously slows down the circulation even more. Sometimes broken veins, troublesome varicose veins and bruises can also be a problem. Your acupuncturist will work on the spleen meridian to help digestion and the distribution of fluids in the body.

Try setting one day a week aside for a cleanse, taking only fresh fruit juice with water: half and half. Drink approximately two quarts a day. Use cleansing herb combinations such as comfrey and pepsin, alfalfa, slippery elm and cascara sagrada. Adjust the latter until you can obtain two bowel movements per day.

If you continue the fast for three days it will be necessary to do one or two cleansing enemas. It is also important to rest for at least one hour during the day, walk or take light exercise, and have hot and cold showers.

Remember to break a fast gradually. Over a period of three or four days after the juices, include whole fruit for breakfast, vegetable salad for lunch and for supper, and diluted juice or broth (homemade from potatoes in their skins, celery, beetroots, carrots and herbs). On the seventh day you can include eggs, nuts and soured milk products, and start back on mild food on the eighth day.

You will also find it helpful to devise a 'spot' exercise that you can do isometrically at frequent intervals during the day. For instance, if it is the hip and thigh area which is troubling you, you can do the following exercise while sitting down: With your knees together, squeeze your buttocks hard and tense all your muscles down to the knees. Hold for five seconds or more. Repeat often. This type of 'unseen' exercise makes good use of the time spent immobile at a desk or in front of television and, best of all, provides greater body-awareness.

When you have mastered this contraction, why not add the peri-anal (pelvic floor) lift described earlier? In this way your remedy and prevention are simultaneous! The bulges should also be kneaded and massaged and the skin brushed daily with a dry bristle bath brush.

TOUCH FOR BEAUTY — A Summary for a Suggested Morning Programme

On Waking
Stretch before getting out of bed.
1 counting backwards whilst holding the breath. Start from 10–1 increasing until you can hold from 50–1
2 repeat selected positive affirmation for the day whilst holding the breath: i.e. 'I am healthy' or other requirements, worded simply and in the present tense
3 move wrists, ankles, fingers while stretching
Benefits: spine/nerves/lungs/brain   *Time:* 2 minutes

In the Shower (or at other times of the day on an empty stomach)
1 rib roll   *Time:* 9 seconds
2 stomach lift. 5–20 contractions for each exhalation. Work up to 50 lifts per day minimum   *Time:* 50 seconds
Benefits: stomach/bladder/diaphragm/abdominal muscles

After the Shower
1 massage the tender reflex areas of the feet   *Time:* 60 seconds
2 facial acupressure and isotonic exercise with normal skin care. Breathe deeply.

During the Day
60-second energy boost as required
Benefits: overall

CHAPTER 9
DEEP TISSUE MUSCLE THERAPY
John Cottone

Deep Tissue Muscle Therapy (DTMT) is a therapeutic and curative massage process which deals with the problem where it is manifesting in the body and traces it to its origin. It is a scientific, specific and systematic method of eliminating toxic wastes, blocks, tension and fibrous connective tissue throughout the muscular system.

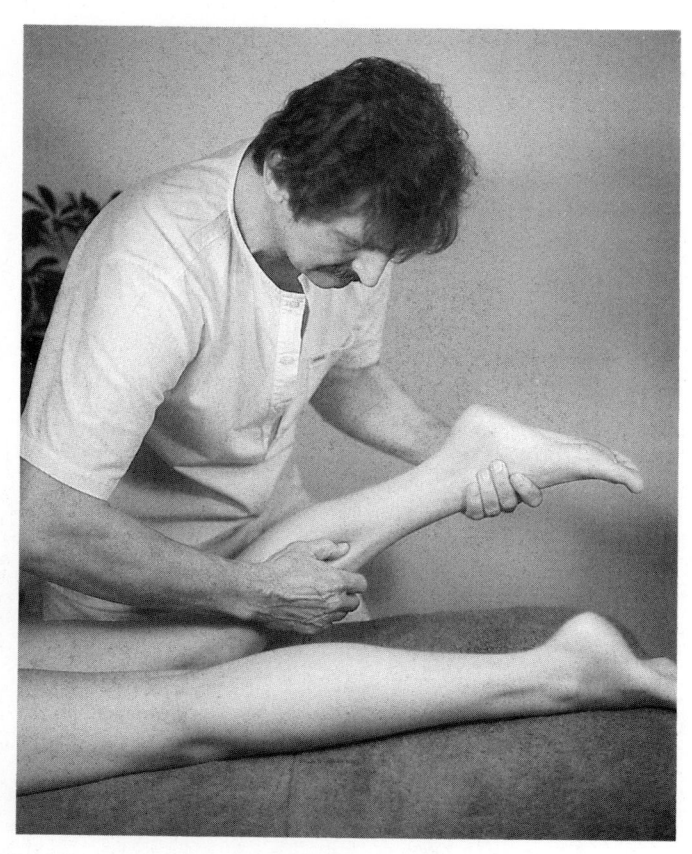

The tibia or shin-bone being sculptured by separating the muscle from the bone (posterior application)

THE SIGNIFICANCE OF THE MUSCLES

DTMT is the study of muscles. Its theory states that the muscles are the number one priority in healing the body and the initial factor in positive or negative health. The muscles are the movers of the body, for not only do they move the parts of the body, they also move blood, air, food and waste. Approximately 70 per cent of the bulk of the body consists of muscle tissue and muscles are part of, and interact with, the respiratory, digestive, circulatory, elimination, nervous, skeletal and sensory systems.

According to DTMT theory, a major cause of disease begins with 'dis-ease' in the muscles. The body's density is composed mostly of muscles. They travel the full length, width and depth of the body like a major highway travels across a country, with its interconnecting roads and byways and must be maintained in the same manner in direct perspective to how much the system is used. Muscles contract, shrink and go into spasm (interlock) in accordance with the amount and type of use, exercise, nourishment and abuse they receive. Over-acid conditions caused by diet, stress and chemical reactions within the body cause the muscles to shrink, harden and become excessively fibrous, which limits their movement and elasticity. This shrinking of muscle in turn pulls the skeletal structure closer together, creating further limiting body movements and causing irritations in the joints, vertebrae and bones of the body.

The physical goal in DTMT is to 'sculpt' the skeletal system and return the natural postural alignment and full rotational movement to all joints. In order to accomplish this, the body's muscular systems are relaxed, separated and elongated while dissolving layer upon layer of individual excessive, tight, fibrous, contracted and spasmodic tissue. Consequently, proper circulation to *all* parts of the body is enhanced, providing blood, nourishment and energy. The body can heal itself only when proper circulation is restored to it.

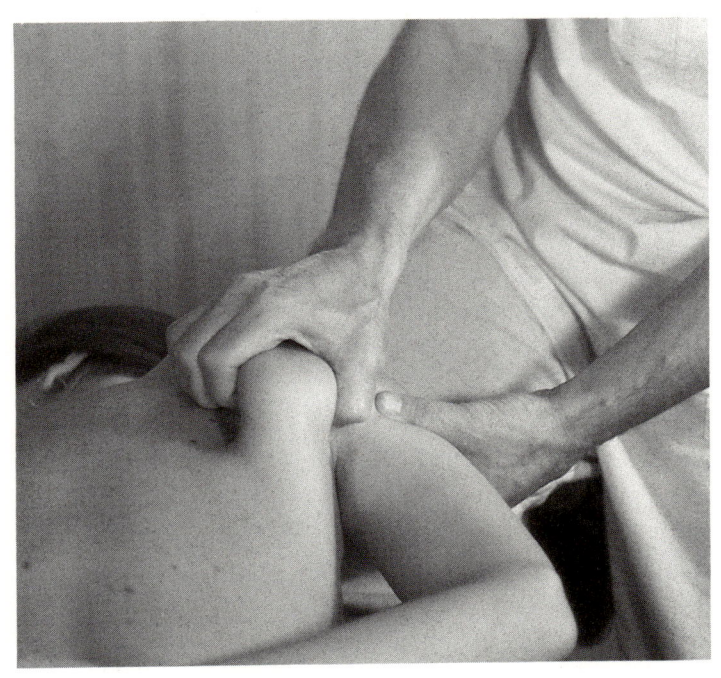

The scapula or wing-bone being sculptured and liberated from anterior and bilateral aspects

YIN AND YANG BODIES

DTMT recognises two basic systems of muscles that are a key to our optimum health:

1   An exterior group of large muscles that act as a buffer between the exterior world and our interior world. These muscles control our major movements and relay the energy of the outer world into our inner reality. In Taoist terms, this is the expression of the *Yang* body (physical body).

2   A set of lighter, interior muscles that join the skeletal structure together and control the expansion and flexions of the skeletal structure. These muscles relay the internal feelings of the body to the outer muscles, to be expressed to the external world. This is the expression of the *Yin* body (emotional or 'psychological' body).

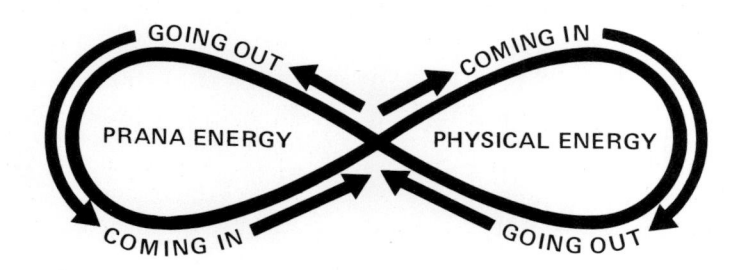

In my experience, there is always this exchange of *Yin* into *Yang* and *Yang* into *Yin*, that creates the balance that we all look for in our lives. To understand the interior and exterior reality of our bodies we also need to understand the universal concept 'As above, so below'. We take oxygen and solid matter into our blood and digestive systems (inner body/below the surface) and we eliminate waste from our bodies (outer body/above). One is a continuous reflection of the other, returning to itself, as in the sign of infinity. We take in, in order to give out: energy comes in to the body, goes out, and comes back in recycled.

It is possible to draw a parallel between massage and ecology, comparing the planet Earth (water and land) with the body (liquid and flesh). If we put waste into rivers over a period of years, that waste will inevitably pollute the water and wash back on us. However if the chemical constituents can be digested and assimilated by the water and its living inhabitants they will not become pollutants.

The process in the human body is similar. What we can easily digest and assimilate becomes pure high grade fuel for us to use as energy. What we cannot, becomes waste that must be removed from the body in order for us to remain healthy. When we take in substances that are difficult or impossible to digest or assimilate, they become irritants, obstacles or pollutants in the body. The body must then use a lot of its energy in the neutralisation and elimination of the substances concerned. This overtaxes the body and can result in tiredness, lack of energy, the feeling of being 'blocked' and numerous other symptoms that set up the context for 'dis-ease' and disease.

MUSCLE TONE

In order to experience optimum health the muscle tissue of the body must be pliable, flexible and in good tone. Ligaments, tendons, organs, skin and muscles are all part of muscle tissue. Muscle tone comes from the constant contraction and elongation of muscles that results from the flow of non-conscious stimuli from the brain and spinal cord to each muscle, and the voluntary physical movements of the body. The involuntary constant stimulation increases or decreases depending on the level of activity of the nervous system.

When the body takes in any substance that creates stress, it can result in the nervous system becoming over-active. The muscles may contract excessively, go into spasm, harden, lose elasticity, or become over-fibrous.

When a muscle goes into spasm and cramps it is easily noticeable and can be dealt with immediately. However if, over the years, a muscle continuously shortens, hardens and loses its elasticity and tone, it slowly strangles the passage of the circulating blood, food, energy, impulses and messages that constantly pass through it. The entire body begins to receive less nutrition. We begin to feel tired and don't know why. We eat more, feeling the need for nutrition, but this usually only results in over-eating habits and excessive body weight. We begin to feel old and sick, and yet we know that we shouldn't feel that way.

PHYSICAL AND EMOTIONAL FACTORS

The most common, and sometimes least noticed, stress comes as a result of physical intake into the body. Food, liquid and air can make the human body feel alive, vibrant, energetic and tingling with well-being, or it can make it feel dead, flat, irritable and ill.

In an attempt to simplify the fairly complex subject of stress in relation to physical intake we can identify three categories:

1 Substances without nutritional value.
2 Substances which are easily digestable and assimilated.
3 Substances which should not be combined, and which may trigger body allergies.

The most commonly used substances which lack nutritional value or which remove more energy from the body than they put in, are tobacco, alcohol and drugs. These substances give us temporarily altered states of consciousness by affecting the blood, and can make us light-headed and free from the realities of our day to day lives. However their overall effect is to drain, leach and irritate the body's organs, chemicals, vitamin and mineral supplies. This situation creates an internal stress which results in muscle tension and contraction.

Muscular shrinkage also occurs from emotional and psychological holding patterns. The muscles adapt to the level of elasticity required to make the elongation and rotation movements used in our daily activities. Emotional upsets that have really affected us can be related to the pains we might have felt in our chest or heart areas. When this happens we 'close off' and protect our chests. Our shoulders come forward, our backs become round and our chests withdraw as we try to protect this area from further exposure to the pain and sorrow we feel impinging from the outside world. In this process the ribs are brought closer together and the muscles shrink and adapt to this new body posture. Years later, as our emotional instincts become more mature and stronger, we try to 'open up' again and we feel restricted and blocked in our emotional expression. We want to be expressive and receptive with our emotions but somehow that flow just isn't there.

In this situation, the muscles have formed a band of protective 'armament' to help us avoid unwanted emotional stimuli from the outside world which our immature emotional instincts were unable to handle at the time. It is as if the outside energy bounces off the body, instead of entering and creating more emotional pain. The major

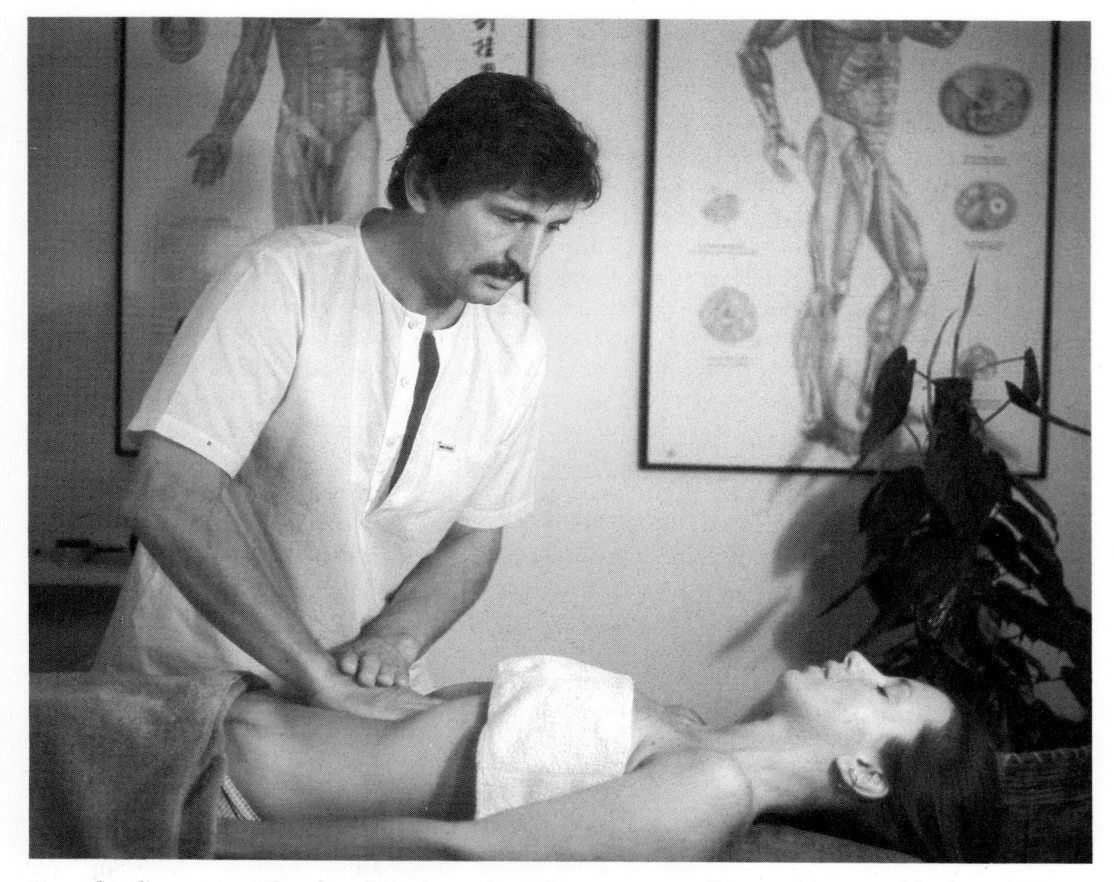

Here the therapist guides the client into a breathing pattern while working on a blockage in the solar plexus area. The solar plexus is a trigger point in uniting both the upper and lower, and the inner and outer, bodies

problem with this armament is that while at an early stage it is protective and keeps outside energy from coming in, it also locks in emotional energy that we need to let out. It becomes increasingly more difficult to express our emotions and we feel more and more internal pressure which begins to manifest itself as pain or confusion.

PHYSICAL AND EMOTIONAL UNITY

As the body becomes blocked from physical and emotional responses, more dependency is put on our intellectual powers. We begin to *think* we are feeling and doing and a state of confusion arises. It has been said, in many ways, by scientists and psychologists that 'what the mind believes to be truth, sooner or later becomes our truth'. However, the physical, emotional and psychological bodies must work in co-operation and balance with each other for the body to experience an authentic sense of unity. A common example of 'a body out of balance' is provided by a person making a decision involving a loved one. The mind might say, 'I need to get out of this relationship, it isn't good for my growth, it holds me back — I just need to leave.' The heart might feel, 'That sounds right, but I love that person, I can't just leave, it would bring pain to one or both of us.' With that internal dichotomy going on, whatever decision that person makes is certain to lead to a feeling of dissatisfaction. It becomes a no-win situation. It satisfies only one of the instincts while another instinct is left unresolved. As one learns to live with that imbalance the more characteristic response becomes stronger and the body armament becomes more solidified around the weaker instincts, further protecting and inhibiting them. This results in a further contracting of the muscles, and poorer circulation of fuel and energy to all parts of the body.

When we close off, and the smaller interior skeletal muscles shrink, inhibiting the extension and rotation of the skeletal bones, we feel this a sense of compacture as a lack of energy in an otherwise healthy body. It is as if a restricted body was living inside a healthy exterior flexible body, with our feelings unrelated to our physical reality. When the thicker exterior muscles begin to shrink and become fibrous we feel old in our external movements and energy levels, and we feel we have 'aged' like a healthy young person living inside an old body. So in the care and maintenance of the human body, it must be looked at as a whole. All of the interactions must be taken into consideration. In many cases, when a problem is manifesting in one area of the body, it becomes at least as important to trace it to the place of origin and solve the problem in reverse. If, because of emotional problems, the body has contracted and developed a physical problem, it must be treated through the physical manifestation right back to the emotional origin — in order to totally free the body from the possibility of the problem returning.

THE CELLULAR MEMORY LEVEL

Ordinary massage may relieve some of the pressure from the muscles but it will not reach the emotional and psychological fears stored deep in the body at cellular memory level.

DTMT, on the other hand, deals with fears stored deep in the body. Long after the mind has stopped thinking about past fears, avoidance and injuries, the body still carries these fears at a deep muscular level. These muscles form a bond of armament around the body that blocks out or buffers pain and fear from the outside world. This armament also 'locks in' psychological and emotional energy that needs to be released into the outer world. The DTMT process works through the armament and liberates the body, allowing the blocked emotional and psychological energy, and cellular memory fears to be brought to the surface and dissipated. Locked energy and fear in the body will inevitably attract injury, illness and failure to itself.

DTMT theory states that:

1 There are fears stored in the body at cellular memory level. Anywhere that there is pain in the body is a direct reflection of fear stored in that area. Pain is the method through which fear expresses itself.

2 Cellular memory can be stored in the adult or adolescent body as a result of physical, emotional or psychological fear and pain. These are usually the easiest to diagnose and deal with. Cellular memory can also be a result of the time spent in the womb prior to birth. It has been proven that the unborn child experiences emotional agitation whenever the mother thinks of smoking or doing anything that affects the oxygen supply to the foetus. Therefore, agitation, depression, poor nutrition, toxins, etc. all have a physical and psychological effect at the cellular memory level.

3 The possibility exists that cellular memory can be brought into the body through the genes of the parents. The cells have a positive memory of how to reproduce themselves and grow. They might also contain a negative memory that has been worked out through the family chain over generations, for many people have fears and pains that they cannot relate to in any way.

HOW DTMT CAN BE EFFECTIVE: TWO CASE-HISTORIES

Two examples of how emotional and psychological blockages are held in the body at cellular memory level occurred recently in a DTMT Advanced Practitioner class. Two volunteers had agreed to be treated by me while the class observed. I asked one of the volunteers, Ms. Z. B. aged 46, to describe any problems she was having, her past medical history and what she would like to have treated. She explained that she had persistent migraine headaches and that she clenched and ground her teeth to such an extent that she was wearing out all her fillings and had to resort to sleeping with a mouth guard. She had a continual neck problem that was very painful and had been seeing a chiropractor for adjustments on a weekly basis for the past year.

I decided to start with her feet to unblock her energy channels and to diagnose through the individual toes. When I finished the work with her feet she felt at peace and went into a deep state of rest. Her breathing became very slow, almost imperceptible.

I then began working on her abdomen and solar plexus area and asked her about a scar which was visible on her stomach. She said she had had a Caesarian delivery. As I continued working on her abdomen area, her breathing tempo started to speed up with hard explosive exhales, and she began moaning and pushing down as if she was in labour. When I completed working on that area I then massaged the bottom of the back of her skull (*occipital area*) and her masseter muscles (jaw hinge), and she began to cry out, as if in pain. Her whole body began to shake as she cried and moaned. The overall energy of the session was as if she was re-experiencing a difficult birth.

After the session was over and she was relaxing, she looked like a little girl who was very happy. Afterwards she said that during the work on her abdomen she kept hearing

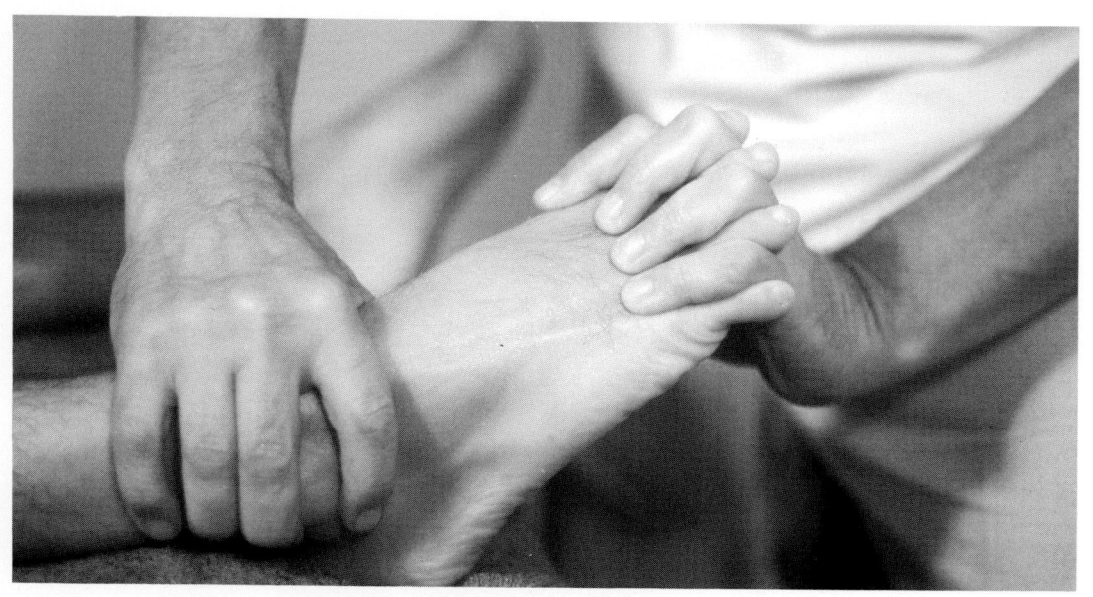

Exploring and flexing the ankle channel while the toes are separated and exercised

the nurse who was attending her during the labour period of her first son's birth. The nurse was saying, 'Hang on, the doctor is coming soon', but she felt trapped and helpless. She explained to the class that her doctor who was on vacation had left instructions for the locum doctor to give her a trial labour. She described agonising shooting pains which coursed down her legs as the baby's head hit the region at the base of her spine. When the doctor arrived he immediately performed an Episotomy (cutting the wall from vagina to rectum) and delivered the baby.

Ms. Z. B. spent a year after that going to physical therapy classes, learning how to walk again and how to bring tone back to the muscles that had been cut.

Through her tears and laughter she said it was the first time she had talked about it in over twenty years. As she left she said she felt exhilarated, light, free and very young. She certainly looked vibrant, alive and happy. When she returned for another session the following week, she told the class that she hadn't experienced a single headache all week and that her jaw felt much more relaxed.

Two months later, she still hadn't experienced any headaches. Ms. Z. B. has had a small recurrence of neck tension which she is able to deal with by her own means but the pain in her jaw has been eliminated. There is still some sign of clenching, but the grinding seems to have subsided.

The diagnosis: The emotional and psychological fear and pain at the cellular memory level seems to have cleared but there is still some work needed to eliminate the last of the muscle tension. She is currently undergoing treatment.

Another example of the physical impact of DTMT work was provided by Mr T. P., also aged 46. For the past four years he had suffered from cold feet and hands and had begun to lose sensation in his feet. This effect had spread up into his legs and he felt he was in danger of falling over when showering. He used to enjoy running, but in the past year had been trying to run for exercise — however, it had been painful to do so. In his own words, 'He didn't have any power in his legs and it felt like his legs were dying — it was like old age'.

Upon examination of his feet and legs, I found his muscles to be tight and in a contracted fibrous condition. He also had weak, fallen arches. There was little energy flow and poor circulation in his legs.

After seven treatments of DTMT Mr T. P. said that his feet were warm once again. 'There's a lot of feeling in them ... They are like my hands, and I actually feel a sense of dexterity in my feet.' He explained that running has become a joy again, and he can now use it as a form of public transportation. Any short errands within a couple of miles, he just runs instead of using his car. His posture and structural alignment is much straighter, his legs feel powerful, his arches are stronger and feel like they are reshaping. He can now run for ten miles and finds it relaxing and rejuvenating. He has a whole new body awareness and does a lot of self-massage and exploration of his muscles.

The case of Mr T. P. is a good example of a characteristic situation. When the muscles become tight and fibrous, the circulation is blocked and this condition in turn creates the context for physical, emotional and mental discomfort and disease.

IN SUMMARY
DTMT is designed to free physical blockages, and to stimulate and to guide the releasing of blocked emotional and mental energy. The body therapy is done with complete awareness of the muscular/skeletal/neural resistance levels and systemati-

cally massages layers of *body armour*. While accomplishing this, there is also an examination and exploration of the body's electro-magnetic fields, circulation system, nervous system, elimination system, *chi* meridians, energy channels, and organs, right down to the skeletal systems. One can then understand the Oriental philosophy of health-care: 'With the examination and exploration of the body is the cure'.

The result is an elongated, toned body with the muscular and skeletal structures working at optimum elasticity and rotation, uniting the physical, emotional and mental bodies in a state of health and well-being.

CRYSTALLISATION

Figure 1 shows the energy channels and their interconnecting paths throughout the body. The *prana* (or life-energy) comes in through the crown *chakra*, circulates through the body and eliminates mainly through the hands and feet. Because of muscle fibre, involuntary holding patterns, and stress, this energy sometimes becomes blocked somewhere along the channel and crystallises. This creates discomfort, physical pain and low body energy. We diagnose and treat this problem through the feet and hands. Each channel represents an element, instinct and *chakra* (See Figure 2). The channels on the left side of the body represent the *Yin* or receptive channels and the channels on the right side represent the *Yang* or assertive channels. The *Yin* and *Yang* aspects of the body must be in balance for us to feel well-being in our daily lives. Whether we are being *Yin* or *Yang*, it must be from a position of pure action. Action in this sense can be defined as the natural flow of human energy in the sense of self-perfection and service to the general pattern of human evolution. If we don't come from this point of view we can become passive instead of receptive, or aggressive instead of assertive. This can stagnate or irritate the channel from under- or over-use and lead to crystallisation in that channel.

We diagnose and treat these channels by first rubbing and kneading the foot to warm and relax it. We explore all the channels between the bones and joints as a preparation for the energy-moving work. You'll find if you sit down and spend 15 to 20 minutes with each foot that continuous rubbing and exploring will seem very familiar and enjoyable to you. When the foot is warmed and relaxed, you should grip the small fifth toe firmly and pull it straight out, elongating the joint that attaches it to the foot — (See Figure 3). This attracts the energy towards the toes and aids in draining old stagnant energy from the body. Hold this position for approximately one minute. You can let a little pressure off the stretch if it is too painful or stretch a little more if it feels too easy. For maximum result do not let go of all the pressure or pull too hard or quickly at any time during the self-treatment. You can do this yourself or exchange a treatment with a friend, after the minute is up, giving gentle, loving strokes to the toe as if milking the energy out the end of it. Then take the toe and bend it down towards the sole of the foot (See Figure 4). This shuts off the elimination of the energy and backs it up toward the head. If there is any crystallisation in the channel, the energy backs up and burns into it, dissolving it and allowing it to flush down and out. Wherever there is a blockage, you may feel it in that part of the body. If there isn't any blockage you may feel the energy move up into your arm and hand. Hold the position for one to two minutes. Whether the channel is blocked or not, using this treatment will stimulate the usage of that energy channel. After the holding period again give loving, 'milking' strokes towards the end of the toe. Continue the treatment through the rest of the toes.

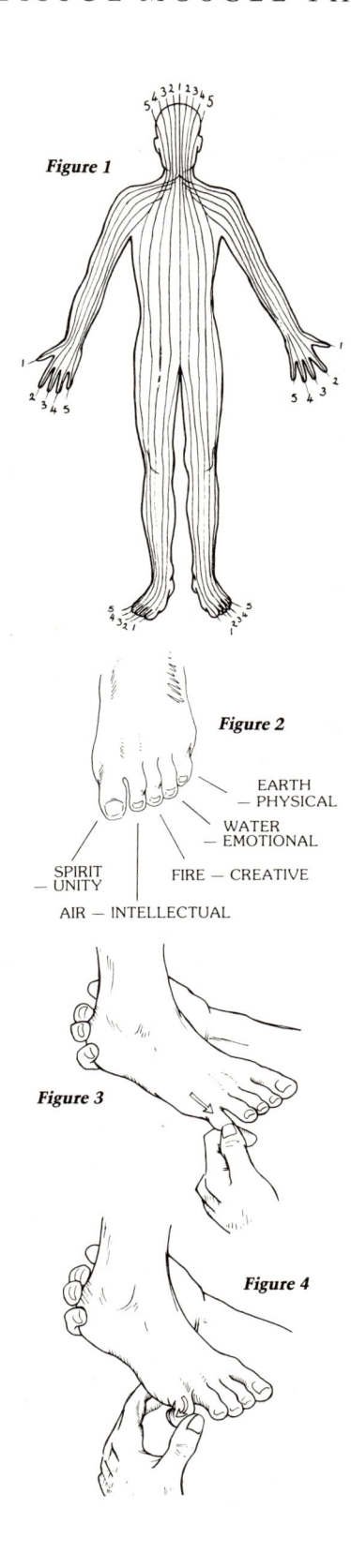

DEEP TISSUE MUSCLE THERAPY

Figure 1

Figure 2

EARTH — PHYSICAL
WATER — EMOTIONAL
FIRE — CREATIVE
AIR — INTELLECTUAL
SPIRIT — UNITY

Figure 3

Figure 4

This treatment will enable you to get a better *Yin/Yang* balance in your lifestyle and increase your overall energy. However, the treatment shouldn't be done more than one or two times per week.

We can use the toe associated with the element water and the emotions as an example of how to diagnose (See Figure 2). If after treating both feet you may have found that on the left foot the Water toe was painful with a burning sensation running through the energy channel. However at the same time the Water toe on the right foot experienced a feeling of well-being when it was being worked on. The diagnosis would be: an imbalance in the receiving and giving of emotions or expressing love. With these symptoms you could have a difficult time in receiving emotions or dealing with your own inner feelings. Emotional displays could easily make you frightened or 'closed off'. The physical massage treatment helps in stimulating and balancing the channel, therefore aiding in more or less use of that energy and integrating your emotional balance.

A PERSONAL NOTE

I try not to be subjective in my writing but I feel compelled to share a reality I have discovered in my travels. In both the alternative and traditional healing sciences, enthusiastic amateurs with good intentions can often leave a patient or client confused as a result of their therapy. I have personally come across body therapists who have read about or had some slight exposure to DTMT work, and who have begun to use more pressure in their normal massage, calling their work 'deep muscle therapy'. It takes a fully trained practitioner many years of dedicated service to reach the technical and practical skills needed to work at this level of consciousness. Keep in mind that it is *your* body that they are practising on! Ask questions and become fully informed with regard to what they are doing, their experience, and their background. It is a physical reality that, 'You only have your body,' and 'Your body is your temple.'

CHAPTER 10
REICHIAN AND NEO-REICHIAN THERAPY
Lew Luton

In Vienna, last year, I visited Freud's house. After viewing the exhibits I was chatting to one of the elderly women running the museum. She asked me if I was in the field.

'Yes, I am one of those renegade Reichians.'

'Reich's influence seems to be extending. He is much followed in Germany. He is taught in the universities there.'

'By the way,' I asked, 'in the picture collection I did not notice any photographs of Reich.'

She smiled, 'Oh, the Jungians come and say there are no pictures of Jung. The women come and say there are no pictures of women. The Reichians come and say there are no pictures of Reich.'

I said I had seen plenty pictures of women, I had seen one of Jung, but I was hard pressed to remember any of Reich. Still, considering the cloud under which he left the Psychoanalytic Association, it was not remarkable.

WILHELM REICH: PROFESSIONAL BACKGROUND

Wilhelm Reich for most of his professional life was at the leading edge of his field. As he followed the implications of his scientific findings he extended his area of interest to encompass not only psychotherapy but also sexuality, childbirth, childrearing, holistic health, functional science, work democracy, self-regulation and alternative education. By the 1940s he had gone beyond psychoanalysis and psychology to orgonomy.

Wilhelm Reich began to be interested in Freud's libidinal theories from his days as a medical student at Vienna. He started a seminar with fellow students to examine, not sexual pathologies as taught by the university, but what happened in normal sexuality, or, as his daughter Eva once explained, 'What happens to your guts in spring'.

In 1920, at the age of twenty-three, Reich was admitted to the Vienna Psychoanalytic Society. He was recognised as a brilliant clinician. Two years later he was appointed clinical assistant to Freud's psychoanalytic clinic. Before many years had elapsed he was training young analysts.

In his training seminar Reich got his young analysts to bring the cases in which they had no success. His premise was that everyone could have presented learned papers on their successes but if they learnt how to overcome their failures they would learn more.

Reich also researched the successful cases. He learnt that a common factor in successful analysis was the establishment, in the subject, of a satisfying sexual/emotional relationship. From these findings he developed the concept of the 'func-

Wilhelm Reich photographed in his laboratory at Orgonon in Rangely, Maine, during the 1950s. Reich wrote on the back of this photograph, 'I am thinking of how to fight the emotional plague'

tional' orgasm: Orgasm not limited to physiological activity but accompanied by deep emotional commitment.

Further research led him to write his first book on the function of the orgasm, *Die Funktion des Orgasmus (1927)* — not to be confused with his English Volume I of *Discovery of the Orgone, The Function of the Orgasm (1942)*. He suggested neurosis could not exist in the person for whom 'functional' orgasm was possible. He felt that he had furthered Freud's work.

Freud and his circle did not seem to think so. Referring to the staid, older analysts, Reich said he felt like a 'shark in a pond full of carp'. The older men had some well-recorded fallings-out with Reich. He had joined the Communist Party, and had begun store-front clinics for the Viennese workers.

Reich's concern at the poor social impact of psychoanalysis, led him to begin the mass movement Sexpol (Sexual Politics). Its aim was to liberate the libidinal restraints of the masses. With Roheim and Marcuse, Reich had been seen as one of the Freudian sexual radicals; one who tried to bridge between Marx and Freud.

Reich also changed his approach to patients. His first deviation from standard psychoanalytic practice was through 'resistance analysis'. He was convinced that free association could in itself be a resistance. He began to work at the point of resistance, and would turn and face his patients and allow himself to be observed, while observing them. He noticed characteristic muscular tension while patients were presenting their material and developed from these insights his concept of 'Character Analysis'.

Through his 'Character Analysis', Reich began to deal with material in an orderly manner. Today some of the neo-Reichian techniques have returned to the old psychoanalytic practice of dealing with material as it is presented — 'Going with the flow', some call it. I feel that they have lost some of the advances Reich made.

The next step from Character Analysis was Vegeto-therapy — the vegetative system being another name for the autonomic nervous system. Breaking another psychoanalytic rule, that 'you must never touch your patients', Reich loosened off their muscular tensions by massage. He found through manipulating these chronically tense muscles that much material was released. Working directly with the body became, as dreams had for Freud, 'the royal road to the unconscious'.

Later Reich used deepened and freed breathing to spark off the autonomic response. 'Reichian breathing' has been used as a name for hyperventilation techniques which have more to do with Leonard Orr than Reich. Hyperventilation techniques overcharge the organism, producing a muscular stiffness and sometimes a profoundly altered state of consciousness. This has a tendency to defeat the therapeutic purpose, in that it impacts the neuroses and reinforces the muscular hardening effect which Reich called 'armouring'. In fear, the client 'splits off' from 'grounded bodily sensations.

Reich joined the staff at the Institute of Psychology at the University of Oslo in 1934. Hitler's assumption of power in Germany in 1933 had caused him to flee Berlin with a suitcase full of scientific papers. In much the same way he had fled his family's farm in 1915 when the Russians over-ran it and burned it. Reich had left Vienna for Berlin in 1930. He had become estranged from his first wife Annie Reich, who was also a psychoanalyst.

1933 was also a momentous year. Reich had published *Character Analysis* and *The Mass Psychology of Fascism*, had been expelled from the Communist Party, and was soon to be expelled from the International Psychoanalytic Society. Annie Reich, left behind in Vienna, allegedly began to spread the rumour that Reich was mad. In the midst of all this upheaval, Reich discovered the biological function of 'tension and charge'.

REICH'S RESEARCH ON ENERGY

From clinical investigation Reich learned that neuroses resulted from a stasis of sexual energy. This stasis resulted from a disturbance of the discharge of high sexual excitation in the organism. He therefore suggested that 'the elimination of the sexual stasis by the orgastic discharge of biological excitation removes every kind of neurotic manifestation'.

From his sex-economy research, Reich produced the 'orgasm formula'. He found the orgasm revealed a four-beat rhythm:

Mechanical tension → *Bio-energetic charge* →
Bio-energetic discharge → *Mechanical relaxation*

This is the function of tension and charge (or TC function).

Further investigation revealed this four-beat pattern applied to all functions of the autonomic system. Even cell division followed this four-beat pattern. Reich was to propose that the orgasm formula was the formula of life itself.

By 1935 Reich was lecturing on character formation and its biological basis. It was during his time in Oslo that he worked with protozoa and made his time-lapse film of their function. The films have been transferred to video tape and are now part of the scientific exhibition at Orgonon, in Rangely, Maine.

He also spent much time investigating *bions*, which he described as microscopically visible energy vesicles. They were the vesicles into which all matter disintegrated if made to swell. They represented transitional forms between living and non-living matter. Reich suggested that 'the bion was the elemental function unit of all living matter'.

In bio-electrical experiments (1934–1936) Reich recorded changes in potential from pleasure to anxiety in millivolts. But he was not satisfied that bio-energy was solely electrical. Reich found experimentally that the small bio-electrical charge was actually supported on a platform of a huge biological charge of energy — orgone (life) energy.

Orgone energy was discovered by Reich (1939–1940) after he found samples of SAPA (sand packet) bions luminating with a greyish-blue light in the darkened laboratory in Oslo. Previously workers in the laboratory had developed conjunctivitis and began to sport sun tans in the depth of the Norwegian winter. Reich found the radiation phenomenon was present everywhere, indoors and out, varying only in the density and intensity of the energy. He was able to quantify this energy; demonstrate it electropically, photographically, thermically, magnetically; and to accumulate it. He found also:

1 Organic materials absorb orgone energy
2 Metallic substances reflect it
3 Blockage of the kinetic energy by any metallic obstacle causes a rise in local temperature

He was able to design a device which accumulated this cosmic mass-free energy. He called it an orgone energy accumulator.

A single unit of orgone was called 1 org. An org was defined as the quantity of orgone energy in a space of one cubic foot which corresponds to the maintenance of a temperature difference 1°C higher in the orgone energy accumulator than in the air outside the accumulator.

1 org = T (o) − T of 1°C for one hour
T (o) = temperature in an orgone accumulator (ORAC)
T = temperature outside of ORAC

Reich also noted that the temperature difference changed according to atmospheric conditions. This led later to his weather modification work. He built a 'cloudbuster', a simple machine which he used to produce rain and reverse drought conditions.

Reich found stasis of orgone energy appeared in the body as a result of repressing emotion; this stasis also occurred atmospherically. He named this condition 'D.O.R.' (deadly orgone energy). He was able to describe it and reduce its effect. Recently it has been observed experimentally that a significant correlation exists between atomic testing and temperature difference, suggesting that these tests affect the terrestrial orgone energy envelope, not only at the location of the tests. After the oranur* experiment Reich became concerned that atomic tests would increase D.O.R. and thus increase desert formation and it is interesting to note that international bodies are at present concerned at the increase in desert formation.

Reich also noted that life forms (orgonomes) could be understood in terms of being formed by the spinning wave of orgone energy. He hypothesised that this spinning

---

* A word coined by Reich and meaning 'orgone energy and uranium'.

Reich's famous 'cloudbuster' located at Orgonon

wave (the *Kreiselwelle*) formed matter according to its pattern of travel in space: that is, bions formed in loops of the wave.

The *Kreiselwelle* can be described mathematically. Reich observed that in a metal-lined dark room, placed within a Farady cage to shield out any electromagnetic effect, the eyes, after they had adapted to the dark (thirty minutes), perceived light displays. Observers reported spinning streaks of light, as the wave moved across their field of vision, or pulsing spots of light if the wave was seen coming towards them.

Reich's experimental work on the formation of matter predated the morphogenetic field theory of Rupert Sheldrake, which is the subject of lively debate at present. Reich perhaps offers the vitalists an experimental method by which to examine the energy of morphogenetic fields.

There may in fact have been one occasion when matter was created in the laboratory at Orgonon. During the oranur experiments, when needles of radium were introduced into a highly charged orgone field, they went wild. Eva Reich reported that a 1 cm deposit of waxy greyish matter was found in the laboratory each day. Although no experimental work was done on this deposit because of other pressures in clearing off the deadly effects of the oranur experiment, this result could offer support for Reich's theory that matter is created by the interplay of two energy streams. He called this process 'cosmic superimposition'. He saw the same process occurring in the sexual embrace, in cyclone formation and in the shape of galaxies. I will deal more fully with this later.

Vitalism suggests that a non-material force which overrides the laws of science controls behaviour and other activities of the living organism. Most biologists are reductionists or mechanists, that is, they hold that living things are complex, organised, computer-like machines. Reich entered the vitalist debate against the mechanistic scientific view. 'The experience of pleasure, of expansion,' he said 'is inseparably connected with living functioning'.

Biologist Rupert Sheldrake, with his theory of morphogenetic fields, is on the side of the vitalists. Support from the computer world comes from Benoit B. Mandelbrot, who for the past twelve years has been an IBM fellow at the Thomas J. Watson Research Centre, New York.

Mandelbrot has suggested that Euclidean geometry was incapable of describing the shapes of clouds, coastlines, mountains and trees. Reich found much the same. He had to develop a new mathematics to describe his work. 'Nature', Mandelbrot says, 'exhibits, not simply a higher degree, but an altogether different level of complexity'. Euclid left these aside as formless.

However Mandelbrot accepted the challenge and investigated the morphology of the amorphous. He has named this class of shapes 'fractals', meaning broken or fragmented. Fractals have 'self-similarity' which means, as in a hologram, the closer you look, you find more of the same.

There are many applications of this fractal measurement: description of wind formations, the branching of river systems, the clustering of galaxies — the things Reich was looking at in his later work. More fascinating is the capacity for describing the human body in terms of fractals: its vascular system, the alveola structure of the lungs and the convolutions of the brain. Mandelbrot discarded the smooth Euclidean universe for one that is flaky, bumpy and *wriggly*.

This leads us back to Reich's understanding that the shapes of objects conform to the flow of orgone energy in and around them. He looked at the *wrigglyness* of the org reflex; the peristaltic movement of a worm, and understood this life-filled similarity. He laughed, 'I have turned man into a worm.'

Reich described forms in terms of 'orgonomes' — the microscopic bionous shapes that he saw repeated macroscopically in life-forms, cyclones and galaxies. He saw that the giant spinning tails of a cyclone or nova were the same, energetically, as people making love. The cosmic superimposition was the same as bodily superimposition. This understanding was reached through the process of 'functional thought' by which Reich sought to unify all processes of Nature and human behaviour. Reich has been accused of 'too muchness' in his work. 'Functionally' it is relatively simple and whole. Like the hologram, the smallest piece of his work is a record of the whole.

THE HOLOGRAPHIC PARADIGM

The holographic theory began with a lens-free photographic process (holography) for which Dennis Gabor received a Nobel Prize. A wave of light scattered by an object was recorded on a photographic plate as an interference pattern. When the plate was read by coherent light, a three-dimensional image appeared. If any piece were snipped off, the original plate would still read in the same manner — the whole image would be reconstructed in three dimensions.

The holographic paradigm states that 'our brains mathematically construct "hard" reality by interpreting frequencies from a dimension transcending time and space. The brain is a hologram, interpreting a holographic universe'. This was proposed by Karl Pribram (1969) and David Bohm as a paradigm for physics (1971) and synthesised by Pribram (1975) to describe the organisation of the universe. The holographic paradigm suggests that a cell could possibly contain all the information of the universe. Which begins to match Reich's process of functional thinking for understanding the micro and macro cosmos and their interlinking.

It is significant that the new paradigm suggests that in psychotherapy, 'Figurative descriptions of a sense of flow, love, joy, confidence, creativity may reflect states of consciousness in resonance with the "holistic wave" aspect of reality. Anxiety, hostility, "stuckness" may represent fragmented states'.* These match descriptions of the 'free function' supplied by Reich, which was supported by his clinical observations of orgonotic 'streamings' reported by patients, and the 'stasis' observed as a deadening process in the body.

Reich's *Character Analysis* was used as a text book for many years by a large number of tertiary institutions and to establish the extent of his influence on psychotherapy today is impossible. His influence keeps appearing in disassociated modalities: Fritz Perls — the founder of Gestalt Therapy — worked with Reich; Reality Therapy — founder William Glasser, in conversation with me, volunteered his debt to Reich; Elisabeth Kubler-Ross uses 'beat-outs' with a rubber hose on telephone books to enable clients to express rage. Stan Grof has incorporated with his non-psychedelic therapy, 'Reichian Breathing' (though I noticed recently at Esalen he now calls his technique 'Grof Breathing'). Frank Lake, in his work on the 'Foetal Distress Syndrome', used 'Reichian Breathing' with guided phantasy.

Because of the difficulty of establishing the limits of Reich's influence on psychotherapy, I will focus mainly upon the mainstream therapeutic modalities attributed to Reich: Orgonomy, Bioenergetics, Radix, Biodynamic Psychology, Biosynthesis and L.E.T. (Life Energy Therapy).

ORGONOMY

Orgonomy was Reich's name for the science and therapeutic modality based upon his discovery of orgone (life) energy. Before his death he appointed Dr Elsworth Baker to train Orgonomists. Dr Baker is still in this practice, although he is over eighty at the time of writing.

Orgonomy is restricted to doctors with psychiatric training and is taught by the American College of Orgonomy. The therapy aims at establishing orgastic potency by releasing characterological armour through the seven segments of the body, ocular to pelvic, from facade to core.

BIOENERGETICS

Bioenergetics was established by Alexander Lowen, John Pierrakos and William Walling, three of Reich's students. Alexander Lowen has published extensively, and, as a result, is one of the most influential of all body therapists internationally.

'Bioenergetics', says John Bellis, a prominent practitioner, 'is a therapy which aims at the development of ego strength and resilience to both the body and psychological level'. The Bioenergeticists focus upon secondary 'grounding' via the pelvic segment. They work from the pelvic segment to the eyes, in opposition to Orgonomy. Reich found that energy flowed in the body from the perineum up the spine and over the head, in a strong stream. Then the stream, like a fountain, flowed gently down the front of the body, as if pulled by gravity. Reich worked with this 'soft' stream, with the client lying down. Reich encouraged them to give into their feelings. Lowen can be said to work with the 'strong' stream up the back. He has his client stand and engage in stress exercises — encouraging the body to give up and thus contact the emotions.

---

* See Ken Wilber (ed.) *The Holographic Paradigm* Shambhala, 1983

RADIX

Radix is a neo-Reichian modality developed by Chuck Kelley, who proposed a new characterology: pain, anger and fear blockers. He also proposed an educational model rather than a medical model. Kelley's practitioners are called teachers and employ a non-verbal technique. Kelley uses Bioenergetic exercises and 'charge'-building exercises. Then teacher and student engage in a one-to-one. The technique is highly interventive and abreaction is left as the outcome. Radix works from the ocular to the pelvic segment of the body.

BIODYNAMIC PSYCHOLOGY

Gerda Boyensen's major contribution to the field presently seems to be a psycho-peristaltic massage. That is, massage employing the understanding of the peristalsis as having a psychic draining effect as well as that of physical elimination.

A stethoscope monitors the peristalsis as the massage proceeds, and the trained practitioner can tell from the different sounds what is occurring for the client. The effect is below the level of the client's awareness.

I have attended a training workshop with Ebba Boyensen and found many of the concepts learnt there useful in practice. Much Jungian understanding has been incorporated into the work.

BIOSYNTHESIS

Biosynthesis is David Boadella's name for his work. Boadella publishes a neo-Reichian magazine, *Energy and Character*, and teaches his techniques in workshops around the world. I have attended one of his workshops and was impressed by his gentle skill at a bodily level. He encourages an abreaction through allowing the clients to access what is 'ripe' for them. He uses emotional flooding and draining techniques. David Boadella has published two books on Reich's work.

THE AUSTRALIAN SCHOOL

Groups of Australian therapists followed Reich's work through his publications during his life-time and applied their own understanding. This is the school I come from, having stumbled across Reich in 1956. My first contact was through my work with Sydney-based therapist, Tom Larkin. Through the 1960s after Reich's death, the workers scattered and not much occurred until the republication of Reich's work in 1967.

Peter Eedy introduced Biodynamic Psychology to Australia in the 1970s. He initially invited Eva Reich, Dr Reich's eldest child, to Australia. She has toured Australia several times since introducing her work, expecially with neonates.

In the last five years a number of practitioners of Biodynamic Psychology have become resident in Australia and in the last two years several therapists trained in Bioenergetics have also become residents.

L.E.T. (LIFE ENERGY THERAPY)

Though close in spirit to Orgonomy, my work — L.E.T. (Life Energy Therapy) — has several distinguishing features. I have added group work, whereas Orgonomists work only in individual sessions, and have found the accelerated learning of a group beneficial for individual members. I work with the 'worried well' — or 'well worried', as some would have it. Orgonomists accept those who are more profoundly disturbed.

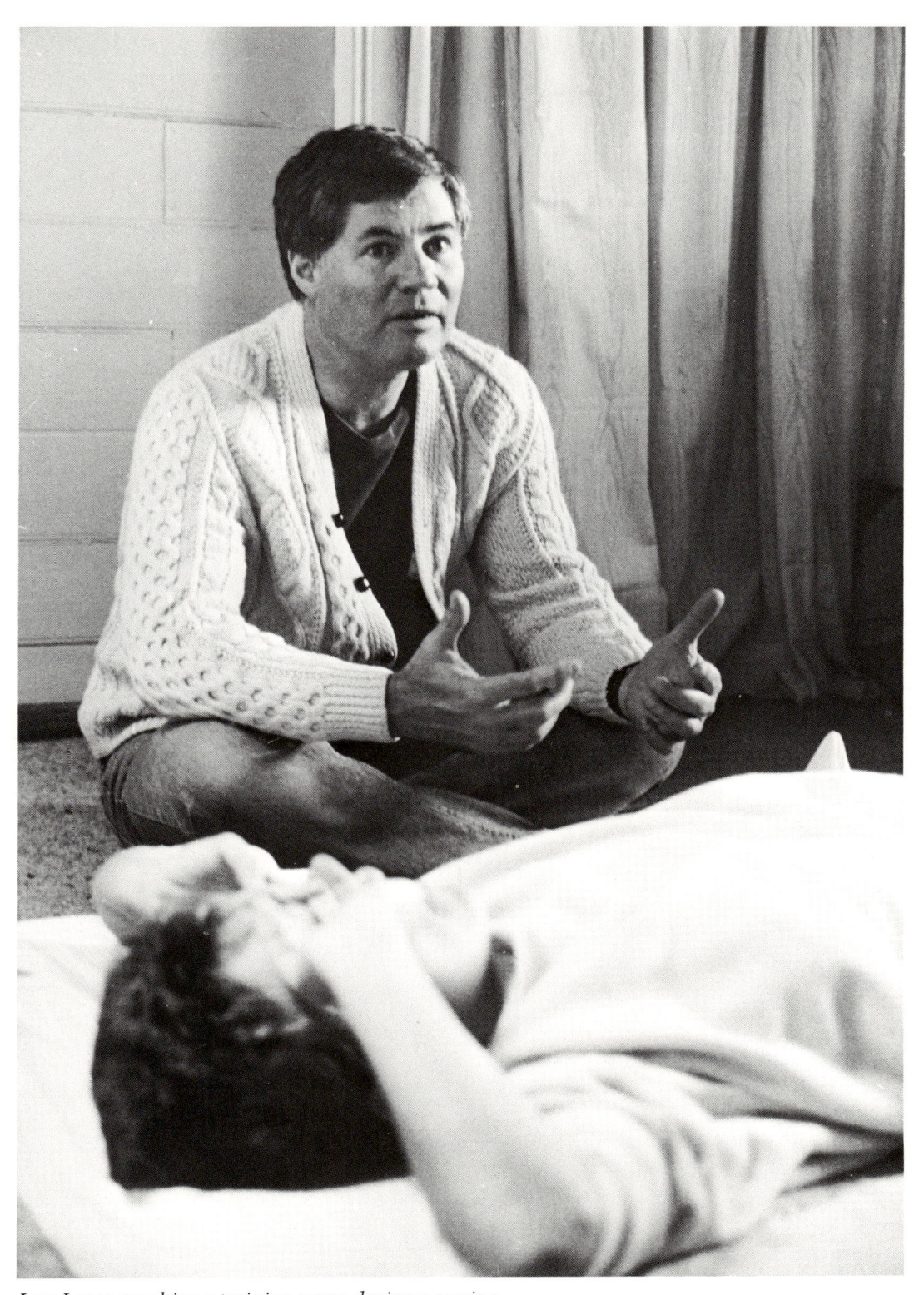

Lew Luton teaching a training group during a session

REICHIAN THERAPY

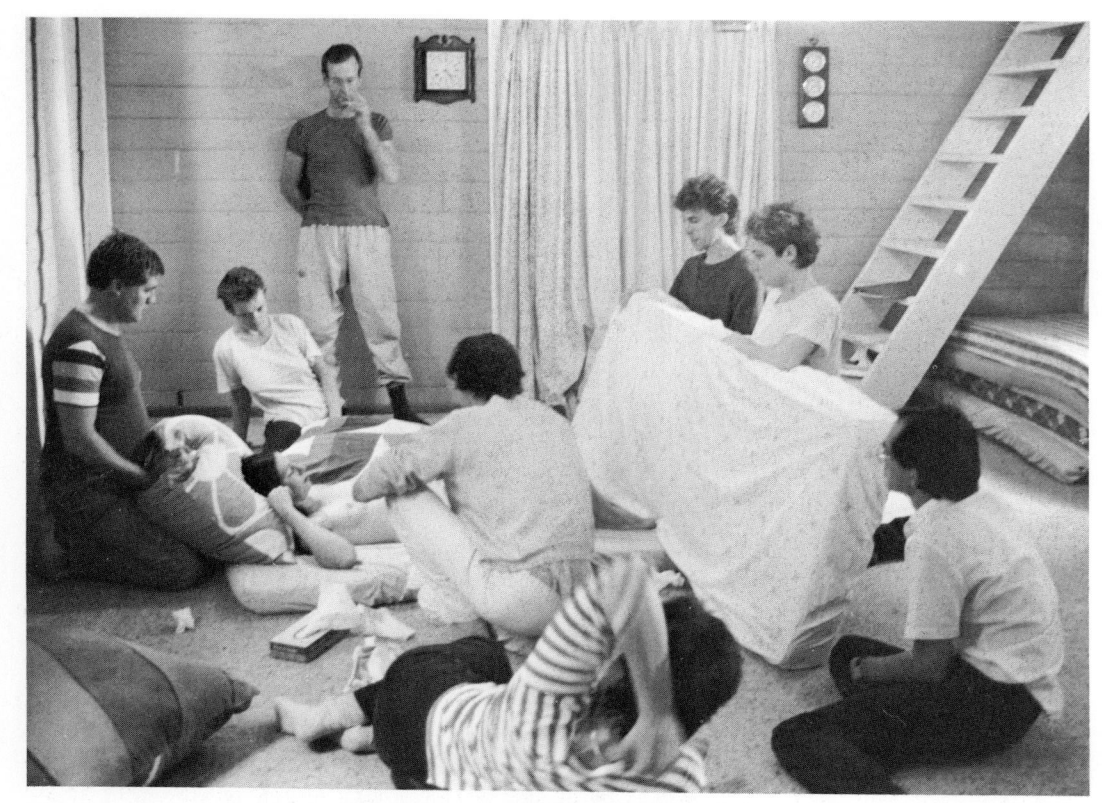

A training group in session. Workers are usually unclothed to the waist to permit unhampered breathing and observation of micro-movements of the body.

I work in an educational model as distinct from the medical model of Orgonomy. I see the 'worker', as I call him, as having had some maladjustive learning process during the developmental period, which can be corrected through a re-education process.

Frank Lake's work on the 'foetal distress syndrome' and the understanding that long-term memory is cellular, suggests it is possible to extend the development period to include interuterine life. It seems reasonable to hypothesise, given clinical evidence of conception memories, that the development period may extend for a far greater period than we had assumed. Direct access to these memories is available through the autonomic response, produced by heightened breathing, a technique introduced by Reich. The holographic theory of brain function plus the theory of morphogenetic resonance may require that we look beyond the development period to what is popularly known as 'past lives'.

If some of the Eastern wisdom teaching proves to be correct, maybe we will have to consider past lives as having a developmental influence on this life. In conversation with me, Lobsang Dolma, a leading Tibetan doctor, advised that Tibetan medical practitioners believe that over 400 diseases have their genesis in past-life experiences.

Much of what has been hitherto judged as mystical may have some scientific justification. Fritjof Capra and other 'new physicists' seem to be of that view. As an adjunct to my work, I have used a non-hypnotic past-life regression technique relying on

Brandon sentences.* Also I have found useful a rebirthing process developed in New Zealand and introduced to me by Eva Reich.**

REICHIAN THERAPY THROUGH THE SEVEN BODY SEGMENTS

Reich developed a concept of the body divided into seven segments. The segments, which correspond the enervation of the autonomic nervous system are: ocular, oral, cervical, thoracic, diaphragmatic, abdominal and pelvic. Below is a brief description of the segments and a brief description of therapeutic strategies relating to them. These should be undertaken only by trained practitioners and are not intended for 'social' use.

Warning: This modality is not a self-help modality. With certain breathing techniques it is easy to spark the autonomic response in many cases; *it is what is done with that response that is of paramount importance.* Serious difficulty can be experienced by the person in unskilled hands, leading to what would be described in LSD terms as a 'bad trip'. If the practitioner is not skilled, that can be disastrous for the worker.

THE OCULAR SEGMENT

The ocular segment contains our distance receptors, eyes, ears, and nose. The sense of smell enables us to contact distance in a way that is complementary to our sight and hearing.

The ocular segment can armour at birth — bright lights, harsh stares, silver nitrate drops in the eyes are some of the causes. A baby born in subdued light and quiet surrounds is able to remain relatively unarmoured in the ocular segment. Schizophrenics, Reich suggests, armour in the ocular segment in the first seven days of life. If trauma occurs perinatally, it has been noted that it is up to six weeks before the eyes resume their natural function.

Received medical wisdom has argued that infants do not focus for six weeks. However, Robert Fantry (1963) testing infants ten hours to five days old found they showed an innate ability to perceive form. Peter Wolff and Burton White (1965) showed that 'infants will (visually) pursue a moving object at birth.'

---

* Thematic sentences used in verbal communication.
** The rebirthing process is carried out by at least six people. There are two people to a side, one at the feet and the helper at the head. Each person on the sides is equipped with a large soft cushion (total = four cushions). The person at the feet has a solid cushion or mattress to give firm support to the worker's feet. (We use an old punching bag at the feet; it yields but the leather is quite firm.) There should be several mattresses butted together to form an area of about 12 feet by 12 feet.
 To commence the process, the worker lies in a foetal position on a central mattress. The helper sits at the head and firmly massages the crown of the head of the worker. The people at the sides place their cushions across the body of the worker, and then lie across the cushions, allowing their dead weight to be the only restriction to movement — no smothering or heavy restraint is permitted. The remaining person applies firm pressure to the worker's feet, following them as they move.
 To achieve the rebirth, the helper orchestrates the others to simulate contractions by applying pressure and releasing it. This is done without words.
 Depending on the type of birth the worker originally had, it is usually sufficient to engage in the pressure/release process for very few minutes before the worker will be reliving his rebirth physically, mentally and emotionally.
 The process is then orchestrated by the helper to become a positive life-enhancing re-creation. Usually the support group engages in a positive welcoming process and may offer massage or other comforting strokes to the 'new baby'.
 Reports of participants are usually positive with the only contraindications arising from poor health, whether physical or emotional.

REICHIAN THERAPY

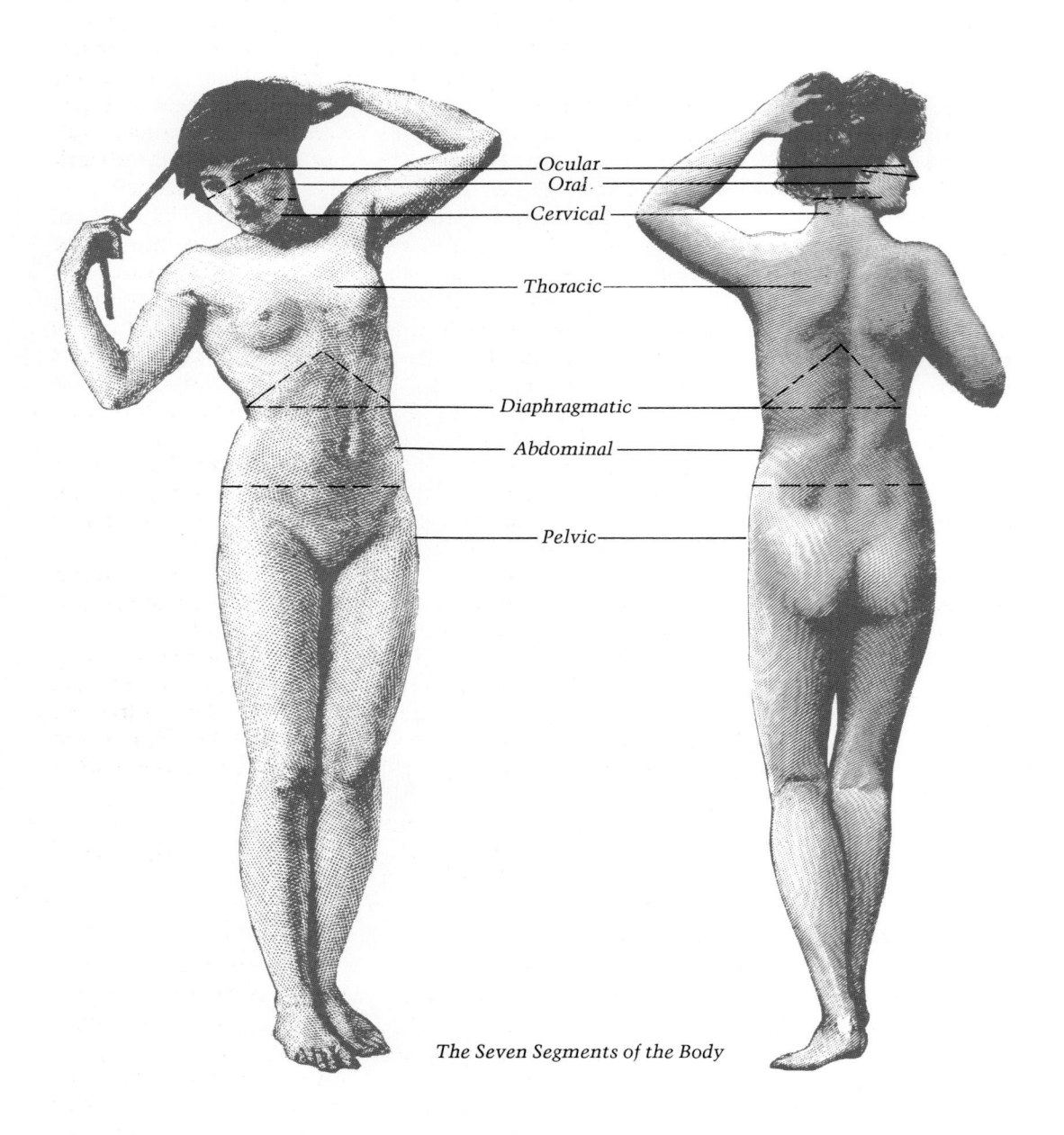

- Ocular
- Oral
- Cervical
- Thoracic
- Diaphragmatic
- Abdominal
- Pelvic

The Seven Segments of the Body

Reichian body segments

Therapy
Dizziness is caused by more energy in the head than can be tolerated by the armouring. In therapy, dissolving the armouring of the ocular segment is assisted by having the 'worker' pull faces to mobilise a frozen face or forehead. Snap the eyes open wide, while sucking in the breath, close them down tight and exhale making a growling sound. Maintaining eye contact over a twenty-minute period by having the helper seated above the head of the worker who is lying down, is a useful diagnostic tool for schizoid states.

Dr Barbara Goldenberg-Koopman developed deep photic stimulation by using a pen-light torch as the target in a darkened room. From her work and Chuck Kelley's work in Radix with 'segment one', I have developed the 'Goldenberg Torch Exercise'.

A lighted penlight is held ten inches in front of and below eye level. The eyes are closed and the breath is mobilised by encouraging deep breathing for at least three minutes. The eyes are then opened and it is suggested that the 'worker' track the passage of the torch from left to right. This is done with an easy pendulum-like swing by the helper. After several minutes the worker is asked to walk, then run into the mattress. The torch for the walking section of the activity describes a figure of eight in a flat plane parallel to the worker. When running starts, the torch is passed randomly and rapidly over the 'worker's' field of vision. Usually an abreaction has occurred by this time. The tantrum should be allowed to die down.

The attention of the worker is then directed back to the lighted torch. The helper synchronises the rising and falling of the torch to the worker's breath so that on the out-breath the torch rises, and on the in-breath it falls — but not as far as it has risen. In this fashion the torch recedes from the worker.

This often produces deep sadness and longing. After the torch has risen out of reach the worker is encouraged to reach out for the torch with the eyes, lips, arms and pelvis. On occasion he may be encouraged to use the words 'Mummy' or 'Daddy'.

The helper, synchronising with the breathing of the worker, allows the torch to drop more than it rises until it is within reach of the worker's hands. He then may take the torch and lay it on his heart. Sometimes a further abreaction takes place. After the abreaction has subsided the worker is encouraged to roll onto his left side. This is the 'soft side'. Lying this way feels more protected. The helper moves behind the worker and rocks him very, very gently at the level of kinesthetic awareness.

This exercise takes over an hour and is best done only where an open-ended format permits such time. The activity, though described mechanically and linearly, should be performed organically — in response to the needs of the worker.

THE ORAL SEGMENT

This segment includes the muscles which control the chin and throat, the muscles of the occiput and the annular muscles at the mouth. It does not include the tongue. Armouring may be a fixed grin, a sardonic smile, a tight jaw or pursed lips. Other signs may appear as a slack jaw, or a continuously open mouth.

The client may talk little, or in orally unsatisfied cases, quite a lot. The tone of the voice may be flat and monotonous — dead. Alternatively, the client may whine or be over-bright, smiling fixedly. Sometimes if one contrasts the eyes and the mouth one can observe sad eyes atop a bright smile. I an reminded in cases like this, of the Doré Previn song, 'I danced to please my father — and I smiled and smiled and danced and danced.'

Therapy
Some modalities, such as Radix, inhibit the workers from talking. The suggestion is that this can be a defence against bodily sensations. With over-verbal character struc-

tures it is wise not to encourage talk. Certainly with clients whose character structures show them 'being in their head', it is perhaps best as a strategy to inhibit the verbal content of the work for some time. However, those who are softly spoken or who exhibit silent character structures, should be encouraged to verbalise.

Growling with the jaw and pelvis thrust forward, and the fists made and held, can begin to mobilise the oral segment. This is best done as a standing exercise. Stamping and the words, 'I won't', can accompany this activity.

Biting a rolled-up towel, while screwing it up with both hands, will release the tension in the masseters and upper thoracic segment.

The gag reflex may be elicited — not to make the worker vomit, just to produce one pelvic counter pulsation. Then the breathing should be encouraged to stream from the genitals. If a coughing spasm (fear) takes hold of the worker, the gag reflex should be elicited in most cases.

Sometimes if a spasm of coughing takes place the client may be encouraged to spit repeatedly into a bucket — spitting out words as well — until the energy for such an activity is discharged.

A warmed baby's bottle is useful for oral deprivation. Water or apple juice is a suitable filler. Milk sometimes proves unsuitable. In some growth groups women have been generous enough to wet-nurse a member who has contacted unsatisfied oral longings. This is not often possible, so the bottle has to suffice. However, the natural generosity and nobility of human beings to others in distress commonly surfaces when group members contact core experiences.

THE CERVICAL SEGMENT

The deep muscles of the neck, the platysma, sternocleido and tongue are included in this segment.

Sadness is often the most held emotion in this segment. Fear of being chopped in the neck, or having your throat cut, often masks the need to do it to someone else. A case in which the father or mother of a family always responded with threats of cutting the child's throat produced fear and intense rage and a wish from the child to do that to the parent. The phantom penis lodged in the throat is found in some cases, as is the feeling of being choked by the father's power or 'always having it rammed down my throat'. A stiff neck may be symbolised in the dynamic language of the body — the expression 'Trying to keep your head above water', uses water to represent the engulfing emotions.

Therapy
Included in the strategies to release the armouring of this segment are tongue mobilisation exercises: the tip of the tongue is extended to the nose, then to the chin and both sides of the mouth. Screaming and yelling may be elicited.

A Japanese martial arts exercise which I call the 'wall shout' is also very effective. Stand six inches off a smooth wall, focus on a spot on the wall, then with a deep breath fill your lungs full of air. Shout at the top of your voice, to the end of the breath.

Note: It is important in this exercise, as in every mobilisation exercise, that the safety of the client be carefully taken care of. Have a smooth, solid wall, a mattress to fall on, and huge cushions between the wall and the worker's foot — in case they want to kick. Remember that at all times unblocking armour in one segment produces a shift in the armouring in all segments.

As an illustration of this, Feldenkrais suggests that for lower back pain, clamp your protruded tongue between your teeth and say loudly your name, address, telephone number. By the time you have finished (laughing) your lower back pain will probably be gone.

Often if people are holding out on sadness, they will appear at the session in a roll-necked pullover, using their clothing as additional armouring. Clothing and glasses may be examined as armour.

THE THORACIC SEGMENT

This segment incorporates the chest, intercostal muscles, pectorals and deltoids. It also includes the scapular and spinal muscles, plus the contents of the chest cage. The hands and arms are also included.

Holding the rib-cage high and locked is a sign of fear blocking. I have seen cases of inflation of the rib-cage to twice the width of the rest of the body. Every other part of the body was shrunken in pain.

On the other hand, an asthmatic's chest will be held as if at the end of expiration and frozen there. Rage has to be released before the asthmatic loosens up. Reich suggested that every asthmatic has a phantasy penis in his throat.

A deep depression of the sternum between the breasts usually denotes infantile mother deprivation. If the position of the mother and father are reversed, that is, if the father is found in the heart, one needs to look at the role of the father as the nurturer in infancy. Fathers often have to step into the mother role if mothers suffer from post partum psychosis or are hospitalised after a difficult birth and are separated from their babies. Some babies are separated from their mother for far too long and are damaged by this. Even a post partum separation of some hours to 'let mother have a rest' is too long.

Therapy may alleviate some of the outcomes but not always successfully. This is particularly evident in children who have been held for adoption over a six-week period as neonates. At present a tragic situation is occurring in Melbourne, Victoria, in which premature babies requiring special care are being sent interstate for a period of weeks.

Therapy
The chest may be mobilised by beating out with a towel or tennis racquet, imitating wood-chopping or skiing; placing two fists behind the rib-cage and flapping the arms like a rooster crowing. In all these exercises making large sounds is important.

The act of reaching out to the ceiling, while lying down, as described in the 'Goldenberg Torch' exercises, mobilises a lot of the heartfelt longing and grief at separation. Using another worker as a bearer, standing, or on his hands and knees, can open up the chest as well. Anger, pain, fear or love may be blocked in this segment.

It is important to have this segment as free as possible so that the respiration is natural and little interfered with.

THE DIAPHRAGMATIC SEGMENT

The diaphragm and the organs under it comprise this segment. They include the contraction ring over the epigastrium and the lower end of the sternum, along the line of the lower ribs, to the tenth, eleventh and twelfth thoracic vertebrae. The diaphragm, stomach, solar plexus, pancreas, liver, gall bladder, duodenum, kidneys and two muscle bundles along the lower thoracic vertebrae are also contained in this segment.

Lordosis of the spine (hollow under the back) is an expression of armouring in this segment. Also the abdomen balloons out and breathing is an effort. Anxiety — as opposed to fear — is held here. Upon release it re-converts back to murderous rage.

What people misname 'heart burn' is often found to be located at the diaphragm. Knots in the stomach are usually associated with an armoured diaphragm.

This segment can be seen as separating the upper and the lower parts of the body, the conscious from the unconscious. A poetic way of seeing this is that the diaphragm symbolises the horizon, the sun, the self. The sun arises from the depths of night — the unconscious — below the diaphragm, to above the diaphragm, into the 'day' of consciousness.

Baker suggests peptic ulcers, gall bladder disease, liver conditions and diabetes are associated with blocking of orgone energy flow in this segment.

Therapy

Jumping vigorously or gagging are two of the ways of freeing this segment. As well there are many stress activities which produce a freeing-up in the diaphragm. Opening of this segment is often accompanied by vomiting.

Though Baker suggests that the first four segments should be opened before work is undertaken on the diaphragmatic segment, Kelley suggests that in Radix teaching the respiration often has to be opened first.

In L.E.T., if the diaphragm is blocked heavily an attempt is made to gain some mobility as a first objective. Freeing the respiration is vital and of prime concern.

THE ABDOMINAL SEGMENT

The abdominal segment includes the large abdominal muscles, the rectus, the transversis abdominus, the latissimus dorsi and the sacrospinalis. If someone has not had an adequate discharge of sexual energy for some time a tension is likely to develop in the flanks. These become ticklish under stasis and will produce spite when freed.

This is a segment that is much attended to in psycho-peristaltic massage.

Elsworth Baker was found that masses may appear and disappear during treatment of the abdominal segment. He holds, however, that treatment is simple if other higher segments are open.

Therapy

Massage and standing exercises in which the breathing is imagined as taking place low in the abdomen have been found effective in my work. A free belly will exhibit a wave-like motion during orgasm.

THE PELVIC SEGMENT

In Chinese traditional medicine, the genitals are the seat of fear. This lends support to the argument that this segment should be approached last. The segment contains all muscles of the pelvis and legs and, of course, the genitals.

The armouring appears in tight or flaccid buttocks: the muscles above the symphysis and the deep and superficial adductors of the thighs are painful and tense.

Often the pelvis is pulled back. I have even noted that what was explained initially as a congenital condition, where the pelvis was rocked well back and held, changed gradually. As the work progressed, the overall tension of the body changed and the pelvis began to swing forward. The client for the first time in his adult life began to seek a full relationship. At the time of writing, he has had a permanent relationship for over twelve months and at the age of 32 will marry shortly. The pelvic fear shows no sign of return.

Therapy

To open this segment one can encourage pelvic rage by standing exercises which involve pushing the pelvis violently forward while shouting. Another way is to place a large soft cushion on the mattress and encourage the worker to beat into it with their pelvis.

The 'jelly-fish' may also be used. Lying on a mattress, the worker bends the knees up and places the soles of the feet close together. On expiration he allows his knees to flop apart. On inspiration he brings his knees together again. Abreaction usually takes place within 5–10 minutes.

Another activity is 'Rock around the clock'. In this, the worker is lying in the 'grounding position' (knees up, feet close together but not touching). The worker begins to rock the pelvis around the face of a large clock upon which it rests. This can be accomplished effectively by allowing the eyes to circle a similar large clock-face at the same time.

LAYERS OF PERSONALITY

Armouring was seen by Reich to appear in two or three layers of the personality:

1 The facade, or the social veneer
2 The secondary layer, where repressions build up murderous rage, spite, hate, contempt etc.
3 The core; always healthy, rational, happy, self-regulating. The decent, simple happy self

The three layers of personality proposed by Reich do not have their equivalent in the psychoanalytic model. They deal more with the dynamics of armouring.

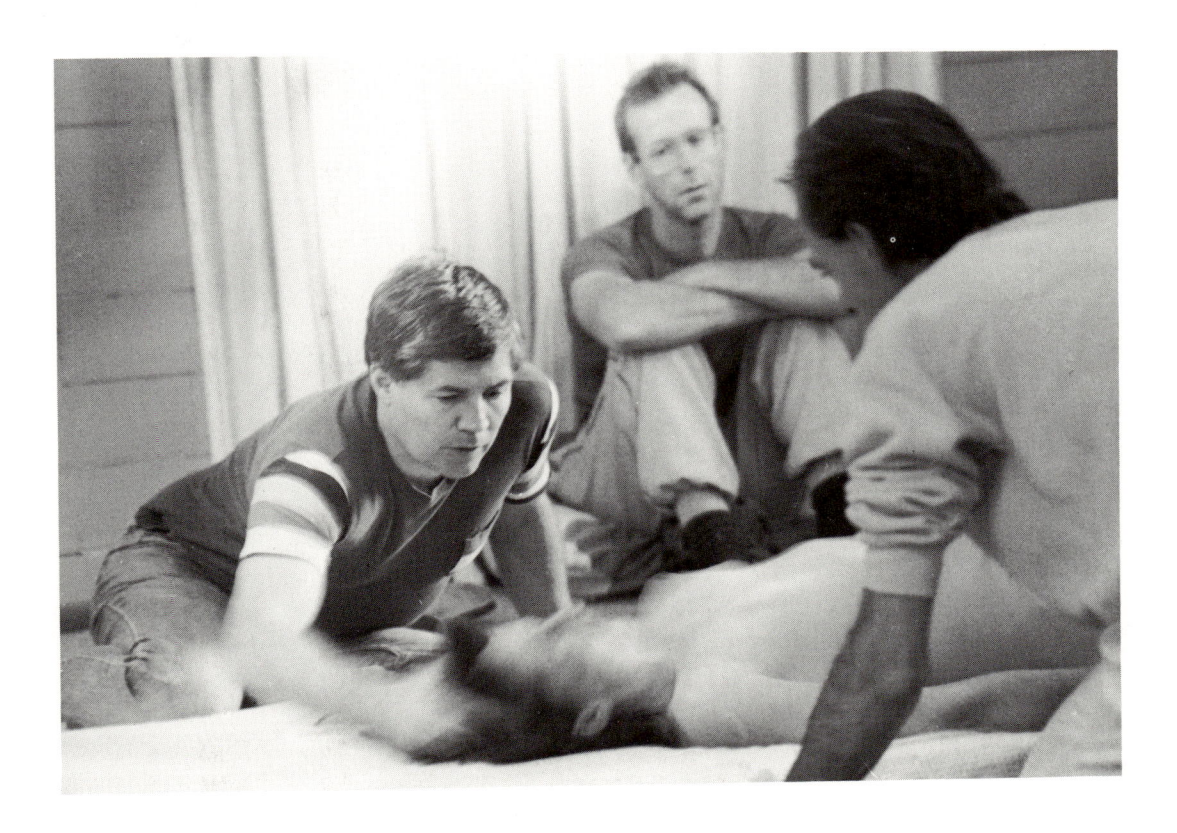

Alexander Lowen maintains that babies are born 'all core'. However, the work of Frank Lake and Stanislav Grof suggests that the interuterine life or the perinatal experience may have already armoured in the infant. This suggests that we need to attend not only to a positive birth experience but a positive period for the mother during pregnancy. David Boadella maintains that, therapeutically, it is important in every session to attain some contact with and expression of the core feelings. He suggests that this ameliorates negative transference. The core may be understood physically as a central streaming of energy from the tip of the tongue via the heart to the perineum.

Armour
The armouring in the body corresponds to a record of past trauma. 'The body is frozen history', suggested Reich. This frozen history corresponds to a standing wave. Chuck Kelley has suggested that stasis is a result of the conflict between feeling and purpose. It has been suggested that long-term memory store is cellular. Certainly Reich's finding that emotional history was released from the musculature in some way supports this.

If long-term memory is indeed cellular and pain causes cellular shrinkage, as Reich found experimentally, then it can be seen that pain is an armouring of the cell — a protective device to prevent dredging up old painful memories from their cellular repository.

Field
Reich found through electrical measurement, that the emotions were accompanied by an energy flow in the body. Dr Thelma Moss has produced a series of Kirlian photographs and movies that appear to support this. Reich was able to record the flow of energy associated with the emotions by placing electrodes on the body and recording the skin galvanic response. Moss has shown that emotions also produce energetic charges associated with the energy field around the body.

In his dark-room experiments, Reich reported an energy envelope visible after dark adaptation (30 minutes). Reich was also able to measure this energy envelope with a field meter. He found, as has been supported by Moss's Kirlian photographs of an anger exchange, that the field can extend four inches beyond the visible body. Dr Moss has also managed to take what might be the first photograph of the orgone energy-field using non-electrical means.

Method of working
In working I observe the four-beat Orgasm formula: Tension → Charge → Discharge → Relaxation

1 In one-to-one situations, the client is asked to report on the week. This in most cases permits the session to be focused on the prime issue. In groups we have the first 'go-round' which deals mainly with problem-solving and transference issues. A contract is then made for what is needed by the worker from the group work on this occasion.

2 The worker strips to his underclothing. This enables visual monitoring of respiration, colour changes and micro-movements of the body which are normally hidden by clothing. With the more repressed workers, clothing is permitted until they feel comfortable in themselves. The worker goes on a mat or performs standing activities, such as charge building. The abreaction generally commences within the first five to six minutes. The abreaction usually swells and, like a wave on a shore, crashes over and recedes. The time for an abreaction which is free, is 5–10 minutes at its peak.

3 There is a refractory time in which the remainder of the charge is discharged. This is much gentler, and depends upon the responses. Tears may be followed by anger, and anger often followed by love. Reich found anger and love ran in the same channels. If we block anger we block love. In our culture open displays of anger and love are not

'Going round' in a group. Verbal material is explored and synthesised.

permitted. In the work we learn, through 'beat-outs', how to release our anger and free our love.

4 This is the cognitive part of the session. The worker is asked to report on what he has learned from the experience. It is most important to synthesise body and mind in order to complete a unit of work.

Duration of work
Generally the work in L.E.T. to restructure the character lasts no more than 400 hours. A one-to-one of 50 minutes or involvement in a week-night group counts as one hour. A weekend intensive counts as three hours. A five-day intensive counts as five hours.

Counter indications
Workers are screened before acceptance into groups. Counter indications are: a current pregnancy, any psychotic episode leading to institutionalisation, a major organ removal, heart or spinal surgery, in certain cases, current and past use of marijuana, LSD or mood changing drugs, a current medical regime including use of pain killers or 'miracle' drugs.

Valedictory
In 1956 I made contact with Tom Larkin who practised Reichian therapy in Sydney and began to work with him. He had his offices in Bligh Street and was known affectionately as the 'beast of Bligh Street'. During this time, Reich lost the court action which had been brought against him by the FDA and was not permitted to market ORACs but while in Arizona, unknown to Reich, co-worker Michael Silvert shipped several ORACs across the State line to New York City. When this was discovered, Reich and Silvert were jailed for contempt of court and Reich's books were burnt under order of the courts (some workers in Australia even hid their books).

I remember sometime towards the end of the first year of my therapy — we did five sessions a week in those days — I was standing out on some rocks at Fairlight Water watching the Sputnik streak like a comet across the night sky. I thought how like Reich that shooting star was. It appeared as a natural event, but really it was a triumph of science.

Two weeks after the Sputnik launch, two days before his parole hearing — on November 3rd, 1957 — Reich was found dead in his prison cell.

CHAPTER 11
REBIRTHING
Michael Adamedes & Alia Paulusz

THE BREATH

Breathing is a meditative and healing technique which has been used for thousands of years. Ancient philosophers have always claimed that breathing affects our mental, emotional and physical well-being.

The oldest known Chinese medical book *Nei Ching* which dates from 2600 BC, states that 'the lungs are the ministers who regulate one's actions', and further describes the lungs as 'the seat of sorrow'. Later Chinese medical texts say that deep breathing can clear the intellect and even prolong life.

The ancient Greeks had a theory of breathing stemming from the work of Aristotle, who wrote: 'The soul is air; air moves and is cognisant. Air that we breathe gives us soul, life and consciousness'. The Pneumatists, inspired by Aristotle's notion, concluded that air was *pneuma* or spirit — the vital force — and that it was the source of all health and disease. Pantanjali, an Indian sage who first codified the rules of Yoga c. 200 AD wrote that 'control of thoughts and emotions is linked to breath control'. That is, by the mastery of *pranayama*, or breath meditation, self-mastery can be achieved.

The importance of breath is also recognised in astrology. Paul Callinan, a contemporary exponent, writes: 'In astrology, it is not the moment of birth which is important but the moment we take our first breath. For the air, like everything in the universe, is affected by the flow of *ch'i* (life energy) and from moment to moment acts as a mirror of its quality. At a deeper level it would show as changes in the rotation, spin and movement of the air molecules. But that first breath stamps the energy field, or aura of the body with its unique quality. It sets, as it were, the celestial energy bandwidths we can tune into, the transmissions we can receive. It unalterably determines many facets of one's being.'

The Book of Genesis states, 'The Lord formed man of the dust of the ground, and breathed into his nostrils the breath of life, and man became a living soul', and Paramahansa Yogananda in his *Autobiography of a Yogi*, writes: 'A human being falsely identifies himself with his physical form because the life currents from the source are breath conveyed into the flesh with such intense power that man mistakes the effect for the cause, and idolatrously imagines the body to have a life of its own'. The Buddhist enlightenment meditation of *vipassana* similarly requires one to learn to watch the breath and in so doing discipline the mind, and transmute the emotions.

Many more examples could be listed: suffice it to say that breathing is an important aspect of physical and mental health and is vital in developing one's consciousness.

Breathing is the most important of the bodily functions and yet it is one of the most neglected. Under normal circumstances it is only possible for a person to live for a few minutes without breathing, before permanent brain damage results, while it is possible to last two to five days without drinking and up to ninety days without eating.

REBIRTHING

Rebirthing is a breathing process aimed at expanding awareness of, and union with one's inner *self*, and in so doing results in healing on the mental, emotional and physical levels.

Rebirthing was developed by Leonard Orr in California during the early 1970s. While lying in a bath and breathing rhythmically, he experienced beneficial, therapeutic effects. At the time he thought it was mainly due to the water: later he realised it was the breathing which was the key to the technique. Orr further refined the breathing technique without the aid of water.

A significant branch of Rebirthing has also been developed by Dr Stanislav Grof, the Esalen-based psychiatrist best known for his research into the LSD experience and birth trauma.

From the holistic viewpoint on health, all illness originates from the separation from one's inner self, source or spirit. It manifests on the mental level as a split between the conscious and unconscious parts of the mind; on the emotional level as an inability to fully feel and express emotions, and finally on the physical level as tension. If the tension becomes chronic, it results in 'dis-ease', or illness.

One of the unique characteristics of the human body is that any inhibition in the organism is reflected throughout the body as a whole. Similar to a hologram, each cell is a microcosm of the entire body. In turn, each organ — which is an organised collection of cells — reflects the tension of the entire body. Therefore any tension held in the body is reflected in the respiratory system. Gradually as tension accumulates in the body the breathing mechanism begins to close down. Most people use only a proportion of their lung capacity.

The Rebirthing process reawakens the breathing mechanism, enabling the body to metabolise, release toxins and function effectively.

The name 'Rebirthing' conjures up images of being 'reborn' or living through the birth trauma. The Rebirthing process is more than integrating and releasing trauma: it is ultimately an integration or union with oneself. The birth experience is highly significant in the development of an individual because it is this initial contact with the external world that establishes life-long behavioural patterns and expectations. The unconscious conclusions formulated by the birth experience programme the ways in which we experience the world and also the ways in which our parents and others relate to us. A typical belief pattern is that to accomplish anything, one must struggle. This can be due to the struggle a baby undertook while being born. Parental conditioning is also a significant factor in personal development which comes to light during the Rebirthing experience.

In the Rebirthing process, there are three important elements: (i) Breathing, (ii) Relaxing and (iii) Awareness.

BREATHING

Breathing is more than the inhalation of air. It is also the main way in which one assimilates life energy. In Sanskrit it is called *prana*, meaning 'the absolute energy' or

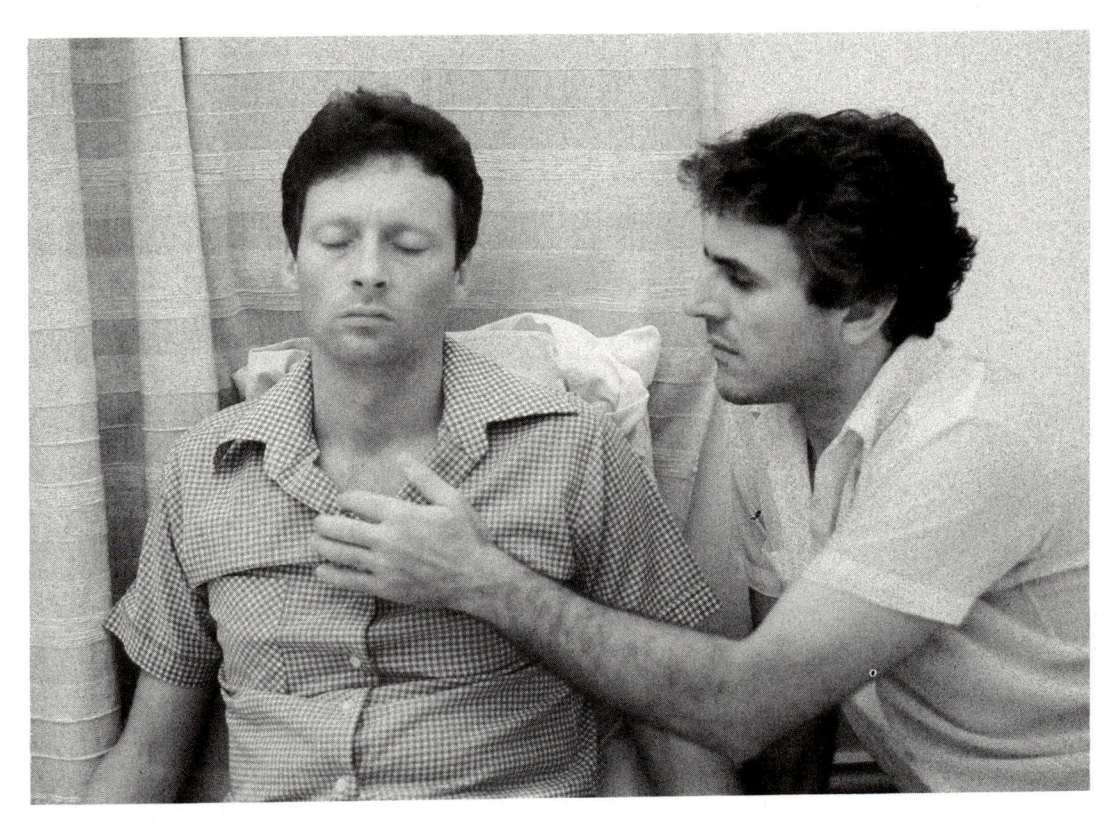

Learning connected breathing

'life-force'. In Chinese it is called *chi*. The Hebrew writer of the *Book of Genesis* knew the difference between the atmospheric air and the mysterious and potent principle contained within it. He speaks of *neshemet ruach chayim*, which translated means 'the breath of the spirit of life'. It is this life energy which sustains all living things. It is in the air, yet it is not the air. *Prana* in its freest and most readily assimilated form is found in fresh air. In ordinary breathing we absorb a normal amount of *prana*: with conscious breathing we are able to absorb a greater quantity of Life Energy which we are able to store in the brain and nerve centres to be available for future use. The supply of *prana* is primarily used by the nervous system. With nervous tension there is an under-supply of *prana*. The Rebirthing breathing is a conscious breathing process which increases the amount of Life Energy assimilated by the body.

When we breathe normally, there is an inhalation — pause — exhalation — pause — inhalation. With the Rebirthing breathing it is inhale — exhale — inhale — exhale. This type of breathing is called connected breathing, and it means inhaling and exhaling without any pause. The breathing develops into a circular rhythm, with the active emphasis on the inhalation, and the feeling of relaxation on the exhalation. The breathing is done only through the nose or only through the mouth, and not through the two together. The act of breathing in and out of only one passageway at a time builds up the energy of the breath. Whether one breathes through the nose or mouth is determined by personal preference and factors like congestion in the respiratory system and the need to energise the body.

Whether a person is encouraged to breathe into the upper or lower parts of the lungs is dependent on the section of the lungs where the breath is being inhibited. As a general rule, a Rebirthee (someone who is undergoing the process of Rebirthing) is encouraged to breathe into that inhibited part of the lungs.

At the beginning of the session, the frequency and depth of the breath is usually faster and deeper than normal 'at rest' breathing. During times of emotional tension, the tendency is to take rapid/shallow breaths. For meditative states the breath is steady and deep, and to energise a person quickly the breath is rapid and deep.

The Rebirther needs to be flexible in approaching the breathing process. The above is a generalisation of the process; the actual frequency and depth of breathing varies with each individual. As long as the breath is connected then there is a wide range in the patterns of breathing.

RELAXATION

A basic belief in Rebirthing is that a person's innate nature is perfection, that one's natural state is that of high energy and happiness. It is the conditioning from the environment which makes us believe that we are not happy with ourselves and tends to make us lose confidence in ourselves.

By relaxing, a person lets go of the conditioning and reconnects with the innate perfect Self. It is when the reconnection with Self takes place that a profound healing occurs. Once a person relaxes and stops 'avoiding', then whatever is in the unconscious will spontaneously come to the surface, enabling it to be integrated and released by the breathing process.

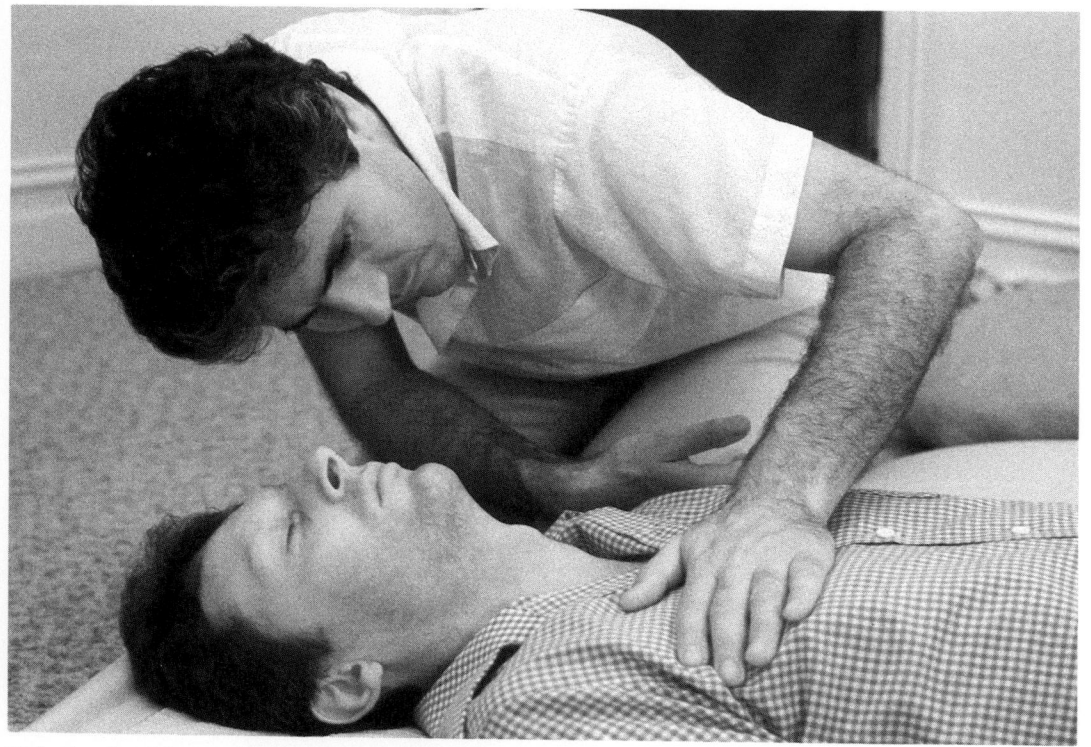

Relaxing is an important part of Rebirthing

AWARENESS

Each night when we go to sleep, it takes approximately two hours from the time of first lying in bed to the point of achieving total relaxation. Yet, within a few minutes of lying down, a person has lost consciousness. What has occurred is a split in consciousness from the normal waking state of awareness to a state of awareness that we call 'unconscious'.

It has been estimated that our unconscious mind represents approximately 95% of our total range of consciousness. The majority of our thoughts and memories are outside our normal awareness and it is these very thoughts which mostly influence our life. While a thought remains unconscious, it will control our life. As soon as it becomes conscious then it is possible to modify and alter it by exercising our willpower.

As deeper and deeper states of relaxation are achieved these thoughts and memories from the unconscious mind become accessible. By remaining fully aware as we breathe rhythmically, and relax, we find that the 'split' in consciousness does not occur and it is possible to connect with the unconscious mind to increase self-awareness and tap long-held unconscious thoughts.

The immediate end result of a Rebirthing session is to achieve a state of deep relaxation, awareness and high energy — and the experience of profound bliss.

It is important not to get too caught up with rigidly applying the technique and understand that *everything works*. The Rebirthing process is a highly intuitive one and it is dependent on the Rebirther being flexible to the needs of the Rebirthee.

PERSONAL RESPONSIBILITY

Another concept fundamental to Rebirthing is accepting personal responsibility. That is: I create my reality and whatever I am experiencing is of my own doing. This is an important idea, for until a person accepts responsibility for his situation, it is not possible for him to be able to change it. While a person continues to believe things 'happen' to him, he will continue to remain a victim, unable to change himself or the situation he finds himself in.

However, the external environment reflects the inner environment. The beliefs a person holds create the situations and people that surround them. Change your beliefs and you change your situation.

BEING REBIRTHED

A typical breath session usually lasts for one to two hours, although the first session is normally preceded by an hour's counselling. During the session, the person lies on a bed, is induced into a state of relaxation and then commences to breathe rhythmically. The breath is a 'connected breath' — i.e. breathing without any pause between the inhalation and exhalation. While the person is breathing in this way, the Rebirther might play music to create a mood, to energise the room and create a sound barrier to outside noises.

As the breathing proceeds gradually the energy level rises, and the person may experience symptoms of hypertension, dizziness, tingling, cramping, tetany, drowsiness or 'going cold'. The extent to which these symptoms occur depends on the level of fear and the ability of the person to let go and to surrender to themselves.

People who are able to accept their feelings and surrender pass through this stage very quickly with a minimum of discomfort, if any at all. For those people who are very afraid, there can be anything from five to thirty minutes of advancing and retreating from the emotions until they eventually 'breathe through' and integrate the experience. Then, almost immediately, there is a release of discomfort resulting in a deep state of relaxation and euphoria. In this state of relaxation, people usually have profound insights about themselves, further helping to release behavioural conditionings. For people who are more experienced, the breathing session is a very relaxing and enjoyable meditative experience.

In the initial stages of Rebirthing, there may be some emotional release. This is a by-product of the body being energised and accepting long suppressed emotions and thoughts. It is the non-acceptance or non-integration of certain thoughts and feelings which creates emotional tension that locks itself into the cellular structure of the body. During the Rebirthing breathing, the body is oxygenated, blood circulation improves, and increased amounts of energy reach parts of the body that have long been held in tension. As the increased amounts of oxygen, blood and energy reach the cells, these stored emotional and mental tensions are brought to the surface to be integrated by the breathing. It can take between three to eight sessions to pass beyond the emotional stage.

Expression of an emotion does not end the suppression of the emotion. To quote Jim Leonard and Phil Laut from *Rebirthing — the Science of Enjoying All of Your Life*:

Drama such as crying, screaming, crawling around, etc. is OK and should not be avoided when it comes up spontaneously, but it does not cause integration. Indeed, very often it distracts a Rebirthee from feeling what is happening and thus makes the integration take longer and be more difficult than it needed to be . . . We recommend that the Rebirther gently remind the dramatic Rebirthee that it is possible to enjoy anything and encourage the Rebirthee to relax completely and continue breathing. If a Rebirthee is being dramatic in a way that includes tensing the throat, such as yelling, sobbing or gasping, it is a good idea to tell the Rebirthee to relax . . . The most dramatic results are produced by the least dramatic Rebirthing.

The process of integration proceeds through deeper and more subtle levels of awareness, like the layers of an onion. It is a process that takes several years, although with Rebirthing, the intention is to complete ten to twenty sessions to reach a level of clarity and competence to be able to Rebirth oneself.

A PERSONAL EXPERIENCE

Alia Paulusz: Here's one of my own rebirthing experiences. The room was prepared by being very clean, tidy and clear. A small candle was lit to assist in purifying and lightening the atmosphere. Curtains were drawn, and a large foam mattress with clean linen was laid out in the centre of the room. There were tissues and towels, sheets and blankets handy. I lay down on my back, my heart pounding with some fearful anticipation. My Rebirther lay down about a metre away from me and propped himself on his elbows. I began breathing, using the connected breath cycle and with my mouth closed. I was very aware that here I was, having the umpteenth breath session, quite able to own my inner feelings and yet scared at another level of the unknown. Perhaps these things would now be revealed. But then, I also had total trust in my Rebirther.

Well! Just about every conceivable breath change and release occurred, skilfully guided by my Rebirther who would gently and firmly insist on my concentration by asking me to use just my lungs and diaphragm and nose for breathing. As I would plateau into a rhythm pattern and begin to move my shoulders and head to push myself along more easily, he would focus me again on my breathing. 'Use fine short breaths', he said, as I breathed longer, deeper and more noisy breaths. As I breathed finely and clearly he would suggest I now see how quietly I could breathe. I felt buzzing in my hands and feet and at the base of my spine as millions of cells were transmuted by the breath. My Rebirther gently touched my right ribcage as I drifted off into another pocket of timeless bliss and forgot to keep breathing. I automatically took a deep breath and shuddered into the next stage. He asked me to roll onto my left side and to breathe fully and very energetically. My shoulders began to heave, and my head moved back and forth as my spine curled and uncurled. A sense of urgency gripped my whole being — then that calm commanding voice ordered me to 'just breathe through your nose and stop all that extra body movement!' So I did. There were many more similar breathings and then as I breathed very fine and clear, my third eye opened. A flash of electric blue triangle ringed with hot pink, backed with the brightness of clear white lights. Every sage, saint, master and avatar I had ever known about and many others besides, appeared in the centre of the triangle. Their eyes locked into mine as they swirled through and whirled away to each side of me, their enigmatic and magnetic smiles sending thrills up and down my spine. My breath broke into gasps as I watched the most spectacular display of 'cosmic Disneyland' and aerobatics performed against swirls of rainbow lights.

My Rebirther now asked me to rest. My body was tingling with energy. I felt 'high', charged with amazing wisdom, perception and 'knowledge', after the most fantastic breath experience I had yet had.

Half an hour later, I opened my eyes from a delicious sleep-trance as my Rebirther gently said 'Have a sip of this'. He held out a cup of steaming rosehip tea. As our eyes met I felt the most inadequate of words, 'Thanks', hovering on my lips. We smiled deeply into each other's eyes, thanking each other for the trust and shared experience. We hugged. I felt honoured to have worked with Leonard Orr.

WET REBIRTHING

Wet Rebirthing is a more dynamic form of Rebirthing and is usually practised after the Rebirthee has gained some experience in Dry Rebirthing. There are two types of Wet Rebirthing: (i) Hot water Rebirthing and (ii) Cold water Rebirthing.

(i) Hot water Rebirthing usually takes place in a hot tub, bath or hot spring with the temperature of the water between 36° to 39°C (98° to 102°F). There are three ways the Rebirth can be carried out: either with the Rebirthee floating face down in the water breathing through a snorkel and supported by the Rebirther; the Rebirthee floating on his back supported by the Rebirther; or the Rebirthee sitting up in the water with or without the aid of the Rebirther. The sensations of floating and the temperature of the water bring up emotions much more quickly and more intensely than dry Rebirthing, and also tend to stimulate memories of the womb. The advantages of this technique are to accelerate the Rebirthing process, to help people who usually have difficulty in contacting their emotions and to reawaken womb and early birth experiences.

(ii) Cold water Rebirthing can be done in a pool, lake, bath tub etc. The temperature is at whatever the Rebirthee can handle. The Rebirthee first stands outside the water and commences to breathe for a few minutes, then steps into the water and gradually lowers the body an inch at a time into the water. You know if you're going too fast if it feels uncomfortable and when the fear that is being brought up by the cold water has not been fully integrated by the breathing. Be gentle and go slowly in lowering yourself into the water. When done properly there is no feeling of discomfort. While breathing the body generates all the heat it needs to keep itself warm.

Wet Rebirthing

Personal note from Michael Adamedes: 'On one occasion it took me more than an hour and a half to fully enter the water. The temperature of the water was about 67°F, while I breathed and did not move I felt comfortable. The only discomfort I experienced was when I tried to lower myself into the water too fast or if I moved my arms about. The experience was pleasant and enjoyable. It left me feeling relaxed and highly energised.

SELF-REBIRTHING

The Rebirthing process is a self-help process. One of its goals is to enable you to Rebirth yourself.

In the initial stages it is necessary to have an experienced Rebirther guiding you because of the fear and emotions that can be generated, and also to give you experience and confidence in the process. Without the help of a Rebirther, it is possible to continue to avoid certain aspects of your personality thus preventing a completion.

Another factor is loneliness. When we were separated from our mothers, most of us interpreted this as a negative thing: most people are afraid to be alone. Having a Rebirther supporting you can help you overcome some of the initial feelings of loneliness. It can take years to completely release the fear of loneliness: as you pass through deeper levels of your personality different aspects of loneliness will emerge.

As powerful as Rebirthing is, no technique can release the accumulated conditionings of a lifetime in a few sessions. By learning to self-Rebirth, it is possible to continue the process on your own. It is recommended that you have at least ten private sessions with a trained Rebirther, for the reasons stated above.

SPECIAL TYPES OF REBIRTHING

There are a number of other ways in which Rebirthing can be used: (i) Eye-to-eye, (ii) Group Rebirthing, (iii) Ambulatory Rebirthing, (iv) Swapping Rebirths.

Eye-to-Eye. This is a form of Rebirthing where two people sit facing each other looking into each other's eyes, and are physically and mentally connected while breathing rhythmically. There are two variations of this method. One is for both people to undergo the experience simultaneously and the other is for one person to be the guide and the other the subject undergoing the process.

There are advantages in both processes. In the first variation, both people experience the process simultaneously, saving the time of having to go through the process twice. The second variation enables the subject to enter the process more deeply, especially if there is any emotional release, as the guide is able to help the subject with the continuous breathing and relax through it.

There are a few points to mention about looking into the eyes. There is a difference between the left and right eyes. The left eye connects to the right side of the brain which is the intuitive, feminine, psychic part. The right eye connects to the left side of the brain which is the rational, masculine, outward going part. When one looks into one eye at a time it is common to notice the two distinct parts of the person — a fascinating experience. Another technique is to look at the spot directly above the centre of the eyebrows (the 'third eye'). This has an entirely different effect. Experiment and discover which suits you best. This is a very powerful and profound form of Rebirthing.

Ambulatory Rebirthing. This type of Rebirthing takes place while you are engaged in other activities such as walking, driving, working etc. Things tend to come up all the time and, rather than suppressing them, it is possible to process and integrate them no matter that you are doing.

The breathing can be done without attracting undue attention and is usually slow and deep. Relax all the muscles you are not using. Remain aware of the details of what is happening in your mind and body, stay in the moment. Allow yourself to enjoy what is happening and be aware that everything works. Stay with what is happening so you can integrate the feeling without becoming unconscious, which was the usual past response. Once mastered, this form of Rebirthing allows you to integrate emotions and thoughts as they are stimulated by your environment.

Group Rebirthing. This is Rebirthing with a number of people under the guidance of an experienced Rebirther. There are two ways of proceeding. One way is by having the group pair off so that half the group is Rebirthed by the other half. Roles are then reversed for the second session. Each Rebirthee is given the individual attention of a Rebirther and everyone gets to experience being a Rebirthee and a Rebirther.

The other way is for all of the group to be Rebirthed simultaneously. The advantage with this is that there only needs to be one Rebirthing session for the entire group. This can either be with everyone lying down or sitting up. If everyone is sitting up it is easier for the group leader to monitor the breathing and keep everyone aware.

Swapping Rebirths. A way of getting Rebirthed regularly without having to pay for it is to swap sessions with another Rebirthing student. This develops experience at being both a Rebirther and a Rebirthee.

It is advisable to pick someone who has had at least ten private sessions so that they are a competent guide. One of the areas Rebirthers commonly experience difficulty with is in Rebirthing their partners and loved ones. Because of the close emotional attachment, while your partner is going through the process it can trigger off responses in yourself. This presents an opportunity for further self-integration.

A word of caution: In some relationships, one or both of the partners may not want the nature of the relationship to change and unconsciously could be inhibiting the process. In this case it is necessary to work on having clear channels of communication. It is a most rewarding experience to be able to regularly Rebirth and be Rebirthed by your partner. It works towards building a more loving and complete relationship.

AFFIRMATIONS

Your thoughts create your reality; by changing your thoughts you change your reality. An affirmation is a positive thought you choose to produce a desired result. Affirmations work in conjunction with Rebirthing to eliminate negative states of consciousness. The following is a concise guide to using affirmations.

1 Be very clear about exactly what you are intending to change.

2 Use positive statements — imagine what you want rather than what you are getting rid of:
Not: I no longer struggle in life, but
YES: Life is easy for me.

3 Use words that are in present tense — always affirm that it is happening *now*.
Not: I will attract my perfect partner, but
YES: I am attracting my perfect partner.

4 Make the statement true for you — find the thought your mind can accept
Not: I now receive a thousand dollars a week, but
YES: I am now willing to receive an abundant income.

5 Use your own name in the affirmation. Usually the best name to use is the name you were called by your family when you were a child.

6 The affirmations will work better for you if you have the attitude that they are fun.

7 Be loving and patient with yourself and the process.

8 The first few times you write an affirmation, use a 'response column' to find out what subconscious resistances you have had that keep the new affirmation from taking root in your consciousness. Anytime you feel stuck, and your affirmations don't seem to be working, try using the response columns.

Example Affirmation — *Response*
I Michael fully believe in my own self worth — Bullshit
I Michael fully believe in my own self worth — Oh yeah
I Michael fully believe in my own self worth — Yeah
I Michael fully believe in my own self worth — Sometimes
I Michael fully believe in my own self worth — I'd like to

9 Affirmations can also be stated in the 1st, 2nd and 3rd persons. Because thoughts are stored in our unconscious in the form of what we think about ourselves, what other people say to us and what other people say about us.

Example
I Michael fully believe in my own self worth.
You Michael fully believe in your own self worth.
Michael fully believes in his own self worth.

'The infinite potential lies within'

A NEW BEGINNING

Rebirthing is a safe, gentle, supportive, self-helping and inexpensive way of discovering yourself. All you have to do is breathe and in so breathing, realise the infinite potential that lies within you. The ultimate aim of Rebirthing is to learn how to unconditionally love yourself and others.

CHAPTER 12
SHINTAIDO
Alexandra Pope

To express 'something invisible' which exists absolutely, without flowing with the passage of time, nor being invaded by the changes of the world, through kata *('forms') which should be developed and reformed as time goes on . . . This is a mission or a destiny with which every 'art' is charged. Its mission is not to create something new or to build up a plausible system by replacing what has been handed down from generation to generation, but to catch sight of something which has always existed somewhere from earliest times without ever being seen by our two eyes, and to express this something with our own body. Its mission is to express through the body's forms or movements some sort of 'perceived world' which visits us with time, while satisfying the limited conditions special to* budo *('martial arts'). We can say that this is actually the pursuit of human life, nothing less than the pursuit of truth. We call the art 'avant garde' which takes these as its goals.*

To every young person who will follow the path of budo *in order to fulfil this cruel and at the same time blessed duty, I can't help crying: 'Be a person of true avant-garde* budo*.' What we have to establish should be a* budo *of new and unknown technique, forms or expressions which must add much more light to the world of* budo *rather than extinguishing its flame. In a strict sense, it is therefore, not a creation but 'an embodiment of secretly hidden cosmic breath.'*

In order to break new ground and create a much better budo we have to overcome many, many obstacles. A time may come when we have to discard all that we have mastered or when we will be repudiated even by our friends. The tradition of our club (which is a stepping stone our predecessors have made for us) may become completely useless. More than that, who can deny that we may have to fight with that 'tradition' in the future? More dangerous for us are the fixed ideas and the temptations within ourselves which would make us look back.

But stick to it! Study, devise and practise with unremitting efforts! Tomorrow is for you.

The world of soul is larger than any exercise hall or any organisation. It is boundless. If we depended only on decaying tradition without seeking after the centre from which springs our fountain of life, our predecessors' words: 'Karate is still immature. Who in the world will complete it?' would vanish unanswered.

I wish that our brilliant future 'karate' might not occupy merely a part of the world, but that, as an infinitely expanding cosmos, it might contain the whole world in it.

SHINTAIDO

Hiroyuki Aoki — founder of Shintaido

(It is uncertain that the term 'karate' will still be used at such a time). 'Karate' would then be no longer budo *as a means of expression, but an art concerned with the problem of Being.*

I am now extremely anxious to express with my body what I have secretly felt, that is, what is thought nearly impossible to express with the body, while asking for a reverberating encounter with an ever unperceived realm.

Hiroyuki Aoki*

* This article was originally written for the junior members of the Chuo University Karate Club shortly after the author graduated. It marks the beginnings of the creative process which led to Shintaido. (*Reproduced with permission of the Shintaido Institute, Tokyo*)

Shintaido is a new art of movement and life expression which incorporates a very dynamic and powerful vision for the well-being of our society today and in the future. Its seeds are in the classical forms of Japanese martial arts but its inspiration is also drawn from the world of Western fine arts and philosophy. So that while its birth place is Japan, Shintaido is strangely unique and new even to the Japanese. The express purpose of Hiroyuki Aoki, the creator of Shintaido, was to develop 'a movement which could go out from Japan and correspond with the imaginations of people all over the world'. But 'in order for Shintaido to be true for all human beings it had to be rooted in the earth, the matrix from which all living things arise. In other words, it had to arise from the Japanese soil. Of course, if it had originated in another country, it would have had its roots in that country's soil'.*

To say that Shintaido is simply a martial art is not enough, yet it lies firmly rooted in that very rich and strong discipline.

BACKGROUND OF THE JAPANESE MARTIAL ARTS

The Japanese martial arts were developed in times when life was incredibly hard for the ordinary person. During the 15th and 16th centuries the whole population was subjected to the ravages of war, people's thoughts were concerned not only with how to survive but also how to accept a death which might come at any moment. According to the needs of the age, certain battle techniques and strategies evolved. However with the introduction of firearms all the excellent skills and tactics that had been developed up until that time suddenly appeared utterly useless. If Budo was to survive it had to change. What began to appear in the 17th century when Japan returned to relative peace was a martial art system taught as a means of cultivating the spirit. 'As an essential element of this training, they studied the art of living perfectly up to the moment of death. As a result, the philosophy of the martial arts became deeper and deeper, adopting the slogan *Shinken Ichinyo* — "developing our mind and sword technique together".'** The other direction the martial arts moved in was the development of battle techniques with even deadlier weapons. This process has not stopped to this day.

The history of martial arts is marked by many famous people who challenged the fixed ideas of their time at the risk of their own lives so that Budo should always remain a vitally living force matching the needs of the times. However the past one hundred years has seen a decline to the point where today it appears almost an anachronism. What we see now is firstly a Budo which is a kind of sport contaminated by 'rationalism' and no longer containing the essence of its philosophy, and secondly, a Budo having no vital energy as a result of too much emphasis on spiritual aspects or mysticism.

THE RESPONSE OF HIROYUKI AOKI

Hiroyuki Aoki sees the martial artists of the Shogun period as spiritual revolutionaries. Although they could not draw the swords freely as they had in earlier times of civil war, they nonetheless staked their lives in one swing of the sword. Mr Aoki feels that 'even in this age of space travel, ... "by crossing swords" we could also develop a new method of exploring psychological sensitivity between two people. By using body movement, we could regain a measure of the genuine communication which has almost disappeared from our lives and at the same time, repair our bodies and minds

---

* Aoki, H., *Shintaido* p. 21
** Ibid., p. 28

Seeking a 'body way' to express truth and beauty

from the damaging effects of modern civilisation . . . that in exploring such a method, we could rediscover the true nature of our bodies and our universe.'***

As a way of looking deeply into oneself, Budo has relevance for all of us today. The study of fighting techniques (how to kill an opponent) is in essence the study of how to live one's own life in very severe circumstances. It is 'a systematic and unparalleled philosophy which states that by facing death itself we can understand and complete our lives.'**** For in such a moment only the most essential things of one's life stand out very sharply in contrast to the other general clutter and we can attain a heightened sense of awareness and vision.

Aoki reached the highest level he could in his study and research of Karate and yet there was a gnawing dissatisfaction in him that the martial arts as they stood were not sufficient to express all that he hoped for.

Throughout his childhood and early student days Aoki showed very strong artistic leanings. That his chosen way in life should become Budo arose initially out of a desire to strengthen his body for his main area of study: *acting*. Two things led him to the

*** Ibid., p. 33
**** Ibid., p. 21

point of wanting to create a new movement art: his desire to express beauty, and the love portrayed by Jesus in the Bible. In his late teens he had been particularly struck by one verse and had become a Christian. The Bible was always a great source of hope and inspiration for him. Karate as it stood was a very exclusive discipline to which few could enter. It no longer fitted with an era in which international communication was of paramount importance.

With such ideas guiding his work he was able to go beyond his present study to create a movement art which would elevate the human condition through forms which would express the simplest, most natural and freest ways of moving. In so doing, this would help people to realise a deeper power or hidden talent. The overriding theme of the martial arts, he realised, must be 'the pursuit of truth to engender love of one's neighbour and the expansion of our consciousness.'*

THE EMERGENCE OF SHINTAIDO

The process for creating Shintaido began about 19 years ago when a group of people from various disciplines within the martial arts, inspired by Aoki's vision, came together. It was through their intense devotion and study under the direction of Aoki that the forms of Shintaido were actually generated. Aoki's desire was to strip away all superfluous movements and ideas to only the most essential and in so doing discover a world of endless possibility. When forms, techniques and movements become simple actions, the real mind and spirit of the technique emerge naturally from the form.

Shintaido is a 'body way' and so therefore its benefits are experienced within the forms. Inasmuch as the body needs a skeleton to support it and any changes in it can affect our whole physical well-being, so form acts in the same relation to ideas. Thought is manifested in form. How we look at life will be reflected in our physical shape and condition. The study of form is a key to development, change and discovery in our lives. Therefore it is vital that these forms should represent the highest ideals.

SHINTAIDO 'FORMS'

The actual practise is divided into quite distinct areas of: *preparation*, the study of the particular Shintaido forms, and *kumite* (practising with one or more partners). However, whether we are stretching an achilles tendon or performing one of the *Toitsukihon* movements, like a holograph, the whole of the practice is expressed in each of its parts.

We begin by forming a large circle and sitting on the floor in *Seiza* position for a few moments of silence. Bowing, we stand and go through a variety of different stretching exercises following the voice of the *goreisha* (the person giving the practice). Even at this rudimentary stage the feeling of the group can change, sensing something in the *goreisha*'s voice or in the electricity in the air just from the fact that a group of people have come together for no other purpose than to move. Bodies that were heavy, tired and lethargic begin to awaken.

The preparation is not designed just as a means for stretching the body but also through it to bring together what may seem a very disparate group of people. There are no barriers to doing Shintaido. Regardless of one's age, sex, religion or physical condition — all are able to join in the practice. Naturally some of the forms are

---

* Aoki, H., Ibid., p. 45

moderated for different physical conditions but this in no way detracts from their effectiveness for that particular person.

Once we have gone through basic stretching exercises we study many different types of jumping which allow for the full expression of our energy and ability or the complete shedding of it. In the process we can release tension and open our bodies, particularly the abdomen area, clear our minds, deepening our concentration and resolve. Our bodies find again a more natural and vital way of moving.

The purpose is not physical endurance but the study of how to change ourselves by going beyond what we normally think we are capable of. The body has tremendous capacities which we can only discover by using it. When we practise Shintaido we soon realise that the normal energy we rely on is quite dispensable.

Often we might start a particular movement for some time. Gradually we start to tire and believe that we cannot continue — a struggle seems to take place between a mind that says 'that is enough' and a body that somehow keeps going. Inspired perhaps by those around and the insistent voice of the *goreisha*, from what seems like nowhere an extraordinarily renewed vigour appears and suddenly the body is moving almost of its own volition as though released from a great burden.

From the preparation we move into the study of the Shintaido forms themselves. In one practice we cannot hope to study the whole Shintaido programme so the instructor will choose what he or she wishes to develop in a particular practice. What follows is an outline of some of the most fundamental forms in Shintaido. *Eiko Dai* and *Tenshingoso* being the most important.

Eiko Dai — *running as freely as we can*

EIKO DAI

In this form we move from the smallest shape we can make to the greatest. As a small ball we imagine ourselves as a lump of clay — unformed — as yet not born to the world of human beings. As we open and stretch upward, we embrace everything around us and stretch our whole being upwards to the sky. This movement is a symbol of communicating with God, the cosmos — an expression of our ideal vision.

From that highest point we slowly lower our arms in one majestic sweeping cut, running as earnestly and freely as we can, with no thought, freeing ourselves from the burdens — real and imaginary — of our past and present and entering the future with the simplest heart and mind. As Aoki says, 'What you have been given from the heavens, you share with others'.*

It is the application of our ideal world to the real one. This form is so incredibly simple, and yet to do it completely really means we have to give up ourselves — and all that we imagine constitutes 'us'. It is a difficult but necessary process, but its implications are so profound when we consider the conflicts within the world today, with each person holding onto his ideas as the 'right' ones. *Eiko* is a way of liberating the imagination and opening a way for renewed understanding as we reach a common ground.

Raising our hands over our heads symbolises complete defeat and surrender. In so doing we admit and approve our powerlessness. Mr Aoki strongly felt that the acts of accepting defeat and crying for help are stronger than the strongest forms in the martial arts, and this was the real point of departure and the image of Shintaido.

TENSHINGOSO

This is a *kata* or series of movements which we can practice wherever we are and in whatever condition we find ourselves, and very quickly experience a state of peace and

Tenshingoso — *we create our world*

* Aoki, H., *Shintaido* p. 66

Tenshingoso

well-being. It contains a universality in clear, simple forms which encompass and express a deep and complex philosophy. It is also a synthesis of martial art technique and simulates the cycle of a human life and even the rhythm of the cosmos. When practising this *kata* we make the vowel sounds 'A' (ah), 'E' (a), 'I' (e), 'O', 'UM' as loudly as possible.

'UM': Tenshingoso begins and ends with this form. As at the beginning of *Eiko*, we try to become as nothing, emptying our minds of all thoughts and ideas.

'A': This movement is similar to the opening movement of the previous form, *Eiko*, and holds the same meaning.

'E': We are creating our world, opening our future, using our own ability to go forward.

'I': We are consolidating the world that we have built.

'O': We are offering up or giving away everything that we have gained before returning to the final movement 'UM', in which our minds are free from all thoughts or ideas.

This is a very basic outline of the meaning of each form. However, with this as a guide, one can gradually discover for oneself a greater range of meanings whilst performing the movements.

Each of the movements is a reflection of some aspect of our lives and so, in performing them, we can understand our true capacities and weaknesses more clearly and work to strengthen the latter through work on the form.

SHINTAIDO

TOITSUKIHON WAZA

The spirit of *Eiko* and *Tenshingoso* is retained even in the most basic forms of the Shintaido programme, and so it is with the *Toitsukihon* which is sometimes called *Eiko Sei*, since it is a formal and condensed form of the *Eiko Dai* movements. Therefore we can proceed naturally from *Eiko* to the *Toitsukihon* forms in all their variations.

Through the practice of the Shintaido movements a strong foundation is laid in our lives. The forms develop unification of our movement, and 'confidence, bravery and courage' (Aoki). Our breathing and contraction naturally deepen and when working with a partner we can adjust our rhythm to theirs. Through the most fundamental means we have — the body — we lay the ground work for a true harmony and genuine communication and cooperation with others.

Mr Aoki wrote that all the Shintaido movements are governed by the principle of *kiri*, or 'cutting':

kiri homi — cutting by pushing
kiri harai — cutting by pulling

These can be arranged in many different ways:

Kiri harai — *cutting by pulling*

Both of these movements can easily be recognised as a condensed form of *Eiko Dai*. After opening and stretching upwards, instead of running we condense the breadth and imagination of *Eiko* into one step, as in *Kiri Oroshi*, by lowering our hips to the ground. Naturally both movements contain the ideas of *Eiko Dai*. They also help us to unify the upper and lower parts of our body — the ideal and the reality — into one movement, developing a good sense of balance.

Through the constant repetition of these clear forms we are able to polish our inner world so that it can shine more brightly. A tremendous sense of well-being and freedom can be generated and a quite unconscious and spontaneous movement is often created. It is necessary to use the total expression of the body in these movements and not just arm power as we cut. Most important of all we should have an open abdomen. This latter point is essential in all aspects of Shintaido training.

By concentrating on opening the body and loosening muscular knots we can unleash blocked emotions and ideas, and develop far greater sensitivity. Suddenly what has appeared as an obstacle in one's life no longer has any significance. There can be a renewal too, of creative ideas.

THE VALUE OF COMMUNICATION

Shintaido also includes the study of *kumite*. Sometimes we utilise simple attack and defence forms in which we do not seek to defeat but to extend our partner's world. Or one person will hold the other partner's wrists very surely and follow with the whole body as he or she performs a *kata* such as *Tenshingoso* or one of the *Toitsukihon* forms, such as *Kirioroshi*. It is very exciting to watch two people build up a dialogue in *kumite* — they come from their own worlds and through movement test their ideas in the reality of communication with each other. At first there appears an awkwardness but the longer they continue the more their movements harmonise, and one is no longer seeing two people but one movement as their worlds merge. To reach such a level takes some time and patience but everyone can experience something on the journey to that point which is fulfilling.

How we breathe is essential to the practice but breathing exercises are not in the main taught as a separate entity. In the process of doing all the forms a pattern develops. Breath deepens naturally and as this occurs so our concentration becomes stronger. In particular, in *kumite*, as your movement starts to harmonise with your partner, you start to breathe as one. The practice always finishes with all the members of the group forming a large circle as they did at the beginning. Sitting in *Seiza* for a few moments of silence they bow and then turn to their instructor and bow again as a form of thanks.

BENEFITS OF SHINTAIDO

It does not matter at what level, or for what reason, we choose to approach Shintaido, great benefits will be experienced. The goal is not mastery of a perfect form because its concept is infinite, but the pursuit of it with all our heart. Through the process of imagination we are able to have soft, open and strong bodies. The key is simply to start. What we come to realise is that it is not merely a physical exercise. As limitations are broken down with the body, likewise one covers new ground in the mind as latent talent is released and drawn out. Body and mind are collaborators in an ever-expanding search to discover life.

The practice of Shintaido is vitally relevant to everyday life. Through the movements we can see our own weaknesses and strengths and we can learn how to develop or

Tenshingoso kumite

utilise them so that we can be more effective and fulfilled. There is a renewal of confidence and encouragement.

Shintaido provides the environment for people to make the desired change in themselves by releasing them from their routine associations, and in a compartmentalised society it brings people of diverse backgrounds and occupations together. It offers us a methodology for the development of our lives. In contrast to the smallness of our daily tasks, Shintaido gives us a glimpse of worlds that are bigger than our imagination. This stretches us to new horizons and gives significance to the smallest of tasks too.

With the simple forms of Shintaido there is little chance of getting caught up in the image of performing elaborate and exotic movements with heady philosophies. Any ideas about our relative strengths and weaknesses and what we want from the practice are irrelevant and, ultimately, a barrier. The only thing that is necessary is simply to *do*, with a strong and open mind. It is hard to indulge ourselves in such an atmosphere and gradually we are able to become the authors of our own transformation.

A movement art must look to the social and environmental issues. Humans do not live in isolation but have responsibility for all that exists in the world. There is a widespread sense of helplessness today that we cannot 'do anything' yet if we imagine each human being as a reflection of the great macrocosm of the world, by changing ourselves, we can indeed have an effect in the world. A genuine communication which seeks to change for the better without destroying our individual identity, is very much needed today.

The great challenge is to love one another despite our differences. A movement art such as Shintaido which can embrace all people in a common dialogue where there are no winners or losers, stronger or weaker persons, is therefore very necessary.

GLOSSARY OF TERMS:

Budo Japanese martial arts.

Eiko Glory. One of the fundamental movements of Shintaido.

Dai Big, expansive.

Gorei Leading or conducting group practice, with or without sound. It may correspond to a conductor's role in a symphonic performance. The practice is completely led by the *goreisha* and the result depends upon him.

Goreisha Person who conducts or leads a group practice.

Kata Forms consisting of stipulated movements which enable us to find ourselves through self-reflection. The essence or heart of *budo* has been transmitted through *kata* without the use of language or letters for explanation. There is no other vehicle in *budo*. Therefore we must, through body movement, explore without any preconceptions what has been transmitted in *kata*. The system of Shintaido also consists of specific *kata*, eg *Tenshingoso*, *Eiko*, *Toitsukihon*.

Keiko In general terms, 'practice', 'training' or 'exercise'. Although these definitions can be used, the term *keiko* is particularly used in regard to the study of Japanese traditional arts such as *Noh*, tea ceremony or *budo*. Through *keiko* we can re-experience how people in the old days lived their lives, how they sought the truth. So in *keiko* what we study is not the practice itself, as it was developed in the past, but the attitude of people who devoted themselves to the practice: how they studied, how they lived. Although Shintaido does not fall into the category of a traditional *budo*, in the sense of *keiko*, Shintaido is no doubt in the stream of *budo*.

Kiriharai Cutting by pulling.

Kirikomi Cutting by pushing.

Kirioroshi Similar to *kirikomi* but cutting lower.

Kumite *Te* means the hand(s), technique, tactics. In Japanese, it originally meant 'to link arms' and later to apply one's technique in *kumite* was a kind of *kata* practised with a partner or partners. It is useful for examining our techniques to see if they are effective and realistic. Furthermore, through *kumite*, we can study many things concerning our relationship with a partner, ways of communicating, etc. In *kumite*, your partner's condition depends directly on you, so that you can see your own reflection through your partner's movement, behaviour, expression, complexion, just like a mirror.

Sei Formal.

Seiza Sitting in a kneeling position keeping one's back straight.

Tenshingoso One of the fundamental movements of Shintaido.

Toitsukihon Common ground technique.

Waza Technique.

ACKNOWLEDGEMENTS

Grateful acknowledgement is made to Writers House Inc., New York, for permission to reproduce 'Self-help Chiropractic' from Nathaniel Altman's *The Chiropractic Alternative* (J. P. Tarcher, Los Angeles 1981).

The editor would also like to acknowledge the assistance of the Australian holistic journal *Nature & Health* in which shorter versions of the chapters on Rebirthing and Shintaido, and the entire chapter on Deep Tissue Muscle Therapy, were originally published.

PHOTOGRAPHY CREDITS

Ralph Hadden: 11, 14, 15, 16, 17, 18; Society of Teachers of the Alexander Technique: 22; Michael Ney: 24, 25, 26, 27, 28, 31, 32; Trager Institute: 35, 36, 39, 43, 47; Kate Wimble: 59, 63, 64, 66, 68, 70, 109, 118, 119, 122, 124, 151, 152, 156, 159, 165, 166, 167, 168, 170; Laurence McManus: 73; East West Centre: 74, 75, 76, 78, 79, 80, 81; Carolyn Johns: 82, 84, 86, 87, 88, 89, 90, 91, 92, 93; Susan Roche: 97, 98, 99, 113, 114, 115; Eva Reich: 130; Lew Luton: 133; Ross Digby: 137, 138, 145, 147; Shintaido Institute: 161, 163.

LINE ILLUSTRATIONS

Society of Teachers of the Alexander Technique: 29, 30; Nathaniel Altman: 50, 51, 52, 53, 55, 56; Nevill Drury: 104; Frances Heath: 127

THE CONTRIBUTORS

MICHAEL ADAMEDES is a Director of the Sydney Healing Centre and Euroa House. A former accountant and social worker he became a Swami with the Satayananda Ashram for two years. In 1981 he was taught rebirthing by Dr Stanislav Grof and since then he has worked as a professional natural therapist and professional rebirther.
Contact Address: Sydney Healing Centre, 236 Darling Street, Balmain, Sydney, Australia. Ph: (02) 810 4699

NATHANIEL ALTMAN lives in New York and works as a professional writer and teacher, specialising in diet and health. He is the author of *The Chiropractic Alternative* (from which the present chapter is extracted) and *Eating For Life*. He is also a contributing editor for *Vegetarian Times* and his articles have appeared in *Health Quarterly*, *Cue* and other food and health oriented journals.
Contact Address: C/- Writers House Inc. Literary Agency, 21 West 26th Street, New York, NY 10010, USA

JEREMY CHANCE was born in Sydney in 1955 and after leaving school became an actor on stage and in television. In 1976 he went to London and worked in the Royal Court Theatre. He became interested in the Alexander Technique because of the help it provided with poise and breath control and subsequently studied to gain a certificate and become a member of the Society of Teachers of the Alexander Technique (S.T.A.T.). He later worked at the Rose Bruford and E15 acting schools in London teaching Alexander's method to actors.
Contact Address: S.A.T.A., 4/150 Holt Avenue, Cremorne, Sydney, Australia. Ph: (02) 90 3424
S.T.A.T., 10 London House, 266 Fulham Road, London SW 10 9EL, England

JOHN COTTONE was born in New York and emigrated to Australia in 1979. He has studied and practised most of the major body/mind therapies including naturopathy, physical therapy, Swedish and therapeutic massage, polarity and zone therapy, shiatsu oriental healing techniques, eastern, western, Mexican and American Indian ceremonial healing, Reichian emotional release and Gestalt counselling. John now specialises in Deep Tissue Muscle Therapy, Ka-Tone Therapy and Advanced Body Therapy and lectures at the Nature-care School of Remedial Therapies in Artarmon and the NSW College of Natural Therapies in Sydney. He has lectured for the National

THE CONTRIBUTORS

Health Federation (USA), is a certified instructor with the Arica Institute, New York, and has given workshops at the Esalen Institute, Big Sur, California.
Contact Address: C/- Naturecare, 1a Frederick Street, Artarmon, Sydney, Australia. Ph: (02) 439 8844

RALPH HADDEN is one of Melbourne's leading massage practitioners and teachers. After completing an Arts degree at Monash University, he trained in naturopathy and osteopathy (at the Southern School of Natural Therapies), and in acupuncture (at Acupuncture Colleges of Australia). He later founded the Melbourne School of Tactile Therapies, which continues today as a successful and respected institution, teaching massage, natural health and personal growth in both short introductory courses and longer certificate training courses.
Contact Address: Melbourne School of Tactile Therapies, Suite 11, 564 St Kilda Road, Melbourne, Australia. Ph: (03) 529 3611

DEANE JUHAN has been a massage therapist at Esalen Institute, Big Sur, California, since 1973, and a Trager Practitioner there since 1978. He lectures on anatomy and physiology for bodyworkers, and is currently writing a book on that subject. He is an instructor for the Trager Institute.
Contact Address: The Trager Institute, 300 Poplar Avenue, Suite #5 Mill Valley, California, 94941, USA. Ph: (408) 388 2688

BARBARA KIMBREY was born in Sydney, studied literature and philosophy at university and, after graduating, became a school teacher. Interested in natural healing, meditation and yoga she later travelled through Asia, the United States and Europe before returning to Australia. In 1979 she began studying oriental health techniques at the East West Centre and in 1981 was invited to study with Masahiro Oki at his Dojo in Mishima, Japan. After training in Oki Yoga with him for a year she returned to teach at East West and she now divides her time between the two centres.
Contact Address: East West Centre, 215a Thomas Street, Haymarket, Sydney, Australia. Ph: (02) 212 4177

LEW LUTON founded the Wilhelm Reich Centre in Melbourne in 1977 and continues to work in private practice. Introduced to Reich's orgonomic therapeutic techniques by Tom Larkin in 1956, Lew has since worked with Glyn Seaborn-Jones, William Glasser, Chuck Kelley, Virginia Satir, David Boadella and Eva Reich. His main professional aim is to include a cognitive component in group work unifying the body/mind experience.
Contact Address: Wilhelm Reich Centre, PO Box 123, Fitzroy, Melbourne, Australia. Ph: (03) 387 6374

ALIA PAULUSZ is an experienced arts and craft consultant now working as a holistic health practitioner. She employs rebirthing, stress management, and life skills counselling in her therapeutic approach.
Contact Address: 4/120 Brighton Boulevarde, Bondi, Sydney, Australia. Ph: (02) 30 6925

ALEXANDRA POPE was originally a teacher of English and Social Studies in England, and is now an instructor of Shintaido. She began Shintaido in England in 1974, initially drawn to it through her love of theatre and movement. She has spent three and a half years in Japan furthering her study and practice of the discipline, and has also been

THE CONTRIBUTORS

closely involved in the setting up and running of the now strong Shintaido group in England. She has recently introduced Shintaido to Australia.
Contact Address: C/- Psychosynthesis Training Centre, 127 Old South Head Road, Bondi, Sydney, Australia. Ph: (02) 389 0193

SUSAN ROCHE was born in Hong Kong, educated in Canada and emigrated to Australia in 1972. Originally interested in yoga, she subsequently studied and qualified as a practitioner of acupuncture and physiotherapy. With Helen Smith she evolved the Touch for Beauty concept which combines acupressure (shiatsu), acupuncture, herbs, energy massage, reflexology, nutrition and meditation.
Contact Address: 25 Sutherland Avenue, Paddington, Sydney, Australia. Bondi, (02) 328 1541

HELEN SMITH is a highly qualified acupuncturist who has been lecturing at the Acupuncture Colleges of Australia in Sydney for the last four years. She has continued to study complementary disciplines including Transactional Analysis, Neuro-Linguistic Programming, Hypnotherapy, Applied Kinesiology, Functional Integration, Reiki energy healing and Superlearning. Her particular interest is in teaching people how to look after their own health more effectively. As well as teaching Touch for Beauty with Susan Roche (now renamed Help Yourself to Health), Helen's classes include Touch for Health, self-hypnosis and practical energy healing work.
Contact Address: 558 Warringah Road, Forestville, Sydney, Australia. Ph: (02) 451 3978

DANIEL WEBER was born in Minnesota and trained to be an actor in Boston. There he met Japanese teacher Michio Kushi of the East-West Foundation. Deeply interested in his Eastern philosophy of life, Daniel studied with him for five years. In the early 1970s he went to England, trained with Dr J. R. Worsley and Dr Van Buren at the College of Acupuncture and subsequently helped establish the East-West Foundation in London. After studying Zen Yoga with Masahiro Oki in Japan, Daniel and his wife Marcea decided to emigrate to Australia. Together they now head the East-West Centre in Sydney and offer a variety of oriental health techniques, including Oki Yoga, shiatsu and macrobiotics.
Contact Address: East West Centre, 215A Thomas Street, Haymarket, Sydney, Australia. Ph: (02) 212 4177

CARL WEBSTER was born in the United Kingdom in 1951 and in his late teens began practising Zen meditation. This led to an interest in the teachings of the Buddha, Lao Tzu and the Zen masters. In his search for a way of practically experiencing these philosophies he was led to the study of yoga and the teachings of B. K. S. Iyengar and eventually began teaching yoga in Cambridge, England. In 1981 he emigrated to Sydney with his wife Gurdive and son Govinda. He is founder and director of The Yoga Centre on Sydney's North Shore, where he teaches yoga and practises oriental medicine.
Contact Address: The Yoga Centre, 1st Floor, 14 Thomas Street, Chatswood, Sydney, Australia. Ph: (02) 43 2657

BIBLIOGRAPHY

1: Sensitive Massage
BENJAMIN, B., *Are You Tense?*, New York 1978. Pantheon
DOWNING, G., *The Massage Book*, New York 1972, Random House
INKELES, G., *The New Massage*, New York 1980, Putnam
MILLER, R. D., *Psychic Massage*, New York 1975, Harper & Row
MONTAGU, A., *Touching*, New York 1978, Harper & Row

2: The Alexander Technique
ALEXANDER, F. M., *Alexander Technique*, London 1974, Thames and Hudson
BARKER, S., *The Alexander Technique*, New York 1978, Bantam
BARLOW, W., *The Alexander Principle*, New York 1973, Random House
JONES, F. P., *Body Awareness in Action*, New York 1976, Schocken

3: Trager Work
Readers are referred to The Trager Institute, 300 Poplar Avenue, Suite #5 Mill Valley, California, 94941, USA, for specialist material on the Trager Approach

4: Self-help Chiropractic
ALTMAN, N., *The Chiropractic Alternative*, Los Angeles 1981, Tarcher
BENSON, H., *The Relaxation Response*, New York 1972, Avon
DINTENFASS, J., *Chiropractic: A Modern Way to Health*, New York 1977, Pyramid
HASSARD, G. H. and REDD, C. L., *Elongation Treatment of Lower Back Pain*, Springfield, USA 1959, C. Thomas
JAUSE, HOUSER, WELLS, *Chiropractic Principles and Technique*, Lombard, Illinois 1947, National College of Chiropractic

5: Iyengar Yoga
IYENGAR, B. K. S., *Light on Yoga*, London 1966, Allen and Unwin
IYENGAR, G. K. S., *Light on Pranayama*, London 1981, Allen and Unwin
LEBOYER, F., *Inner Beauty, Inner Light*, London 1979, Collins

6: Oki Yoga
OKI, M., *Practical Yoga*, Indianapolis 1971, Bobbs-Merrill
OKI, M., *Yoga Therapy*, Tokyo 1976, Japan Publications

BIBLIOGRAPHY

7: Shiatsu

HOUSTON, F. M., *The Healing Benefits of Acupressure*, Northamptonshire 1958, Thorsons
IRWIN, Y. and WAGENVOORD, J., *Shiatsu*, Philadelphia 1976, Lippincott
MASUNAGA, S. and OHASHI, W., *Zen Shiatsu*, Tokyo 1977, Japan Publications
OHASHI, W., *Do-It-Yourself Shiatsu*, London 1977, Allen and Unwin
WARREN, F. Z., *Freedom From Pain Through Acupressure*, New York 1976, Fell
YAMAMOTO, S., *Barefoot Shiatsu*, Tokyo 1979, Japan Publications

8: Touch for Beauty

Readers are referred to Help Yourself to Health, 25 Sutherland Avenue, Paddington, Sydney, Australia for specialised reading lists. See also *Shiatsu* list (Chapter 7, above).

9: Deep Tissue Muscle Therapy

COTTONE, J., 'Physical and Etheric Balance', Sydney 1983, *Nature & Health*, Vol. 5, No. 1
COTTONE, J., 'Deep Tissue Muscle Therapy', Sydney 1984, *Nature & Health*, Vol. 5 No. 3
COTTONE, J., 'The Ka-tone Approach to the Organs of Elimination', Sydney 1984, *Nature & Health*, Vol. 5 No. 4

10: Reichian and Neo-Reichian Therapy

BAKER, E. F., *The Man in the Trap*, New York 1967, Collier Macmillan
BOHM, D., *Wholeness and the Implicate Order*, London 1980, Routledge & Kegan Paul
BURR, H. S., *Blueprint for Immortality*, London 1972, Spearman
FERGUSON, M., *The Aquarian Conspiracy*, London 1981, Paladin
GROF, S., *Realms of the Human Unconscious*, New York 1975, Viking
LAING, R. D., *The Voice of Experience*, London 1983, Pelican
LAKE, F., *Clinical Theology*, London 1966, Darton, Longman & Todd
MOSS, T., *The Body Electric*, Los Angeles 1979, Tarcher
RAKNES, O., *Wilhelm Reich and Orgonomy*, Baltimore 1971, Penguin
REICH, W., *Character Analysis*, New York 1972, Simon and Schuster
REICH, W., *Ether, God and Devil/Cosmic Superimposition*, New York 1973, Farrar, Straus & Giroux
REICH, W., *Function of the Orgasm*, New York 1973, Farrar, Straus & Giroux
REICH, W., *Selected Writings*, New York 1974, Farrar, Straus & Giroux
REICH, W., *The Bion Experiences*, New York 1979, Farrar, Straus & Giroux
REICH, W., *The Cancer Biopathy*, New York 1973, Farrar, Straus & Giroux
SHARAF, M., *Fury on Earth*, New York 1983, St Martins Press
SHELDRAKE, R., *A New Science of Life*, Los Angeles 1981, Tarcher
WILBER, K., (ed.) *The Holographic Paradigm*, Boulder 1972, Shambhala

Readers are also referred to the following journals: *Energy & Character*; *Journal of Orgonomy*; *Offshoots of Orgonomy* and *Radix Journals*.

11: Rebirthing

DRURY, N., *Healers, Quacks or Mystics?*, Sydney 1983, Hale & Iremonger
LEBOYER, F., *Birth Without Violence*, New York 1975, Knopf

BIBLIOGRAPHY

LEONARD, T. and LAUT, P., *Rebirthing — the Science of Enjoying Your Life*, Los Angeles 1983, Trinity Publications
ORR, L., *Rebirthing in the New Age*, Millbrae, California 1980, Celestial Arts
ORR, L., *Physical Immortality*, Millbrae, California 1981, Celestial Arts
RAMACHARAKA, YOGI, *Science of Breath*, London 1932, Fowler
RAY, S., *Celebration of Breath*, Millbrae, California 1983, Celestial Arts
VERNY, T., *The Secret Life of the Unborn Child*, New York, Delacorte
WAMBACH, H., *Life Before Life*, New York 1979, Bantam

12: Shintaido

AOKI, H., *Shintaido*, San Francisco 1982, Shintaido of America Institute

Readers are referred to the Shintaido of America Institute, PO Box 22622, San Francisco, CA 94122, USA, for specialist material on Shintaido.